RICHARD LEDERER

DVENTURES OF A VERBIVORE

POCKET BOOKS

New York   London   Toronto   Sydney   Tokyo   Singapore

For the idea of the game "The Difference a Word Makes," pp. 181–85, and some of the examples I am indebted to Maxwell Nurnberg, *Questions You Always Wanted to Ask about English but Were Afraid to Raise Your Hand* (Washington Square Press, 1972).

Versions of some material in this book have appeared in *Writer's Digest, Verbatim, Word Ways, The Farmers' Almanac, Sky Magazine,* and the *New York Times.*

POCKET BOOKS, a division of Simon & Schuster Inc.
1230 Avenue of the Americas, New York, NY 10020

Copyright © 1994 by Richard Lederer

Design by Stanley S. Drate/Folio Graphics Co., Inc.

Library of Congress Cataloging-in-Publication Data

Lederer, Richard, 1938–
    Adventures of a verbivore / Richard Lederer.
       p.   cm.
    ISBN: 0-671-70941-0
    1. English language—Lexicology. 2. English language—Usage.
I. Title.
PE1571.L43   1994
428—dc20   93-32287
                                                                CIP

First Pocket Books hardcover printing March 1994

10 9 8 7 6 5 4 3 2 1

POCKET and colophon are registered trademarks of
Simon & Schuster Inc.

Printed in the U.S.A.

To my verbivorous children
Howard, Annie, and Katy

$\mathcal{A}$CKNOWLEDGMENTS

Thousands of thanks to my "Looking at Language" readers for their many submissions and letters; to Gloria Rosenthal not only for creating and running the Wonderful World of Words weekend but for helping so much with the writing of the chapter; to my son, Howard, for his poker lore; to Barbara Bushy for permission to use excerpts from my appearance on the "Jim Bohannan Show"; to Al Greengold, William Ward, and Miriam Espinosa for their many homophonic contributions; to Rabbi Robert Schenkerman for his partnership in the joys and oys of Yiddish; to my daughter Katy for help in unlocking the code of prep school slanguage; to *Writer's Digest* senior editor Tom Clark for permission to share and expand my Grammar Grappler columns; and to my Pocket Books editor, Jane Rosenman, for her blissfully thunderous joy in my work.

ℰONTENTS

I

LEDERER IN WORDLAND

II

THE GRAMMAR GRAPPLER

I

*L*EDERER IN WORDLAND

ℋeels Over Head in Love with Language

𝒪ne day I received a letter inviting me to come visit Marilyn Frasier's sixth-grade class at Broken Ground School, a progressive elementary school on the east side of my town. I drove out to Broken Ground and chatted for about forty-five minutes with the students about the joys of language and the challenges of the writing life. During the question-and-answer session that followed, one of the boys in the class asked me, "Mr. Lederer, where do you get your ideas for your books?"

Ever since I became a writer, I had found that question to be the most difficult to answer and had only recently come up with an analogy that I thought would satisfy both my audience and me. Pouncing on the opportunity to unveil my spanking new explanation for the first time, I countered with "Where does the spider get its web?"

The idea, of course, was that the spider is not aware of how it spins out intricate and beautiful patterns with the silky material that is simply a natural part of itself.

3

Asking a writer to account for the genesis of his or her ideas is as futile as asking a spider to explain the source of its web and the method of its construction.

So, when the young man asked his question, I replied, "Where does the spider get its web?"

He shot right back, "From its butt!"

Since that visit, I've checked out the boy's assertion, and, sure enough, spiders do produce their silk in glands located in their posteriors. The glands open through the tiny spinnerets located at the hind end of the abdomen. Well, it may be that for lo these many years I've been talking and writing through my butt, but that doesn't stop me from being a self-confessed and unrepentant verbivore.

Carnivores eat flesh and meat; piscivores eat fish; herbivores eat plants and vegetables; verbivores devour words. I am such a creature. My whole life I have feasted on words—ogled their appetizing shapes, colors, and textures; swished them around in my mouth; lingered over their many tastes; let their juices run down my chin. During my adventures as a fly-by-the-roof-of-the-mouth, user-friendly wizard of idiom, I have met thousands of other wordaholics, logolepts, and verbivores, folks who also eat their words.

What is there about words that makes a language person love them so? The answers are probably as varied as the number of verbivores themselves.

Some word people are intrigued by the birth and life of words. They become enthusiastic, ebullient, and enchanted when they discover that *enthusiastic* literally means "possessed by a god," *ebullient*, "boiling over, spouting out," and *enchanted*, "singing a magic song." They are rendered starry-eyed by the insight that *disaster (dis-aster)* literally means "ill-starred" and intoxicated by the information that *intoxicated* has toxic poison in its heart. They love the fact that *amateur* is cobbled from the very first verb that all students of Latin learn—*amo:* "I love."

Wordsters of etymological persuasion also hope to be sitting in the catbird seat when it comes to locating the origins of colorful phrases. In the phrase *to make both ends meet,* what are the ends and how do they come together? Answer: Here *meet* is actually *mete,* an adjective meaning "equal." The two ends are assets and liabilities that nineteenth-century bookkeepers had to make mete, that is, to balance. Does *a flash in the pan* derive (*de + rivus,* "from the river") from the way prospectors pan rivers for gold? Answer: No, *a flash in the pan* refers to the occasional misfiring of the old flintlock muskets when the flash of the primer in the pan of the rifle failed to explode the charge.

But why has the catbird seat come to signify a position of advantage? My reading of a number of ornithology books reveals that the catbird does not usually sit high up in branches, where it could get the best view, but rather lurks half-hidden in shrubbery. What is so special about the catbird and its vantage point? Intrepid phrase-hunters will never rest until they track down the answer.

Still another denomination of logophile sees words as collections of letters to be twirled, juggled, and shuffled. They look at the four points of the compass and note a pattern: *north* and *south* end with the same two letters, and so do *east* and *west.* They look at the words that signify the four seasons and observe a similar symmetry. *Winter* and *summer* end with the same two letters and can be converted into verbs of opposite meaning; with a different twist so can *spring* and *fall.*

Inspired by the word *bookkeeper,* with its three consecutive pairs of double letters, these logologists fantasize about a biologist who helps maintain raccoon habitats: *a raccoon nook keeper*—six consecutive sets of double

6 ADVENTURES OF A VERBIVORE

letters—and another biologist who studies the liquid se-
creted by chickadee eggs. They call this scientist a *chickadee egg goo-olist*—and into the world is born three consecutive sets of triple letters!

With a rare kind of vision, these word nuts see that
if you add a *lie* to *a nation*, you get *alienation;* if you take
the *id* out of the verb *intimidate*, you get the adjective
intimate. That kind of parallax view of words is part of
their *identity*, which they epiphanously see as their *i.d.
entity.*

Then there's the breed of wordster who enjoys trying to turn the brier patch of pronoun cases, subject-
verb agreement, sequence of tenses, and the indicative
and subjunctive moods, into a manageable garden of
delight. Such devotees of correct usage often explore the
nuances of confusing word pairs—*take* vs. *bring* (you
take out the garbage; you bring in the newspaper), *podium* vs. *lectern* (you stand on a podium; you stand behind a lectern), and *comprise* vs. *compose* (the large comprises the small; the small composes the large).

Among my favorite wordmongers are those who
prowl the lunatic fringe of language, *lunatic* because the
ancients believed that prolonged exposure to the moon
(Latin *luna*) rendered one moonstruck, or daft. These
recreational wordplayers wonder why we drive in a
parkway and park in a driveway, why the third hand on
a clock is called the second hand, and why, if adults
commit adultery, infants don't commit infantry. Why is
it, they muse, that a man puts on a pair of pants but a
woman puts on only one bra? Why is it that a man can
call a woman a vision, but not a sight—unless his eyes
are sore?

Finally, there are the legions of pundits, punheads,
and pun pals who tell of the Buddhist who said to the
hot dog vendor, "Make me one with everything."
That's the same Buddhist who never took Novocain

when he had teeth extracted because he wished to transcend dental medication. These punderful verbivores become even bigger hot dogs when they tell about Charlemagne, who mustered his Franks and set out with great relish to assault and pepper the Saracens, but he couldn't catch up. (Frankly, I never sausage a pun. It's the wurst!)

At rare times, all these elements come together in a single word. Has there ever been another word as human as *usher?* In sound and meaning it is not a paragon among words, but it accommodates the full spectrum of humankind. Words and people have always hung around together, and within the brief compass of the five letters in *usher* we find the pronouns *us, she, he,* and *her.* Like humanity, *usher* has a long history, going all the way back to the Latin *ostium,* "door," related to *os,* "mouth," because a door was likened to the mouth of a building. So there again is that iron link between things and human beings.

Usher winkingly reminds us that all words are created by people and that language unfailingly reflects the fearful asymmetry of our kind. Thus, even though writers write, bakers bake, hunters hunt, preachers preach, and teachers teach, grocers don't groce, butchers don't butch, carpenters don't carpent, milliners don't millin, haberdashers don't haberdash—and ushers don't ush.

There are as many reasons to love words as there are people who love them. As a self-confessed, unrepentant, and lifelong wordaholic, logolept, and verbivore, I salivate when I discover that my name means "wealthy leather worker" and that the New Hampshire town I live in, Concord, is both a homophone of *conquered* and a capitonym, that is, a word like *polish* and *job* that changes pronunciation when it is capitalized.

I am heels over head in love with language. When I say "heels over head" rather than "head over heels," I am not two letters short of a complete alphabet or a syllable short of a coherent statement. "Head over heels" is the normal position, sort of like doing things ass backwards, which is the way we do everything. I don't know about you, but when I flip over something, my heels are over my head.

When I say *language*, I mean by and large the English language. That's because in matters verbal I am unabashedly lexist. Just as among many other things, the Italians do food well and that, among their many other accomplishments, the French do style and fashion well, I believe that we English speakers do language especially well. This book chronicles my heels-over-head love affair with the English language and my personal adventures with the people, ideas, books, and events that have made English a perpetual joyride for me. May you have a wordaholic, logoleptic, and verbivorous time sharing that junket with me.

𝒜 Wordy Weekend

𝒯 all and majestic on a mountaintop in New Paltz, New York, sits the stately, turreted Mohonk Mountain House, looking as if it belongs somewhere in the Swiss Alps rather than within a throne's stow of New York City. Set amidst the natural beauty of enormous old trees, wooded trails, glaciated rock cliffs, and a crystal blue lake, the national landmark also exudes the Victorian charm of gazebos, gatehouses, and greenhouses outside, and paneled rooms, hand-carved furniture, and fireplaces inside. For the more active guests who prefer doing to seeing, Mohonk offers a succession of more than forty theme programs that include a music weekend, a mystery weekend, a comic-strip weekend, and even a chocolate weekend.

It is mid-November of 1991, and I have returned to this mountaintop resort for the second time to speak at and romp through the annual Wonderful World of Words weekend. It is Friday night, and the front desk is busy checking in hotel guests, but the guests checking in are even busier. While the clerks merely have to sign in the guests and hand out the keys, the guests now have a Packet of Puzzlers, and apparently they can't wait to get started. They attack the word games in the Packet even as they head for the elevators, or they sit right down in chairs nearby and start writing at once. Here is the shortest of six posers that will be served up during our wordy weekend. Give it your best before consulting the answers in the chapter "Answers and Explanations I."

Each of the following crypticlike words represents a well-known motto, phrase, or saying. For example, KDI would be the abbreviated version of "crazy, mixed-up kid," and TIME TIME would be "time and time again."

1. Business

2. Timing timing

3. Rhutt fiction

4. Writiting

5. Wa ys

6. Bsoduyl

7. **Blood**water

8. Jump jump sheriff

9. I right I

10. Well enough

11. Bucdropket

12. Her buck

Gloria Rosenthal, all five feet two of her, bustles about greeting regulars and welcoming newcomers. A self-described "word buff, puzzle nut, and language lover," Gloria is a Long Island writer and lecturer who is the originator, creator, coordinator, gamesmonger, and absolute wordmistress of the Wonderful World of Words weekend. When she is not putting this event together, creating word games for magazines and puzzle books, or writing fiction and articles, she is busy being a wife, mother, and grandmother.

Gloria's support staff for the weekend comprises her husband, Larry, her sister Babe and brother-in-law Sonny, and her daughter Amy, who has flown in from Minneapolis to help. They all wear the Wonderful World of Words sweatshirts.

When I ask Gloria to describe the typical person who attends this wordy getaway, she says, "Over the years I've discovered that a love of language does not necessarily have anything to do with one's profession or occupation. Avid word buffs come from every field. They're lawyers, doctors, teachers, retired people, secretaries, nurses, insurance brokers, salespeople, housewives, and househusbands. I know a bridge builder, a real 'dese' and 'dose' kind of fellow, who loves language as passionately as any of us.

"There are different types of word-lovers—those who play with words, those who turn a phrase, those who pop a pun, and those who solve a puzzle. It calls for a trick of the mind that has little to do with education. Someone with a passion for words sees a sign, as I once did, that says 'Laundry Palace' and immediately drops some letters to come up with 'Land Dry Place' and then keeps beheading so that *place* becomes *lace* and then *ace*. For true word-lovers, even the simplest word can tickle their punny bone and get them going."

Marcia Hillman, a lyricist from Manhattan who has attended eight of the ten Wonderful World of Words weekends, tells me, "I love this stuff. I write lyrics, which means my head is forever spinning, which is why I like to do puzzles. Attending the Wonderful Weekend of Words is like going to a health spa for your brain. The whole experience is yoga for the brain cells— a joyous stretch for the mind."

Jeannia Yapczenski, a fourth-grade teacher from Carteret, New York, has made the pilgrimage to New Paltz all ten years of its existence. "I'm a wordaholic," Jeannia tells me. "I find this weekend to be therapy, and so do others. People who meet here have occasional reunions in New York throughout the year. I love the games approach to life, and I wish there were more games and puzzle books for children."

The first gathering, in the spacious, oaken main hall, is for my opening talk, "From Bard to Verse," on the mind-boggling contributions of William Shakespeare to our English tongue (including the phrase *boggles the mind*). Other speakers who have been similarly inspired to lend their talents to the Wonderful World of Words weekend include Dick Cavett, Maura Jacobson, Edwin Newman, Will Weng, Willard Espy, Thomas Middleton, Peter Funk, and Paul Dickson. I can see why. It is always a pleasure to talk to word-lovers, but this eager, attentive, rollicking assemblage seems "gift-rapt" for a speaker who wants to share words about words. It is a rare honor to live and move and have one's being among such inveterate verbivores.

After my presentation, everyone gathers for an ice-breaking game (*break the ice* is another phrase that Shakespeare bequeathed us) invented by Gloria and Larry. Scramble Scrabble® is a team form of Scrabble allowing up to seventy-seven gamesters to play using giant tiles. Each team forms its word collectively, holds up the tiles, and receives a score.

A casually attired, bright-eyed man with a salt-and-pepper beard and keen gleam in his eye has not joined a group but is very much caught up in the game. In a crowd you would not pick him out as Stephen Sondheim, the brilliant, award-winning composer and lyricist, but when he talks about words and puzzles, you just know that this fellow does extraordinary things with language every day of his life.

Stephen walks around the Scramble Scrabble® room looking at everyone's words, obviously trying not to show approval or disapproval. At one point, clearly in considerable anguish, he rushes over to Gloria and laments, "That team has a seven-letter word and they don't know it!"

The next morning, Stephen lectures briefly about "Puzzles, Lyrics, and Other Word Games." "As a kid," he tells us, "I was always fascinated with words. Even before I could read, I could recognize songs by the length of the words. I have always seen words as collections of letters, a quirk in the head, like being double-jointed."

Most of Stephen's presentation is a question-and-answer session, and both the questions and the answers are scintillating. "To fit the meanings and syllables to the rise and fall of music is akin to constructing a crossword puzzle and fitting letters into grids," he explains. Such is this music man's fascination with creative word puzzles that we learn that *West Side Story* could have been completed two weeks earlier if Stephen and his collaborator, Leonard Bernstein, had not spent so much time working on cryptic crossword puzzles.

Mary Higgins Clark is the next Saturday-morning speaker. She is a thoroughly charming and down-to-earth woman, so friendly and sharing that it's hard to imagine her sitting alone plotting and writing about murders, which she accomplishes with considerable success—if you want to call being America's most widely read suspense writer a success! She talks about "The Mystery of Words," and she enthralls her audience.

Mary explains that she "was born into an Irish family, where words were the stuff and credence of life. How does an Irishman propose? He says, 'Would you care to be buried with me, mother?'

"Words are my business. I started reading from the time I could interpret two words together. And I've always been a writer. I started writing from day one."

I ask Mary how she got started as a writer. "I remember being asked by my sixth-grade teacher, Sister Mary Lorenzo, to write a paragraph using all twelve spelling words of the day. Then my teacher took me around to read the paragraph to all the classes. And it made me feel wonderful."

The next weekend attraction is the Saturday-afternoon Great American Will Shortz Team Treasure Hunt. Will Shortz is the senior editor of *Games* magazine and puzzlemeister on National Public Radio's "Weekend Edition." He has been making up posers since he was eight years old and selling them to national magazines since the age of fourteen. At Indiana University, he became the first and only person to major in puzzles and, in 1974, to receive a degree in enigmatology, the art and science of puzzle construction.

"I love to whack people on the side of the head and make them see words and language in a new way," Will explains to me during a brief interview. "Most people's jobs are not creative. They don't use their minds in fresh ways. By solving puzzles, they gain the pleasure of being creative."

Since the Wonderful World of Words weekend began in 1982, Will has been program leader and created and run the Treasure Hunt. The challenge is a tantalizing sequence of puzzles wherein teams must solve one enigma to get the clue to solve another enigma to get a clue, and so on. Contestants are rushing all over the hotel, up and down the stairs, in and out of public places, such as the gift shop, where magazines have been fanned out so that the initial letters of each title subtly spell out the acrostic PIANO IN TV ROOM. Although the prizes for winners of all weekend competitions are just games and books, you would think from the zeal and zest of the players that the big payoff is, at the very least, a trip to Paris.

The Sunday-morning session starts with yours truly expostulating on "The Play of Words"—homographs, homophones, double-sound puns, oxymora, contronyms, and spoonerisms. The verbivorous weekenders should by this time be whacked out on words, but the audience has not lost any of its enthusiasm, and the room is packed. Even those who must leave before lunch are in attendance, holding coats and hand luggage. It is gratifying to see that their joie de lex is not at all dimmed by the promises they have to keep to the outside world.

At the end of my talk Faire Hart, Mohonk's director of public relations, slips a note into my hand. Her dancing homophones and double-sound puns show that this fair heart, with her homophonous name, has thoroughly imbibed the spirit of my presentation: "Deer Rich heard, Eye deed knot no weather two scent ewe eh Lederer too tank ewe four thee wheeze dumb. Aye dee sided knot two. —Sin Sear Lie, eh Neo Fight"

After so many years of overseeing the Wonderful World of Words weekend, Faire is surely more than a neophyte, a down-to-earth word that has grown from two Greek word parts that mean "newly planted." The real neophytes at the wordy weekend have found that they can dig down to the roots of language and draw as much sustenance from words as do the most deeply planted wordophiles.

$\mathcal{T}$our of Duty: Labor of Love

$\mathcal{L}$ike Billy Pilgrim, in Kurt Vonnegut's *Slaughterhouse Five*, I often become unstuck in time.

I suddenly find myself at one o'clock in the morning on a Wednesday, which means that I must have just landed in Los Angeles. I've flown in from Denver, where I did an interview with the *Denver Post* and a signing at a Denver bookstore. On that same day, September 19, I have winged my way to Denver from Chicago, where I had done some radio work and book signings.

Or suddenly I am at the end of a three-week promotional tour for one of my books, having traveled from New York to Boston to Philadelphia to Washington, D.C., to Atlanta to Milwaukee to Chicago to Denver to Houston to Los Angeles to San Francisco to Seattle to Vancouver to Winnipeg to Toronto—one day at a time.

When I am on the road and in the air for one of my books, my life is run by my publicists, who lay out my itinerary with military precision. Incredibly, the plans

16

work. In the world of the book tour, airplanes really do arrive at times like 7:38 P.M., and the interviewers really do await me as my schedule promises.

On a typical day, I get into my hotel around two in the morning and whirl through the aborning day: 7:25–7:30 A.M.—a morning-drive radio show by telephone in my hotel room; 9:00–10:00 A.M.—a local television show; 10:30–10:45 A.M.—a nationally syndicated radio show by telephone; 11:00–11:30 A.M.—cable television; 12:00–12:30 P.M.—another cable television show; 1:30–2:15 P.M.—press interview on the telephone; 2:30–3:00 P.M.—local press interview by telephone; 5:00–5:30 P.M.—local radio show with call-ins; 5:45–6:15 P.M.—radio network taping; 8:00 P.M.—fly to the next city for an equally busy day.

Within the seams of this schedule I sign stock at up to a dozen area bookstores. Whenever I visit a city, I drop in wherever I can to scribble my name on the title pages of my writings. I genuinely enjoy meeting people who work with books, and my personal contact with them helps to purchase real estate—preferred shelf and window space in the Darwinian universe of the bookstore. In addition, signed books sell three times faster than unsigned ones and are far less likely to be shipped back to the warehouse. As publisher Alfred A. Knopf once quipped about the dread specter of returned books, "Gone today, here tomorrow."

Does all this sound like the Book Promotion Tour From Hell? It isn't, believe me. I love it. Sure, my two-to-three-week rips through the United States and Canada have their infernal aspects:

- Luggage that grows heavier each day and comes to weigh a hundred pounds;
- Clothing that becomes a trifle wrinkled and ripe;

- Talk-show hosts with glued-on smiles who start interviews with "Well, Richard, what is your book about?"—and I know that I'll have to slog through a half hour with someone who hasn't read my book or even the press kit.
- Fellow travelers on airplanes who ask me questions like "So you're a writer, eh? What do you do for a living?" and "Oh, you're a writer? I'd love to write a book." I have been an English teacher for almost three decades, and almost nobody has ever said, "Oh, you're a teacher. I'd love to be a teacher." That's a shame.
- The eerily mixed atmosphere of glitz and humiliation: Godiva chocolates on the pillow to greet my arrival at an elegant hotel room and a signing the next day during which I sit in the store for an interminable hour staring bleakly ahead. On the card table laden with my books is taped a sign that beckons MEET THE AUTHOR! Customer after customer enters the store, gives me a bewildered look, and moves on to buy a cat book or a greeting card. Sometimes only a half dozen of them come up to buy my book.

But I stand ready to do it again. A book tour is a wonderful privilege, an arrangement that costs a publishing house at least a thousand dollars a day and indicates its faith in the author's work and ability to promote that work. After sitting in front of a computer writing a book for a year or two, a few weeks on tour is neither a grueling ritual nor a substantial investment of my time.

Here is what I love about book tours:

- Writing is one-tenth inspiration and nine-tenths perspiration. As the novelist Thomas Mann once said, "A writer is someone for whom writing is harder than for other people." Aside from being sweaty and strenuous, writing is lonely work—a human being alone in a room with the English language trying to make it come out right. Some writers enjoy that splendid isolation; I prefer the sound and smell and energy of humanity. On the tour I meet scads of new people—bookstore managers, salespersons, and customers, radio and TV interviewers, cabbies, passengers on planes, and other touring authors. For that relief, much thanks.

◆ The new acquaintances I get to know best are my media escorts. About fifty thousand new books are published in the United States each year, and the authors of approximately a third of these releases tour to some extent. This activity has spawned a burgeoning industry of escorts—helpful outreaching people (almost all women) who meet me in front of my hotel each morning ("Look for a blonde in a gun-metal Subaru!") and trundle me from radio stations to TV stations to bookstores to newspapers, plying me on the run with sandwiches and sympathy. (Some of the guides are a trifle uncomfortable with the title *escort;* I've suggested *godmother* or, in that rare case, *godfather.*)

Kathi Kamen Goldmark, my San Francisco godmother, even provides me with a special "rescue me" pen mounted with a plastic, blond rock guitarist. If someone bothers me during a book signing, I am to take out the pen, a signal for my guardian to step forward and whisk me away to a fabricated telephone call. I have never had to use the pen.

◆ In some bookstores my books are displayed in the

same windows that exhibit the latest from the likes of Tom Clancy and Stephen King.

♦ People actually do show up for most of my book signings, and some of them tell me that they enjoy my work. Teachers are compulsive sharers. When I watch people at these events take away my books, quantities of something that I have *made*, I feel my teaching mission enlarged and replicated, feel the truth of Henry Adams's pronouncement: "A teacher affects eternity. No one knows where his influence ends."

♦ My luggage has never gotten lost.

♦ For the cover of my book *Crazy English* my artist, Dick Anderson, drew a caricature of me with an unapproachably slim body. Deciding that life would have to imitate Dick's art, I went on a diet and shed forty-five pounds. On tour a waist is a terrible thing to mind, but although I sampled every variety of honey-roasted peanut dispensed by America's flight attendants, I didn't gain weight.

Logging so many air miles, I have had ample opportunity to take a lot of notes about "plane talk," the loopy jargon of the airline industry. To learn how bizarre our English language really is, especially in matters of getting to and from airports, take flight with me on a typical tour day:

I wake up in my hotel room for the night, and I take the elevator down. Already that's odd because something that elevates goes up, so how can an elevator descend?

It does, though, and I get in a shuttle bus that goes back and forth to the airport terminal. Actually, it goes forth and back, since you have to go forth before you can go back. And I don't know about you, but that word *terminal* always scares me when it's in an airport.

On the way to the airport, the bus enters rush-hour traffic. Despite the word *hour,* I notice that, in most big cities, rush hour usually lasts more than sixty minutes. The bus gets caught in a big traffic bottleneck. But it's really a *small* traffic bottleneck because, literally, the bigger the bottleneck, the more easily the fluid flows through it. Yet you never hear anyone say, "Boy, this morning I got caught in one of the smallest traffic bottlenecks of my life!"

Now I'm at the terminal, and I go to the podium to confirm my ticket. Actually, it's a lectern. *Podium* issues from a Greek root that means "foot" and gives us the words *podiatrist* and, from the Latin, *pedestrian. Lectern* comes from the Latin root *lectura,* meaning "to read." Podiums (*podia* if you're a purist) you stand on; lecterns you stand behind.

I ask the airline official behind the lectern if I am on a nonstop flight. Fortunately, she says that I am not. That's good because I want the flight to stop somewhere. The trouble with nonstop flights is that you never get down.

At any rate, the voice on the public address system announces that it's time to preboard. *Preboard* strikes me as something that people do before they board, but I notice that those who are preboarding are really boarding.

Then it's time for the rest of us to get on the plane. I don't know about you, but I don't get *on* a plane; I get *in* a plane.

As I enter, one of the flight attendants (they used to be stewardesses, but I think the popularity of the androgynous job description is a useful innovation) cautions me, "Watch your head." I jerk my head around, but I am still unable to watch it. Trying to watch your head is like trying to bite your teeth.

On the flight, I pray that we won't have a near miss. *Near miss* is an expression that has grown up since World War II, but logically a near miss is a collision. *Near hit* is the more accurate term, and I hope to avoid one of those, too.

Then comes the most chilling moment of all. The dulcet voice on the airplane intercom announces that we should fasten our seat belts and secure our carry-on bags because we are beginning our "final descent." *Final descent!* Boy, does that sound ominous. I pray that my fellow passengers and I will live to experience other descents in our lives.

Incredibly, the aircraft touches down with all of us alive and begins to taxi on the runway. (If planes taxi on runways, I wonder, do taxis plane on streets?) Now the same voice asks us to keep our seat belts fastened until the aircraft (never just *airplane*) "comes to a complete stop." That reassures me, as I wouldn't want the vehicle to come to "a partial stop," which, of course, would be an oxymoron.

Finally, the vehicle does stop, and we are told that we can safely deplane. After that, I'll decab, decar, or debus and enter another hotel. The next morning I'll wake up to face another day of plane talk.

After forty-eight continuous, contiguous, consecutive years of being in a classroom as a student or teacher, I, like the poet in the yellow wood, have taken the divergent road. As Robert Frost tells us, that makes "all the difference." So far, I'm loving that difference.

*A*ll-American
Dialects

*I*n addition to going on book tours, I run around the country speaking to groups of teachers, students, librarians, women's clubbers, guild professionals, and businesspersons. These good people go to all the trouble of putting together meetings and conferences, and I walk in, share my thoughts about language in their lives, and imbibe their collective energy and synergy. I will go anywhere to spread the word about words, and in going anywhere from California to the New York Island, from the redwood forest to the Gulf Stream waters, I hear America singing. We are teeming nations within a nation, a nation that is like a world. We talk in melodies of infinite variety; we dance to their sundry measures and lyrics.

Midway through John Steinbeck's epic novel *The Grapes of Wrath*, young Ivy observes, "Ever'body says words different. Arkansas folks says 'em different, and Oklahomy folks says 'em different. And we seen a lady from Massachusetts, an' she said 'em differentest of all. Couldn't hardly make out what she was sayin'."

23

One aspect of American rugged individualism is that not all of us say the same word in the same way. Sometimes we don't even use the same name for the same object.

I was born and grew up in Philadelphia a coon's age, a blue moon, and a month of Sundays ago—when Hector was a pup. "Phillufia," or "Philly," which is what we kids called the city, was where the epicurean delight made with cold cuts, cheese, tomatoes, pickles, and onions stuffed into a long, hard-crusted Italian bread loaf was invented.

The creation of that sandwich took place in the Italian pushcart section of the city, known as Hog Island. Some linguists contend that it was but a short leap from *Hog Island* to *hoagie,* while others claim that the label *hoagie* arose because only a hog had the appetite or the technique to eat one properly.

As a young adult I moved to northern New England ("N'Hampsha," to be specific), where the same sandwich designed to be a meal in itself is called a grinder—because you need a good set of grinders to chew them. But my travels around the United States have revealed that the hoagie or grinder is called at least a dozen other names—a bomber, Cuban sandwich, Garibaldi (after the Italian liberator), hero, Italian sandwich, rocket, sub, submarine, torpedo, wedge, wedgie, and, in the deep South, a poor-boy (usually pronounced "poh-boy").

In Philadelphia, we wash our hoagies down with soda. In New England we do it with tonic, and by that word I don't mean medicine. Soda and tonic in other parts are known as pop, soda pop, a soft drink, Coke, and dope.

In our little corner of the country, we take the term *milk shake* quite literally. To many of us residing in these parts, a milk shake consists of milk mixed with flavored syrup—and nothing more—shaken up until foamy. If you live in Rhode Island or in southern Massachusetts and you want ice cream in your milk drink, you ask for a cabinet (named after the square wooden cabinet in which the mixer was encased). If you live farther north, you order a velvet or a frappé (from the French *frapper*, "to ice").

Clear—or is it clean?—or is it plumb?—across the nation, Americans sure do talk "different." Perhaps you've heard about the senior editor of a dictionary of American dialects who assumed room temperature, bit the dust, bought the dirt condo, bought the farm, breathed his last, came to the end of the road, cashed in his chips, cooled off, croaked, deep-sixed, gave up the ghost, headed for the hearse, headed for the last roundup, kicked off, kicked the bucket, lay down one last time, lay with the lilies, left this mortal plain, met his maker, met Mr. Jordan, passed away, passed in his checks, passed on, pushes up daisies, returned to dust, sleeps with the fishes, slipped his cable, sprouted wings, took the last count, traveled to kingdom come, turned up his toes, went across the creek, belly-up, the way of all flesh, to glory, to his final reward, and west— and, of course, died.

What do you call those flat, doughy things you often eat for breakfast—battercakes, flannel cakes, flapjacks, fritters, griddle cakes, or pancakes?

Is that strip of grass between the street and the sidewalk a berm, boulevard, boulevard strip, city strip, devil strip, green belt, the parking, the parking strip, parkway, sidewalk plot, strip, swale, tree bank, or tree lawn?

Is the part of the highway that separates the northbound lanes from the southbound lanes the centerline, center strip, mall, medial strip, median strip, medium strip, or neutral ground?

Is it a cock horse, dandle, hicky horse, horse, horse tilt, ridy horse, seesaw, teeter, teeterboard, teetering board, teetering horse, teeter-totter, tilt, tilting board, tinter, tinter board, or tippity bounce?

Do fisherpersons employ an angledog, angleworm, baitworm, earthworm, eaceworm, fishworm, mudworm, rainworm, or redworm? Is a larger worm a dew worm, night crawler, night walker, or town worm?

Is it a crabfish, clawfish, craw, crawdab, crawdad, crawdaddy, crawfish, crawler, crayfish, creekcrab, crowfish, freshwater lobster, ghost shrimp, mudbug, spiny lobster, or yabby?

Depends where you live and who or whom it is you're talking to.

I figger, figure, guess, imagine, opine, reckon, and suspect that my being bullheaded, contrary, headstrong, muley, mulish, ornery, otsny, pigheaded, set, sot, stubborn, or utsy about this whole matter of dialects makes you sick to, in, or at your stomach.

But I assure you that, when it comes to American dialects, I'm not speaking fahdoodle, flumaddiddle, flummydiddle, or flurriddiddle—translation: nonsense. I'm no all-thumbs-and-no-fingers, all-knees-and-elbows, all-left-feet, antigoddling, bumfuzzled, discombobulated, flusterated, or foozled bumpkin, clodhopper, country jake, hayseed, hick, hillbilly, hoosier, jackpine savage, mossback, mountain-boomer, pumpkinhusker, rail-splitter, rube, sodbuster, stump farmer, swamp angel, yahoo, or yokel.

The biblical book of Judges (12:4–6) tells us how one group of speakers used the word *shibboleth*, Hebrew for "stream," as a military password. The Gileadites had defeated the Ephraimites in battle and were holding some narrow places on the Jordan River that the fleeing Ephraimites had to cross to get home. In those days it was hard to tell one kind of soldier from another because soldiers didn't wear uniforms.

The Gileadites knew that the Ephraimites spoke a slightly different dialect of Hebrew and could be recognized by their inability to pronounce an initial _sh_ sound. Thus, each time a soldier wanted to cross the river, "the men of Gilead said unto him, Art thou an Ephraimite? If he said, Nay, then they said unto him, Say now Shibboleth: and he said Sibboleth: for he could not frame to pronounce it right. Then they took him and slew him at the passages of Jordan: and there fell at that time of the Ephraimites forty and two thousand."

During World War II, some American officers adapted the strategy of the Old Testament Gileadites. Knowing that many Japanese have difficulty pronouncing the letter _l_, these officers instructed their sentries to use only passwords that had _l_'s in them, such as _lallapalooza_. The closest the Japanese got to the sentries was _rarraparooza_.

These days English speakers don't get slaughtered for pronouncing their words differently from other English speakers, but the way those words sound can be labeled "funny" or "quaint" or "out of touch." In George Bernard Shaw's play _Pygmalion_, Prof. Henry Higgins rails at Liza Doolittle and her cockney accent: "A woman who utters such depressing and disgusting sounds has no right to be anywhere—no right to live. Remember that you are a human being with a soul and the divine gift of articulate speech: that your native language is the language of Shakespeare and Milton and The Bible; and don't sit there crooning like a bilious pigeon!"

Most of us are aware that large numbers of people in the United States speak very differently from the way we do. Most of us tend to feel that the way "we" talk is right, and the way "they" talk is funny. "They," of course, refers to anyone who differs from us.

If you ask most adults what a dialect is, they will tell you it is what somebody else in another region passes off as English. These regions tend to be exotic places such as Mississippi or Texas—or Brooklyn, where *oil* is a rank of nobility and *earl* is a black, sticky substance.

It is reported that many Southerners reacted to the elections of Jimmy Carter and Bill Clinton by saying, "Well, at last we have a president who talks without an accent." Actually, Southerners, like everyone else, do speak with an accent, as witness these tongue-in-cheek entries in our *Dictionary of Southernisms:*

ah: organ for seeing
are: sixty minutes
arn: ferrous metal
ass: frozen water
ast: questioned
bane: small, kidney-shaped vegetable
bar: seek and receive a loan; grizzly
bold: heated in water
card: one who lacks courage
farst: a lot of trees
fur: distance
har: to employ
hep: to assist
hire yew: a greeting
paw tree: verse
rat: opposite of *lef*
reckanize: to see
tarred: exhausted
t'mar: day following t'day
thang: item
thank: to cogitate

Any glossary of Southernspeak would be incomplete without *"yawl:* a bunch of you's." When I visited Alex-

andria, Louisiana, a local pastor offered me proof that
y'all has biblical origins, especially in the letters of the
apostle Paul: "We give thanks to God always for you all,
making mention of you in our prayers" (First Epistle to
the Thessalonians, 1:2) and "First, I thank my God
through Jesus Christ for you all" (First Epistle to the Romans, 1:8). "Obviously," the good reverend told me,
"St. Paul was a Southerner." Then he added, "Thank
you, Yankee visitor, for appreciating our beloved Southernspeak. We couldn't talk without it!"

An anonymous poem that I came upon in Louisville
clarifies the plural use of the one-syllable pronoun *y'all:*

> *Y'all gather 'round from far and near,*
> *Both city folk and rural,*
> *And listen while I tell you this:*
> *The pronoun* y'all *is plural.*
>
> *If I should utter, "Y'all come down,*
> *Or we-all shall be lonely,"*
> *I mean at least a couple folks,*
> *And not one person only.*
>
> *If I should say to Hiram Jones,*
> *"I think that y'all are lazy,"*
> *Or "Will y'all let me use y'all's knife?"*
> *He'd think that I was crazy.*
>
> *Don't think I mean to criticize*
> *Or that I'm full of gall,*
> *But when we speak of one alone,*
> *We all say "you," not "y'all."*

If the truth about dialects be told, we New Englanders also have accents. Many of us, particularly in eastern
New England, drop the *r* in *cart* and *farm* and say *caht*

and *fahm*. Thus, the Midwesterner's "park the car in Harvard Yard" becomes our "pahk the cah in Hahvahd Yahd." A number of New Englanders, including the famous Kennedy family of Massachusetts, add *r*'s to words, such as *idear* and *Cuber*, if the sound comes before a vowel or at the end of a sentence.

When an amnesia victim appeared at a truck stop in Missouri in the fall of 1987, authorities vainly tried to help her discover her identity. Even after three months, police "ran into a brick wall," according to the *Columbia Daily Tribune*. Then, linguist Donald Lance of the University of Missouri–Columbia was called in to analyze her speech. After only a few sentences, Lance recognized the woman's west-Pennsylvania dialect, and, within one month, police in Pittsburgh located the woman's family.

Among the clues used to pinpoint the woman's origin was the west-Pennsylvanian use of *greezy*, instead of *greacey*, and *teeter-totter*, rather than *seesaw*. Dialectologists know that people who pronounce the word as *greezy* usually live south of a line that wiggles across the northern parts of New Jersey, Pennsylvania, Ohio, Indiana, and Illinois.

Linguist Roger Shuy writes about the reactions of Illinois people in a 1962 survey of regional pronunciations, including the soundings of *greasy*: "The northern Illinois informants felt the southern pronunciation was crude and ugly; it made them think of a very messy, dirty, sticky, smelly frying pan. To the southern and midland speakers, however, the northern pronunciation connoted a messy, dirty, sticky, smelly skillet."

Now is the time to face the fact that you speak a dialect. When you learned language, you learned it as a dialect; if you don't speak a dialect, you don't speak. *Dialect* isn't a label for careless, unlettered, nonstandard speech. A dialect isn't something to be avoided or cured. Each language is a great pie. Each slice of that pie is a dialect, and no single slice is the language. Don't try to change your language into the kind of English that nobody really speaks. Be proud of your slice of the pie.

In the early 1960s, Steinbeck decided to rediscover America in a camper with his French poodle Charlie. The writer reported his observations in a book called *Travels With Charlie* and included these thoughts on American dialects: "One of my purposes was to listen, to hear speech, accent, speech rhythms, overtones, and emphasis. For speech is so much more than words and sentences. I did listen everywhere. It seemed to me that regional speech is in the process of disappearing, not gone but going. Forty years of radio and twenty years of television must have this impact. Communications must destroy localness by a slow, inevitable process.

"I can remember a time when I could almost pinpoint a man's place of origin by his speech. That is growing more difficult now and will in some foreseeable future become impossible. It is a rare house or building that is not rigged with spiky combers of the air. Radio and television speech becomes standardized, perhaps better English than we have ever used. Just as our bread, mixed and baked, packaged and sold without benefit of accident or human frailty, is uniformly good and uniformly tasteless, so will our speech become one speech."

Thirty years have passed since Steinbeck made that observation, and the hum and buzz of electronic voices has since permeated almost every home across our nation. Formerly, the psalmist tells us, the voice of the turtle was heard in the land, but now it is the voice of the broadcaster, with his or her immaculately groomed diction. I hope that American English does not turn into a bland, homogenized, pasteurized, assembly-line product. May our bodacious American English remain tasty and nourishing—full of flavor, variety, and local ingredients.

Radio Days

"I love radio people," says Richard Lederer ex-statically. In the hundreds of in-studio and on-the-telephone interviews that I have done with radio broadcasters around the United States and Canada, I have discovered that the English language is in good mouths with radio people. Almost all the radio folk who have interviewed me have actually read the book we're supposed to be talking about and have been genuinely excited about the material. I have been delighted, but not surprised; words are the stuff that radio is made on, and radio broadcasters earn their livings painting pictures with words.

Thanks to the magic of teleconferencing, often the format for a given show is call-in, and the phones and airwaves crackle with logolepsy. I am often asked if I miss teaching; my happy experiences on the radio have led me to answer, "I haven't left teaching." In a less intimate but broader way, I now reach more people in a month than in a lifetime of teaching, especially through my regular shows on New York, Wisconsin, St. Louis, Los Angeles, and New Hampshire public and commercial radio.

At times, the teacher becomes the student, and I learn something new from the callers. Once on "New York and Company," the popular New York public-radio call-in show hosted by Leonard Lopate, a listener called wanting to know my opinion of the origin of the phrase *the spitting image.* I offered two possible explanations: One theory maintains that *the spitting image* is derived from *the spirit and image* (the inner and outer likeness) and that in Renaissance English and Southern American speech *spirit* became *spi'it,* with the *r* dropped. A second hypothesis proposes that *spitting* really means what it says and that *the spitting image* carries the notion of the offspring's being "identical even down to the spit" of the parent.

Immediately the WNYC switchboard calls lit up with listeners eager to expound their theories. Quoting idioms from various languages, callers demonstrated that the metaphor is truly salivary. In French, for example, the expression is *C'est son père tout craché.* ("He is his father all spat out.") Great expectorations! For the first time I could be certain that the second explanation of *the spitting image* was the correct one.

While I was doing a show via telephone with host Davis Rankin on KURV, a small station in southwest Texas, a listener called to ask about the origin of the word *malarkey.* I responded that I had consulted many reputable dictionaries about this word, and all had sighed "origin unknown." A few minutes later a caller named Lynn got on the line to disagree. She claimed that she was descended from an Irish family named Malarkey, in which the men were reputed for their great

size and athletic feats. As tall Irish tales about the Ma-
larkeys' prowess spread, *malarkey* came to be a synonym
for *blarney*, another word of Irish descent, originating
with the Blarney stone, at Blarney Castle, near Cork.
Those who are courageous enough to hang by their
heels and kiss the stone are rewarded with the gift of
persuasive gab.

Who knows? Lynn's explanation could be a bunch of
malarkey, or she could know whereof she speaks. If she
is right, she has enriched our knowledge of the origins
and development of a beguiling English word.

One of my favorite forums (or *fora*, if you're a purist)
for interviews and call-ins is the "Jim Bohannon Show,"
on which I've had the great pleasure of appearing several times. Jim is the exuberant and highly verbivorous
host of the three-hour talk show that airs from Washington, D.C., on the Mutual Broadcasting Network. The
"Jim Bohannon Show" is on a clear channel that reaches
almost every state in the USA, and when Jim opens the
lines for callers, the in-studio telephone board incan-
desces. From Maine to California, from Florida to Washington State, one can hear the multifold accents and
concerns that reflect a sprawling and diverse nation of
speakers. Best of all, Jim doesn't just interview me; he
himself enters into the spirit of the wordplay. Here, just
about verbatim and with a minimum of cutting and pol-
ishing, is a swatch of call-ins and responses that illustrate just how lively and well is the state of the English
language in our states. Jim's opening interview with me
has just ended, and we go to the call-in segment of the
show:

JB: All right, your turn. Let's go to the phones right
now. The number is 703-685-2177. Hello, Portland,
Oregon.

Caller: Hi. Why does no word rhyme with *orange?*

RL: It's not true that no word rhymes with *orange*. You see, Jim, there are a number of words that are famous for being unrhymable, and the two most famous are *orange* and *silver*. However, there was a man—I'm not kidding—named Henry Honeychurch Gorringe. He was a naval commander who in the midnineteenth century oversaw the transport of Cleopatra's Needle to New York's Central Park. Pouncing on this event, the poet Arthur Guiterman wrote:

> *In Sparkhill buried lies a man of mark*
> *Who brought the Obelisk to Central Park,*
> *Redoubtable Commander H.H. Gorringe,*
> *Whose name supplies the long-sought rhyme for* orange.

Or you can bend the rules of line breaks and sound as Willard Espy did:

> *Four eng-*
> *ineers*
> *Wear orange*
> *brassieres.*

So *orange* is rhymable.

Caller: And I have a pun for you: Why is Daffy Duck so daffy? Because he smokes quack.

RL: Very good. Now, I've got a duck pun for you. Who was the only duck president of the United States, sir?

Caller: Abraham Lincoln?

RL: Pretty close. Mallard Fillmore. You can't duck that one.

JB: And there was the great duck explorer—Francis Drake. . . . Philadelphia, you're on the air.

Caller: What is a thirteen-letter word in which the first eight letters mean "the largest," and the complete word means "the smallest"?

RL: Oh, boy, you've got me.

JB: Oh, I know—*infinitesimal.*

Caller: Correct. You're too good, Jim.

JB: Kansas City is next as we talk with Richard Lederer.

Caller: There was a little country that was chastised by all the other countries because it was a bad little country. The other countries wouldn't throw any commerce the little country's way, so it kept yelling, "O grab me! O grab me!" Well, all the other countries thought that turning the tables was fair play, so here's what they did: "Embargo."

RL: That's a very clever semordnilap, a palindrome that reads backwards. *Embargo* is "O grab me" reversed.

JB: Nashua, New Hampshire, you're on the air.

RL: Woooo, Nashua, one of *my* people.

Caller: Yes, a fellow Granite Stater.

RL: We take nothing for granite there. Go ahead.

Caller: What's the deal between "I could care less" and "I couldn't care less"?

RL: The deal is that logically you couldn't care less. If you say that you could care less, then you care to some extent and are being careless about "care less." But remember, sir, that negatives are very unstable in English, so we say "Let's see if we can't do it" when we mean "Let's see if we can do it." Or "I really miss not seeing you" really means "I really miss seeing you."

JB: We go to Houston next, hello.

Caller: I'm a big fan of puns. We use them a lot at work. They're good for cutting the seriousness away from things. One of the little things we do at work: We take a phrase like *the leading edge of technology,* and we say, "Bakers are on the kneading edge of technology," "Taxicab drivers are on the fleeting edge of technology," and "Lawyers are on the pleading edge of technology."

JB: And doctors are on the bleeding edge of technology.

RL: Stockbrokers are on the greeding edge of technology.

Caller: And gardeners are on the weeding edge.

RL: Or on the seeding edge.

JB: And very shortly after this show, we're going to have an announcer on the reading edge. He's going to update us on the news. Sault Sainte Marie, Canada, you're next with Richard Lederer.

Caller: I just wanted to ask Richard a couple of spelling words. What do the letters M-A-C-D-U-F-F spell?

RL: Macduff.

Caller: And what does M-A-C-I-N-T-O-S-H spell?

RL: Macintosh.

Caller: And what does M-A-C-H-I-N-E-R-Y spell?

RL: I don't want to ruin your night, ma'am, but it's *machinery,* not *MacHinery.*

JB: We go to Hamden, Connecticut.

Caller: Heaveno, Jim; heaveno, Richard.

JB: This is a man who does not like to say "hello" because this is a family program. He prefers to say "heaveno."

Caller: There are three groups of words: *sun* and *fun,* which are similar; *woo* and *wound,* which are opposites; and *toast* and *coast,* which are unrelated. It seems that in a good language words that sound the same should mean the same.

RL: I beg to differ. Language reflects the fearful asymmetry of the human race, and you can't get that kind of logic. In a perfectly logical language, if *pro* and *con* are opposites, then is *congress* the opposite of *progress*? I mean we have a language in which "What's going on?" and "What's coming off?" mean the same thing, while a wise man and a wise guy are opposites, a language in which the third hand on a clock or watch is called the second hand, and your nose can run and your feet smell. I'm not looking for logic in language because human beings, not computers, make language, and we're not logical.

JB: Indianapolis, you're on the air with the "Jim Bohannon Show."

Caller: Why did they use to name hurricanes with female names? Because otherwise they'd have been him-icanes. The reason I called is—I thought you'd get a kick out of this—I can't see, and every once in a while I meet a young lady that I'd like to get acquainted with, and my favorite line is, "Would you like a blind date?"

RL: Very funny. You are sightless, sir?

Caller: Yes, I am. And I have run into—oops, there's another figure of speech—some short women. I'm presently dating a girl who's four foot three, and I told her that it's better to have loved a short girl than never to have loved a tall.

RL: Oooooh, this guy is very good. Have you heard about the blind fellow who takes his Seeing Eye dog into a store and the man picks up the dog and whirls it around over his head. The shopkeeper asks, "What are you doing?" And the blind man says . . .

Caller: "We're just browsing."

JB: This is Baltimore next.

Caller: Mr. Bohannon, I'd like to ask Mr. Lederer a question about words. There are three words in the English language that end in G-R-Y. Two of them are *angry* and *hungry*. What is the third?

RL: Thank you for asking that, sir. You have given me a wonderful opportunity to perform a great service to the American people because what you are quoting is one of the most outrageous linguistic hoaxes in this country.

The answer is that there is no answer, at least no satisfactory answer. May I advise anybody who happens on the *angry plus hungry plus what?* poser, which slithered onto the American scene around 1975, to stop wasting time and to move on to a more productive activity, like counting the number of angels on the head of a pin or searching for a way to write the sentence "There are three *two*s (*to*'s, *too*'s) in the English language."

There are at least fifty *-gry* words in addition to *angry* and *hungry*, and every one of them is either a variant spelling, as in *augry* for *augury*, *begry* for *beggary*, and *bewgry* for *buggery*, or ridiculously obscure, as in *anhungry*, an obsolete synonym for *hungry*; *aggry*, a kind of variegated glass bead much in use in the Gold Coast of West Africa; *puggry*, a Hindu scarf wrapped around the helmet or hat and trailing down the back to keep the hot sun off one's neck; or *gry*, a medieval unit of measurement equaling one-tenth of a line.

A much better puzzle of this type is, name a common word, besides *tremendous*, *stupendous*, and *horrendous*, that ends in *-dous*. Why don't we invite the callers to submit their opinions on this one?

JB: West Palm Beach, Florida, you're next.
Caller: Yes, Mr. Lederer, does a person graduate college or graduate from college?
RL: Or is the person graduated from college? Logically, one is graduated from college since the college confers the degree on the students. That has changed, and educated people are perfectly comfortable with

the active-voice "graduate from college." I'd avoid "graduate college." It's awkward and sounds as if the person is doing the graduating of the institution.

JB: Athens, Georgia, you're on the air.

Caller: I have two for Mr. Lederer. A member of a New York state family had committed a murder and been electrocuted in the electric chair at Sing Sing. To put the best face on the affair, this man's descendants would say that the man once occupied the chair of applied electricity in one of the state's leading institutions.

RL: A wonderful example of a euphemism, calling a spade a heart. What's your other contribution?

Caller: This is a bilingual pun. There was this snail who came into an inheritance and decided to go to an automobile showroom and asks the price on a red convertible. "Fifty thousand dollars," he's told. So he peels off the fifty thousand and says, "Can you do me a favor?"

"Yes, sir," says the dealer, "what do you want?"

"How about you getting your body-and-paint man to paint me a capital *S*, for *snail*, on each door of this fancy car?" asks the snail.

"Sure, we can do that, but why?"

And the snail says, "When I ride down the boulevard in this fancy car, I want my friends to stare at each other and say, 'Look at the S car go!' "

JB: Gaithersburg, Maryland, you're on the air.

Caller: I want to share a true pun opportunity that came up many years ago. I was coordinating a serious business meeting, the attendance of which was supposed to include a gentleman named Cappella, and at the last minute we got a note that Mr. Cappella was unable to attend the meeting. I remarked that the meeting would have to be held a Cappella—and got nothing but cold stares.

RL: Your colleagues are just jealous. As Oscar Levant once said, "A pun is the lowest form of humor, when you don't think of it first."

JB: This is Clackamas, Oregon.

Caller: I've got one thing to ask. I used to tell quite a lot of puns myself, until I learned that there was some danger to it, so I gave them up. My main fear in the afterlife was eternal punnishment.

JB: We go to Austin, Texas. Richard Lederer is on with you. Hello.

Caller: Good evening. Did you ever get an answer for the fourth word ending in *-dous?*

JB: No, and thanks for reminding us. Okay, *tremendous, stupendous, horrendous*—and . . .

Caller: Hazardous.*

---

*At least thirty-two additional *-dous* words repose in various dictionaries: *apodous, arthropodous, blizzardous, cogitabundous, decapodous, frondous, gastropodous, heteropodous, hybridous, iodous, isopodous, jeopardous, lagopodous, lignipodous, molybdous, mucidous, multifidous, nefandous, nodous, octapodous, palladous, paludous, pudendous, repandous, rhodous, sauropodous, staganopodous, tetrapodous, thamphipodous, tylopodous, vanadous,* and *voudous.*

$\mathcal{J}$est for
the Pun of It

$\mathcal{O}$nce upon a time, the New Hampshire Lawn Tennis Association sponsored a slogan contest. From its beginnings, the organization's letterhead symbol had been two crossed tennis racquets, and the group's president offered a prize, a can of tennis balls, to the member who could serve up the spinniest slogan to go with the logo.

Since I have been an incorrigible (and encourageable) punster all my life, the challenge stirred my blood. As I bounced around a few ideas, I realized what a matchless set-up this contest was. With low overhead I could drive home my point for a net gain.

Immediately from my childhood I recalled the story of the two cats who were watching a tennis match. One turned to the other and said, "You know, my mother's in that racquet."

I was having a high-strung gut reaction.

Then I had a stroke of good luck. I decided to do some research for my slogan by reading the world's

43

greatest writers of tennis books. So I opunned the books of Robert W. *Service* and Miguel *Cerv*antes, Lord *By*ron and Richard *Lovelace*, Honoré de *Balzac* and Joseph *Addison*, and Ivy Compton Bur*net* and Kurt Vonne*gut*. And of course, I read the works of the two greatest authors of all time—Alfred, Lord Tennyson and Tennis E. Williams.

Now I was ready to write my slogans. Linesmen ready? Here they are:

"Shake hands with our racquet."

"We're dedicated to faultless services in New Hampshire."

"We deliver a smashing opportunity."

"Our service will improve your service."

Apparently the panel of judges reacted like a cross court. They wondered what the deuce I was doing writing these base lines. So, as a backhanded compliment, they declared as the winner my fifth slogan, the one that didn't have any pun in it at all: "The sport for a lifetime in the state for a lifetime." And why not? It was the one with the American twist!

Winning a slogan contest and a can of tennis balls isn't the only reward for a lifetime of being a jack-of-all-trades, master of pun. Early in 1989 I received a delicious invitation: "The International Save the Pun Foundation cordially invites you to the Fourth Annual Punsters Dinner at Mareva's Restaurant in Chicago. Special guest speaker John Crosbie, Founder and Chairman of the Bored, and Punster of the Year, Richard Lederer. Come pun, come all!"

Accompanying the invitation was a map of "Oh Pun Territory," marked by such features as Lord's Prairie, Forever Moor, Joan Rivers, Gerald and Henry Fjord, Sit-Up-Strait, Lloyd Bridges, Piggy Bank, Oh-Say-Can-You-Sea, Sexual Peak, Dis-a-Point, Psycho Path, Woody Allen, Gene Autree, W.C. Fields, Air-Plain, and George Bush. The date of the dinner was April Fools' Day, of course.

Yes, Virginia, there really is an International Save the Pun Foundation, a verbal glee club dedicated to wordy causes like preserving the pun as an endangered specious. At the very end of 1988 I received a letter from John Crosbie, the presiding gray eminence of the Pun Foundation and author of *Crosbie's Dictionary of Puns*, a veritable punster's bible. Mr. Crosbie's message began, "We are delighted to confirm that this Foundation has chosen you to receive its Punster of the Year Award for 1989, based on your latest book, *Get Thee to a Punnery*."

Thrilled to be designated as Attila the Pun, the fastest pun in the western world, I immediately sent off a reply that started with this salutation—

—a rebus that translates into "*Dear John Crosbie*." You'll get the idea of the whole letter from its first paragraph: "I am all charged up and positively ec-static about the electrifying news that you are planning to socket to me and plugging me to go on the circuit as your Punster of the Year. To re-fuse such a creative outlet would be re-volting to the point of battery. In short, I am de-lighted."

I know. You're a groan up who thinks that I'm a compulsive puntificator cursed with a pukish, not puckish, imagination. That's all right with me because I amused to wit and always bear in mind the slogan of the International Save the Pun Foundation: "A day without puns is a day without sunshine—There is gloom for improvement."

For all of us who have experienced the loneliness of the long distance punner, the dinner in Chicago was the farce that launched a thousand quips. More than two hundred loaded punslingers attended, pleased to have so many pun pals to go out wit.

Punning is a rewording experience. The inveterate (not invertebrate) punster believes that a good pun is like a good steak—a rare medium well done. In such a prey on words, *rare, medium,* and *well done* are double entendres, so that six meanings are crammed into the space ordinarily occupied by just three.

Punnery is largely the trick of compacting two or more ideas within a single word or expression. Punnery challenges us to apply the greatest pressure per square syllable of language. Punnery surprises us by flouting the law of nature that pretends that two things cannot occupy the same space at the same time. Punnery is an exercise of the mind at being concise.

During a question-and-answer session following a talk I once gave to the American College of Physicians in Washington, D.C., one of the good doctors asked me if there was such a thing as a perfect triple—three meanings inhabiting the same word. Now that is the kind of challenge that sets the true verbivore to salivating. In fact, as I worked on this puzzle over the next two years, I experienced great expectorations.

After hours and hours of diddling, I came up with what I believe is the perfect triple—a quick introduction to the *punch* line, and no forcing of any of the three puns: *Have you heard about the successful perfume manufacturer? His business made a lot of sense (scents, cents).*

With the world's largest vocabulary (more than three times as many words as German, in second place), English is the most marvelous language in the world in which to pun. To illustrate that claim, allow me to take you on a tour of homophones—words that are pronounced the same but are spelled differently and with different meanings.

What do these twenty words have in common?

aisle	llama
hour	psalter
knap	scent
knave	whole
kneed	wrap
knew	wrest
knickers	wretch
knight	wright
knit	write
knot	wrote

The answer is that in each case if the first letter of each word is removed (those who play word games call this process a beheadment), what remains is a homophone of the original word.

Now take a look at another list of twenty words, and decide what the cluster has in common homophonically:

add	flue
bee	fore
belle	inn
block	lamb
borne	lapse
butt	ore
bye	please
canvass	sow
caste	too
damn	wee

The answer is that when the *last* letter of each word is removed (curtailed), what emerges is a homophone of the original word.

What do these twenty words have in common? This time, you'll find the answer on page 161 of "Answers and Explanations I":

bear	reed
break	rude
gale	ruse
great	seer
hide	steak
hose	steel
meet	tale
ore	tear
pare	tide
pride	wear

Now do the same with this list, checking in "Answers and Explanations I":

aunt	maize
boarder	mined
buoy	mooed
callous	mourning
cannon	oar
choral	read
fined	reign
guild	seamen
hoarse	two
lead	waive

One of the flashiest and most pyrotechnic delights of our language is its uncommon stockpile of homophones, all lined up and ready to be pressed into service by the punster. What do you call a naked grizzly? A bare bear. What do you call a raspy-throated equine? A hoarse horse. *Bare-bear* and *hoarse-horse* are among the hundreds of same-sound-different-spelling pairs in the English vocabulary.

How many trios can you think of? It shouldn't be too difficult to capture two or three like the triple homophone lurking in this very sentence.

My pun pals and I came up with more than a hundred tight triads and fabulous foursomes! Notes on the diatonic scale (do, re, mi, etc.) are permitted, but no proper nouns, foreign words, regional pronunciations, archaisms, or letters of the alphabet are allowed, we'll say aloud. We worked into the wee hours of the morning, at which point we shouted, "Whee!" (Aha! Another triple play!) We hope you'll do the same before consulting "Answers and Explanations I."

The pun is mightier than the sword, and often sharper—and at the International Save the Pun Foundation fesitivities, one was much more likely to run into a pun than a sword, as everybody present took a blue ribbin'. The hours fled away because, as one frog said to the other, "Time's fun when you're having flies!" Put that one in your funny pile—and your punny file.

The highlight of the evening was the appearance of the pun made flesh in the person of Joyce Heitler, the president of the Chicago Chapter of the ISPF, who each year comes dressed as the Pun-Up Girl, attired in visual puns that the audience had to decipher. On her head Joyce wore a small weaving mechanism, translating to "frame of mind" or "hair loom." Her dress was splashed with dots and dashes—"dress code." On her finger Joyce wore a ring woven out of red hair—"red hair ring." Around her neck was a lace collar. An easy one: "neck-lace."

Joyce's most enticing sartorial challenge was that she claimed to be wearing a visual oxymoron—an outward and visible sign of two opposite ideas, such as *jumbo shrimp, pretty ugly,* or *old news.* I spotted an airless inner tube slung over Joyce's shoulder and under her arm.

"Flat busted!" I shouted, confident that I had identified the hidden oxymoron. "No, you silly," replied Joyce. "This is at-tire, or, if you wish, a boob tube," at which point this stud re-tired from the competition treading lightly. The oxymoronic solution reposed in the "loose tights" that Joyce was sporting.

Among the evening's delights was a Rap-Pun Contest (someone suggested "Rap-Pun-Sel") in which each table of pundits composed a string of puns to rap rhythms. One of the best raps included these verses of poetree. Try reading it aloud rap-aciously:

> *"Oh, Juniper, grow by my side."*
> *The Oak bent down to plant a kiss.*
> *"Someday we will exchange our boughs*
> *And live our lives in wooded bliss."*

> *Then Juniper axed her lover Oak*
> *In the morning forest dew,*
> *Willow bend your limbs abought me,*
> *Maple I wood pine fir yew."*

It didn't take long for the assembled pun ladies and pun gents to start testing their punupmanship by making up their ideal menu. As Francis Bacon once almost said, without hamming it up, some puns are to be tasted, others to be swallowed, and a few to be chewed and digested. Mareva's is living proof and reproof that a Polish gourmet restaurant is not an oxymoron, and, even though Joyce Heitler proclaimed, "We don't serve soup to nuts," a delicious borscht was brought out, inspiring one punhead to call out, "The heartbeet of America!" (The Foundation initially thought about holding the dinner in a new restaurant on the moon, a perfect place for a bunch of lunatics. But an investigation revealed that while the moonie restaurant has great food, it doesn't have any atmosphere.)

Then, just for the halibut, the international punsters took a Pole and came up with a number of fishy suggestions for an ideal punsters' menu, a buffet of sole food. Among the tour de farces highest on the scales of effishiency were "salmon rushdie," "tuna turner," "poisson ivy," "bass ackwards," "dill pickerel," "brain sturgeon," "combination lox," "porgy best," "turn pike," and "win one for the kipper." That night the world was our roister.

If you are one to carp about these finny lines, you must be hard of herring.

Teacher and author Robert Greenman takes a gamble with an analogy about punsters: "Punning is the natural act of people who like to play with words and who have the impromptu verbal dexterity to make strange, but often pointed, associations from plainly spoken statements. Their minds work like Las Vegas one-armed bandits, with plums and cherries and oranges spinning madly upon someone's utterance, searching for the right combination to connect on a pun."

Words are indeed constantly whirling about in my punster's brain. To most people *Norway, Israel, Pakistan, Uruguay, Jamaica, Germany, Haiti, Hungary, Turkey,* and *Greece* are simply the names of countries. For me they are words ready to be spun and aligned: Little Miss Muffet liked neither curds Norway. Your leather wallet is fake, but mine Israel. My backpack is dark brown, but your Pakistan. I'm a gal and Uruguay. I see your daughter is taking piano lessons. Jamaica do it? An antibody will kill a Germany time. I love coffee but I Haiti. On Thanksgiving I get Hungary for Turkey if it doesn't have too much Greece.

I am always eager that the results of my whirling puns will be fruitful—plums, not lemons. Like many puns, this one hits the etymological jackpot. The sense of *lemon* as "something that turns out badly" can be dated from the introduction of slot machines, on which any combination that includes a lemon is a loser.

I have mined my mind to come up with a game that I'm sure will be a winner. The challenge is the product of the way I hear and see words—words gyrating, words turned inside out, words standing on their heads.

Pretend that you are a newspaper editor and that part of your job is to manufacture clever headlines for news stories submitted to your desk. What punderful headline, for example, would you concoct for a story about a bunch of cattle placed in a satellite that is now orbiting the earth? Your creation might read THE HERD SHOT ROUND THE WORLD.

For another example, suppose you are assigned to headline a story about the fact that the film industry has been churning out lavish productions, such as the story of Peter Pan grown up and the saga of gangster Bugsy Siegel? You might try HOLLYWOOD IS GETTING US INTO THE THEATERS BY HOOK OR BY CROOK.

Here are twenty news stories that I've made up. Using the clues provided, create a punderful headline for each event. Then compare your responses with those in "Answers and Explanations I":

1. Educators argue the merits of using television in the classroom.

HEADLINE: _____ OR NOT _____ .

2. A four-foot-eight-inch clairvoyant is arrested for fraudulent business practices, but she escapes.

HEADLINE: SMALL MEDIUM _____ _____ .

3. Thanks to advances in science, the boll weevil is no longer a threat to cotton crops.

HEADLINE: FARMERS FEAR NO _____ .

4. A fancy new hotel is built featuring a grand ballroom in which to hold evening parties.

HEADLINE: A SITE FOR _____ .

5. Nine children are caught in an ocean undertow. At the last minute an ostrich gallops into the water and, with its long neck and powerful beak, pulls each child from the brine.

HEADLINE: _____ IN TIME _____ NINE.

6. The movie *Robin Hood* is banned in some cities because it contains too many fights, battles, and killings.

HEADLINE: MOVIE DEEMED TO HAVE TOO MUCH _____ VIOLENCE.

7. In front of the New York Public Library on Fifth Avenue, New Yorkers are often found sitting on the steps reading their books. On each side of the steps is a statue of a lion.

HEADLINE: NY'ERS ARE OFTEN FOUND _____ BETWEEN THE _____ .

8. A baker creates a cleaver that can cut four loaves of bread in a single chop.

HEADLINE: BAKER INVENTS A FOUR-_____ _____ .

9. Residents living near the track on which the Indianapolis 500 race is run are disgusted by the noxious fumes emanating from the race cars. They take their complaint to court.

HEADLINE: RESIDENTS SUE TRACK FOR _____ _____ EXPOSURE.

10. Newscaster Connie Chung starts a teakwood company.

HEADLINE: CHUNG _____ _____ .

11. A factory that makes balsa wood products goes up in flames.

HEADLINE: GREAT BALSA _____ .

12. A plant that manufactures small parts for Datsun automobiles explodes.

HEADLINE: IT RAINED DATSUN _____ .

13. A noted senator becomes the target of a merciless political cartoonist who depicts a silly-looking caricature of the man uttering a number of promises that he never kept.

HEADLINE: SENATOR IS DRAWN _____ .

14. A congregation paints its church and, to stay within budget, uses paint thinner. After a hard rain washes away all the paint, the congregants paint the church again, this time without thinner.

HEADLINE: CHURCH MEMBERS REPAINT AND _____ _____ _____ .

15. A music historian discovers that the composer Franz Joseph Haydn once had an affair with an East Indian woman.

HEADLINE: RESEARCHER DISCOVERS A HAYDN _____ AFFAIR.

16. A gardening expert advises homeowners to weed their vegetable patches frequently to achieve bountiful harvests.

HEADLINE: _____ 'EM AND _____ .

17. Queen Elizabeth denies all rumors that Prince Charles and Lady Diana are having marital troubles.

HEADLINE: ELIZABETH IS QUEEN OF _____ .

18. The Mercy Tea Company comes out with a new tea made from the juice of the koala bear. Customers soon discover that hair from the animal floats on top of the tea.

HEADLINE: THE KOALA _____ _____ _____
IS NOT _____ .

19. Lion meat becomes the latest culinary craze in the U.S. The beast is marinated in cognac for six hours before roasting.

HEADLINE: AMERICANS DINE ON THE _____
LION.

20. A national poll reveals that middle-aged men often fantasize about Jane Fonda.

HEADLINE: U.S. MEN HAVE A _____ CALLED FONDA.

$\mathcal{M}$y Son
the Poker Player

$\mathcal{I}$n May of 1987 my son, Howard Lederer, of New York City, made a pilgrimage to that windowless, clockless pleasure dome known as Las Vegas to compete in his first World Championship of Poker. Playing in a packed room at Binion's Horseshoe Casino in downtown Vegas, Howard was one of a record 152 entrants who each bought into the competition for $10,000. I'm pleased to report that my son became, at age twenty-three, the youngest player ever to reach the final table and ultimately placed fifth. Since then, Howard has gone on to win national tournaments with impressive names, such as the 1991 Diamond Jim Brady Texas Hold'em Shootout and the 1992 Four Queens Poker Classic in High-Limit Omaha. In the 1993 World Championships, he placed second in High-Limit Omaha and fourth in Seven-Card Stud.

People often ask me how I, a longtime English teacher at a church boarding school, react to my son's profession as a player of poker. The answer, in a phrase, is with great pride. I believe that each human being is born with a particular microchip in the brain and that we should spend our days applying that gift as fully as we can. I was a premedical student at Haverford College, and I went on to study at Harvard Law School. But I found myself reading the chemistry texts and the legal casebooks for their literary value, and I knew that something wasn't right. I began to realize that the microchip in my brain was calling me to a life of language (the word *vocation* derives from the Latin *vocare*, "to call"), and I decided to become an English teacher. I'm so lucky that I did: a career in medicine or law would have caused me to blush unseen and waste the sweetness of my life on the desert air. We each have but one life to live. For my son, gambling is the iron string to which his heart vibrates, and, for better or for best, it is at the poker tables he can most fully realize his human potential.

All the Lederer children grew up in a house of games. Beginning when the kids were quite young, their mother and I taught them to play verbal games such as ghost, inky-pinky, and Scrabble; board games such as Monopoly, checkers, and chess; and card games such as war, spit, go fish, oh hell, and hearts. In their early teens we taught them the rudiments of poker and bridge.

After graduating from St. Paul's School in 1982, Howard deferred attendance at Columbia University to hone his poker skills for a year. As that time drew to a close, we considered whether he should enter Columbia in September or pursue his poker full-time. I had watched him play and was awestruck by his precocious abilities in the game, so I looked at him and said, "Howard, shut up and deal." He's been doing just that ever since.

As a schoolmaster and my son's first poker mentor, I am button-burstingly proud of the precision with which my son has learned to practice his craft. When he telephoned me each night after his triumphs in the World Championship tournament, I could scarcely restrain myself from flying out to Vegas (without an airplane) to bask in the brightness of his achievement. To think that a child of my loins, a mere slip of a lad, could place fifth in a world championship. Moreover, Howard's $56,250 prize money warms the heart of a father who firmly believes that people should be rewarded for the sweat of their brains.

My son's enterprises at the poker tables of New York, Atlantic City, Las Vegas, and Los Angeles and my own adventures with linguistics may seem worlds apart, but they aren't, really. Both our passions involve a marriage of hardheaded statistical thinking, an intuitive playing of hunches, an endless search for patterns, and a reading of human behavior. Great poker players must have a firm grounding in the statistics of card distribution, but, as my son the poker player explains, "Weak players don't realize that they may hold the best cards in a situation where it appears that nobody has a very good hand. But somebody's got to win, yet the poor player will fold the cards too soon.

"To play poker at a high level is to read people," adds Howard. "If you see a guy in a game and his hands are trembling, he may well be holding real good cards, not the opposite, as you might think. But if a player is breathing irregularly, he's probably pushing his hand very hard. If he expels his breath as he collects his winning chips, you know he's been bluffing and you can make that part of the profile you're forming about him."

As a professional linguist, I have a library of hundreds of books in which to track down word and phrase origins. But, like my son the gambler, I cannot do my best work without staying in constant touch with people. I have always agreed with Walt Whitman, who yawped barbarically, "Language is not an abstract construction of the learned or of dictionary makers, but something arising out of the work, needs, joys, tears, affections, tastes of long generations of humanity, and has its bases broad and low, close to the ground."

I have received a number of inquiries asking the origin of the ubiquitous expression *the whole nine yards,* which means roughly the same as "whole hog" and "the whole ball of wax." Few of my elbow books offer any explanation at all, and those that do are often in conflict.

Some sources contend that bolts of cloth used to consist of nine yards and that only the fanciest dresses would require the whole bolt. Others inform us that some World War II fighter planes carried nine yards of belted ammunition. Pilots often boasted that they had "shot the whole nine yards." A third theory is that *the whole nine yards* refers to the amount of rock from a placer mine that can be loaded by two men during a shift, comparable to sixteen tons of coal. Yet a fourth view postulates that a three-masted square-rigger carried three yardarms on each mast, so the whole nine yards means that the sails were fully set to move the ship along rapidly or to change course.

I have never been completely satisfied with any of these explanations. My memory and my research tell me that *the whole nine yards* is fairly new to the American scene and does not reach far back into the argot of the dry-goods and sailing trades. H. L. Mencken, in his path-breaking *American English* (1919–51), never discusses the expression.

As I have interviewed dozens of workers in many fields, one trade has beckoned more persistently and beguilingly than the others—concrete mixing. A number of respondents in building and engineering have expressed a strong hunch that *the whole nine yards* refers to the huge mixing barrels perched on the backs of trucks at construction sites. The engineers and workers tell me that the revolving barrels attained a maximum volume of nine cubic yards during the 1960s, precisely the time when *the whole nine yards* achieved widespread popularity in American English. Others involved in construction inform me that, for safety reasons, the law prohibits filling a nine-cubic-yard barrel to its full capacity, so that *the whole nine yards* would indeed signify that one is really going all out, even beyond the letter of the law.

I still don't have a definitive explanation of *the whole nine yards,* but I'll keep on keeping on—listening, researching, and interviewing—hunting for a solution that will take the quest out of the realm of the abstract and into the concrete.

My son's poker and my adventures as a verbivore converge in yet another way, for a full deck of vivid words and phrases has made the trip from the poker table into our everyday conversation and writing. The color and high-risk excitement of poker inspired more than 180 players to invest a total of $1.8 million and change in the 1993 World Championships. These same qualities have made the language of poker one of the most pervasive metaphors in the English language that I so love.

The basic elements of poker are the cards, the chips, and the play of the hand. It has been a revelation for me to discover how each has become embedded in our daily parlance.

Beginning with the cards themselves, the verb *to discard* descends from *decard,* "away card," and first meant to reject a card from one's hand. Gradually, the meaning of *discard* broadened to include rejection beyond card-playing. A cardsharp who is out to cheat you may be dealing from the bottom of the deck and giving you a fast shuffle, in which case you may get lost in the shuffle. You might call such a low-down skunk *a four-flusher.* *Flush,* a hand of five cards that are all of one suit, flows from the Latin *fluxus, flux* because all the cards flow together. *Four-flusher* characterizes a poker player who pretends to such good fortune but in fact holds a worthless hand of four same-suit cards and one that doesn't match.

All of these terms originated with poker and other betting card games and have undergone a process that linguists call broadening. A good example of movement from one specific argot to another is *wild card berth* or *wild card player* as used in football and tennis.

Now that I've laid my cards on the table, let's see what happens when the chips are down. Why do we call a gilt-edged, sure-thing stock *a blue-chip stock?* Because poker chips are white, red, and blue, and the blue ones are the most valuable. Why, when we compare the value and power of two things, do we often ask how one *stacks up* against the other, as in "How do the Pistons stack up against the Lakers?" Here the reference is to the columns of chips piled up before the players seated around a poker table. These stacks of plastic betting markers also account for the expressions *bottom dollar* and *top dollar. Betting one's bottom dollar* means wagering the entire stack, and the top dollar, or chip, is the one that sits atop the highest pile on the table. Indeed, the metaphor of poker chips is so powerful that one of the euphemisms we use for death is *cashing in one's chips.*

The guts of poker is the betting. *You bet!* has become a standard affirmative expression in American English, and it is far from being the only betting metaphor that has traveled from the gaming halls to our common vocabulary. If you want to call my bluff on that one and insist that I put up or shut up, I'll be happy to put my money where my mouth is.

Say you're involved in a big business deal. You let the other guy know that you're not a piker running a penny-ante operation and that he'd better ante up big. One theory traces *piker*, one who habitually makes small bets, to westward migrants from Pike County, Missouri. These small farmers were less inclined than hardened veterans to risk high stakes, and the county name became eponymously synonymous with penny-pinching cheapness. *Ante*, from the Latin for "before," refers to chips placed in the middle of the poker table before the betting begins, so a penny-ante game is fit only for pikers.

The business negotiations continue, and you sweeten the pot by upping the stakes. You don't want to blow your wad, but you don't want to stand pat either. Rather than passing the buck, you play it close to the vest without showing your hand, maintain an inscrutable poker face, and keep everything aboveboard. If all goes well, you'll win the jackpot; if it doesn't, you might end up in the hole and in hock.

Stand pat comes from the strategy of keeping one's original (pat) hand in draw poker rather than making an exchange. Because cardsharps are known to engage in chicanery when their hands are out of sight and under the table, or board, *aboveboard* has come to mean open honesty and *under the table* the opposite. *Playing it close to the vest* ensures that no one else will peek at the contents of a player's hand. *Jackpot* originally described the reward to the big winner in a poker game and has gradually expanded to include the pots of gold in slot machines, game shows, and state lotteries.

Pass the buck is a common cliché that means "to shift

responsibility." But why, you may have asked yourself, should handing someone a dollar bill indicate that responsibility is in any way transferred? Once again the answer can be found in high-stakes gaming halls and riverboats. The *buck* in *pass the buck* was originally a poker term designating a marker that was placed in front of the player whose turn it was to deal the next hand. This was done to vary the order of betting and to keep one person from dealing all the time, thus cutting down on the chances of cheating. During the heyday of poker in the nineteenth century, the marker was often a hunting knife whose handle was made of a buck's horn. The marker defined the game as Buckhorn Poker, or Buck Poker, and gave us the expression *pass the buck*.

In the Old West, silver dollars were often used as markers, and these coins took on the slang name *buck* for their own. Pres. Harry S Truman adopted the now-famous motto "The buck stops here," meaning that the ultimate responsibility rested with the President. Before you began reading this chapter, that statement may have sounded like the taking of graft, with dollar bills ending up on someone's desk. But now that you know poker terminology, *pass the buck* and *the buck stops here* make perfect sense.

The hole in the phrase *in the hole* refers to a slot cut in the middle of nineteenth-century poker tables through which checks and cash were deposited into a box, to be transferred later to the coffers of the house. You can still find these holes in modern-day poker tables, and one deeply in debt has most of his or her money in the hole. *In hock* descends from the game of faro, a cousin of poker. The last card in the box was known as the hocketty card. The player who bet that card was said to be *in hock,* at a disadvantage that could lose him his shirt.

The cleverest application of poker terminology that I have ever encountered appears on the truck of a New Hampshire plumbing company: "A Flush Is Better Than a Full House." In poker that isn't true, but a homeowner would recognize its wisdom.

It's in the cards. You can bet on it.

$\mathcal{H}$aunted Words

$\mathcal{T}$o the man or woman who knows its origin, each word presents a picture, no matter how ordinary it may appear. Sometimes the attrition wrought by time and human memory has ravaged the images so that no trace is left. In other instances, surface grime can be wiped away so that the beauty of the details can be restored and the contours and colors can once again be seen.

For me, word pictures are like family snapshots. Discovering the origin of a word or phrase gives me the same pleasure I used to experience when my grandparents, parents, and older brothers and sisters would open up the family album, point to a cluster of sepia photographs, and tell me stories about the people gazing out from the pages. Hearing tales about those who came before me and uncovering those odd, buried, Old World family mysteries helped me to learn whence I came and who I am. Words too are our forebears. Most were born long before we were, and all bequeath us their rich legacies. Illuminating the faded picture of a time-hallowed word or phrase throws light on our history and our customs, our loving and fighting, our working and playing, our praying and our cursing.

Numbering my days figuring out words, I have come to see how the English language plays a figurative numbers game with us and how those numbers offer clues about our past. Hidden in the word *atonement*, for example, is the number one because *atonement*, in its original religious sense, meant "at-one-ment" with God. *Trivial* comes from the Latin *tri*, "three," and *via*, "way," and means literally "like something found at the place where three roads meet." In ancient times travelers and shoppers often tarried at intersections in order to exchange idle chitchat and gossip. Hence the definition of *trivial*, "common, insignificant." *Decimate*, from the Latin *decem*, "ten," arises from the Romans' nasty practice of maiming or slaying one out of every ten captive soldiers or mutineers. Some language purists insist that *decimate* should continue to apply only to situations in which exactly 10 percent of something is destroyed. In common usage, however, the word has come to mean "destroy a large part of," as in "the caterpillars have decimated the maple trees in our neighborhood."

The poet William Cowper once wrote of

> *philologists who trace*
> *A panting syllable through time and space,*
> *Start it at home, and hunt it in the dark*
> *To Gaul, to Greece, and into Noah's ark.*

As an avid wordhunter, I love stalking bestial words through time and flushing out the animals that live in the ark of language. Cranberries acquired their name from the Low German *kranbeere*, meaning "crane," because the plant flourishes in marshy lands frequented by cranes. The original scapegoat was an actual goat upon whose head were symbolically placed all the sins of the ancient Hebrew community. As we read in the book of Leviticus, the animal was allowed to "escape" into the wilderness, bearing the community's burden of sin and atoning for all its transgressions.

If a scapegoat was really a goat, one might wonder, does a dandelion have anything to do with lions? Most certainly. The English used to call the yellow, shaggy weed a "lion's tooth" because the indented ("made jagged, as with a tooth"), pointed leaves resemble the lion's snarly grin. During the early fourteenth century the lion's-tooth plant took on a French flavor and became the *dent-de-lion*, "tooth-of-the-lion." Then it acquired an English accent: *dandelion*.

Toothsome etymologies such as the one for *dandelion* were of great assistance when, early in the summer of 1992, I was invited to address the members of the New Hampshire Dental Society. A number of dentists will tell you that getting me to sit still in a dentist's chair is like pulling teeth. Still, I was delighted to find out that the oral metaphors in our language provided a topic that I could really get my teeth into.

At first I thought that such expressions would be as scarce as hen's teeth. (Hens, of course, don't have any teeth.) As I began collecting ideas for my talk, I vowed that I would give my eyeteeth for some good examples.

The eyeteeth, I discovered, are so called because they are located directly below the eyes in the upper jaw and are called canine teeth because they resemble the pointed teeth of dogs. As such, they are especially useful in holding and tearing food, and they are the most difficult and painful of teeth to extract. Thus, if you would give your eyeteeth for something, you are willing to go through a lot to relinquish something of great value.

Teeth are often cited to indicate strength. We talk about an agreement that has teeth in it and being in the teeth of a battle fighting tooth and nail. We describe strong winds and sarcastic comments as "biting."

Teeth are also associated with duplicity. We talk about people who "lie through their teeth," that is, who force themselves to assume a calm demeanor that will conceal their true feelings. They display a hearty smile, baring and clenching their teeth as a means of controlling their emotions and pretending that "butter wouldn't melt in their mouths." Closely related is the expression *to laugh on the wrong side of one's mouth*, which originally meant to laugh in a forced way, perhaps by opening only one corner of the mouth. "Which side of the mouth is the wrong side?" we wonder aloud.

Many phrases from the book of Job in the Old Testament have become proverbial in our language: "Naked came I from my mother's womb, and naked shall I return"; "The Lord gave, and the Lord hath taken away"; and "My bone cleaveth to my skin, and to my flesh, and I am escaped with the skin of my teeth." This last phrase has been altered slightly to *by the skin of my teeth*.

Despite objections that the teeth don't have any skin, centuries of Bible reading have given the expression a permanent place in our language as a description of a close escape. Many interpret the *skin* in *skin of my teeth* to refer to the enamel covering the teeth, a film as thin as Job's margin of safety.

As with *dandelion*, animals and teeth converge in *mastodon*, the name we assign to those lumbering pre-elephants. *Mastodon* is cobbled from the Greek *mastos*, "breast" (as in *mastectomy*) and *odont*, "tooth," as in *or-*

thodontia ("correct teeth"). Mastodons are so named for the nipplelike protuberances on their molars.

The space I've left at the start of each paragraph in this book is an *indentation*. When we indent a paragraph (from the Latin *dens*, "tooth," by way of the French *dent*), we take a chunk, or small bite, out of the beginning. *Indenture*, from the same root, strictly means "a document with serrated edges," referring to the once-common practice of cutting contracts into halves with jagged edges—one-half for each party to the agreement. By fitting the edges together, one could authenticate the document.

When we describe a golden-ager as "long in the tooth," we are reflecting the fact that our gums recede with age, thereby displaying more and more roots. It is the same with horses. The age and health of a horse can be ascertained by examining the condition and number of its teeth. Although an animal may appear young and frisky, a close inspection may reveal that it is "long in the tooth" and ready for the glue factory.

Still, it is considered bad manners to inspect the teeth of a horse that has been given to you and, by extension, to inquire too closely into the cost or value of any gift. Now you know the origin of *don't look a gift horse in the mouth,* one of our oldest proverbs, whinnying back at least 1,500 years.

But if you decide to pay money to a horse trader, you are advised to determine whether it is a young stud or an old nag by examining the teeth and obtaining your information "straight from the horse's mouth," precisely where responsible etymologists should look.

Tracking phrases to their original sources offers the intrepid wordhunter a journey of adventure and enlightenment, a veritable idioms delight. Late in 1989,

President Bush marked the twentieth anniversary of the first lunar landing by proposing that the United States establish a base on the moon as a stepping satellite for a manned (and womanned?) mission to Mars. Estimates of the total cost of Mr. Bush's expanded space program ran as high as $400 billion, moving House Majority Leader Richard Gephart of Missouri to warn, "Mr. President, there's no such thing as a free launch."

Surely Representative Gephart's waggish pun ranks as one of the wittiest tour de farces uttered by a modern American politician. To appreciate fully the Gephart riposte, one must, of course, be familiar with the claim "There's no such thing as a free lunch," a political aphorism now heard throughout the land.

As soon as I read the Gephart statement in the newspaper, I decided to track down the genesis of "There's no such thing as a free lunch." My search and research through several dictionaries of contemporary quotations led inevitably to Milton Friedman, the Nobel Prize–winning economist and informal adviser to Barry Goldwater and Richard Nixon. Dates of origin ranged from 1973, when Mr. Friedman granted a *Playboy* interview (reprinted in his book *There's No Such Thing as a Free Lunch*), to 1977, when, in the manner of the scholar Hillel, he stated to members of the Knesset Finance Committee in Jerusalem, "There's no such thing as a free lunch. That is the sum of my economic theory. The rest is elaboration."

But something seemed amiss here. Did this ubiquitous expression, I asked myself, really begin life as late as the 1970s? One telling fret in the etymological armor is that the acronym TANSTAAFL (for the more colloquial "There ain't no such thing as a free lunch") was popularized in Robert Heinlein's *The Moon Is a Harsh Mistress*, a science-fiction best-seller that first appeared in 1966.

Deciding to go straight to the source's mouth, I telephoned Milton Friedman's office at Stanford University, interrupting an assistant's lunch, which probably wasn't free. She explained that the staff received many calls and letters asking if Professor Friedman was indeed the maker of "There's no such thing as a free lunch" and assured me that, although he had popularized it in his widely read *Newsweek* columns, he was not the progenitor. She then referred me to *The New Palgrave: A Dictionary of Economics* (1987) and an article therein by Robert Hessen, which she asserted was the definitive statement on "free lunch."

Dr. Hessen does indeed sweep away all misconceptions in a concise, informative four-paragraph disquisition that begins: " 'There's no such thing as a free lunch' dates back to the early nineteenth century, when saloon and tavern owners advertised 'free' sandwiches and titbits to attract mid-day patrons. Anyone who ate without buying a beverage soon discovered that 'free lunch' wasn't to be taken literally; he would be tossed out unceremoniously." Dr. Hessen traces the passing of "free lunch" into the marketplace of ideas, beginning with the time of the New Deal, in which it meant that the welfare state is a "snare" and a delusion, and surviving through the Vietnam War era to the present time. After consulting a number of conservative journalists as possible sources for the quotation, the author concludes, "All efforts to identify the true originator proved unavailing."

That the "free lunch" analogy is at least 90 years old, that Milton Friedman is not its creator, and that its origins are shrouded in the mists of history are typical of my experience in the origins of words and phrases. I have learned not to grab for the easy answer or fall under the thrall of the romantic explanation. The bywords are *caveat lexamator*: word-lover beware.

The Greek *etymon* means "true, original," and the Greek ending *-logia* means "science or study." Thus, etymology is supposed to be the science or study of true and original word meanings. But I have learned that the proud house of etymology is populated by all manner of ghoulies and ghosties and long-leggety beasties miscreated by spook etymologists. (*Spook* reaches back to the Dutch *spooc*, "ghost, specter.") These sham scholars would rather invent a word origin after the fact than trace it to its true source. Spooks prefer drama and romance to accuracy and truth. With spooks it is sentence first, trial never. Listen now to the rattling of some of the most haunted and haunting words in the annals of spookery.

In *Polite Conversations* (1738), Jonathan Swift wrote, "Our King James First . . . being invited to Dinner by one of his Nobles, and seeing a large Loyn of beef at his table, drew out his sword, and knighted it." For the gullible that is indeed how the word *sirloin* came about. Mary Queen of Scots, so another story goes, was temperamental about her fare and, when piqued, would eat nothing but a preserve of oranges, of which she was inordinately fond. The delicacy was therefore nicknamed *Marie malade*, hence *marmalade*.

Despite high marks for ingenuity, these etymological explanations are merely exercises in free association without regard for attribution. *Sirloin* is not so called because James I or Henry VIII (according to Thomas Fuller in 1655) or Charles II (according to *Cook's Oracle* in 1822) knighted his favorite dish, declaring, "Arise, Sir Loin." In truth, *sirloin*, the upper or choicer part of a loin of beef, was borrowed from Middle French *surloigne* (*sur*, "above" + *loigne*, "loin") centuries before any of the monarchs who are credited with honoring the cut of meat. But legends die hard, especially when they are lit by such bright stories, and this particular flight of etymological fancy has survived for more than three centuries as a hoax of word-play foisted on unsuspecting language-lovers. Similarly, *marmalade* did not begin with the tastes and distastes of Mary Queen of Scots. More straightforwardly, the word issues from the Portuguese *marmelada*, "quince," which in turn descends from the Greek *melimelon* (*meli*, "honey" + *melon*, "apple").

More culinary spookery has been served up in the game of tennis, where *love* means "no points." The most charming derivation for the use of *love* in this sense is that the word derives from *l'ouef*—"the egg"—because a zero resembles an egg, just as the American-ism *goose egg* stands for "zero." But *un oeuf*, rather than *l'ouef*, would be the more likely French form, and, any-way, the French themselves (and most other Europeans) designate "no score" in tennis by saying "zero." Most tennis historians adhere to a less imaginative but more plausible theory. These more level heads contend that the tennis term is rooted in the Old English expression *neither love nor money*, which is more than a thousand years old. Because love is the antithesis of money, it is nothing.

One of the most persistent and spookiest of etymol-ogies is the recurrent wheeze that *posh*, "elegant, swanky," is an acronym for "p(ort) o(ut), s(tarboard) h(ome)," a beguiling bit of linguistic legerdemain that has taken in a company of estimable scholars. When British colonial emissaries and wealthy vacationers made passage to and from India and the Orient, they often traveled along the coast of Africa on the Peninsular and Oriental Steam Navigation Company line. Many of these travelers sought ideal accommodations "away from the weather," on the more comfortable or shady side of the ship. By paying for two staterooms—one portside out, the other starboard home—the very rich could avoid the blazing sun and strong winds both

ways, an act of conspicuous consumption that has become synonymous with anything luxurious and ultra-
smart.

While the abundant inventiveness here deserves at
least a sitting ovation, this etymology of *posh* is bosh.
For one thing, neither the travelers' literature of the period nor the records of the famous Peninsular and Oriental line show a jot of reference to *posh*. For another,
an examination of the deck plans of the ships of the period reveals that the cabins were not placed on the port
and starboard sides. For a third, *posh* does not show up
in print until 1918.

The editors of the *Oxford English Dictionary* say nothing
of any connection with the location of cabins on ships and
either ignore or reject outright the acronymic theory, and
all Merriam-Webster dictionaries list the origin as "unknown." Moreover, the monsoon winds that blow in and
out of the Asian heartland shift from winter to summer.
This fickle phenomenon changes the location of the shel-
tered and exposed sides of a ship so that in a given season
the ideal location can be starboard out, portside home
(hence, *soph*). More likely and more mundanely, *posh* hails
from a British slang word of the same spelling that means
"a dandy," but don't count on it.

Wordhunters beware: Eating humble pie has nothing etymologically to do with the word *humble,* "lowly."
The dish was really *umble pie*, made from the umbles—
heart, liver, and gizzard—of a deer. The servants and
huntsmen had to settle for these innards while the lord
of the manor and his guests dined on venison.

Nor does *cop* derive from "c(onstable) o(n) p(atrol),"
tip, in the sense of a gratuity, from "t(o) i(nsure)
p(romptness)," *S.O.S.* from "Save our ship," *babble* from
the Tower of Babel, or *news* from the first letters of
the points of the compass—"n(orth)-e(ast)-w(est)-

s(outh)"—in which case it would be the unpronounce-able *nesw*. About this I am being completely sincere.

The spooks squeak and gibber that *sincere* issues from the Latin *sine cērā*, the idea being that Roman pur-veyors of marble and pottery deviously polished their wares with wax to apply a false luster and conceal cracks and holes. Honest merchants, who did not doc-tor their products, proudly displayed them as being without wax—*sine cērā*. If you believe that, please get in touch with me. I have a bridge, an S&L, and a lovely parcel of swampland I want to sell you.

$\mathcal{R}$eal-Life Linguistics

$\mathcal{M}$any people picture linguists, those who study language scientifically, as gray-bearded professors with their eggheads in the clouds, their bespectacled eyes fastened to the pages of ponderous, dusty dictionaries, and their feet firmly planted on midair. In reality, there are occasions when linguists are very much involved in reality and can apply their knowledge of language to real-life legal and business situations. I know because I am occasionally called upon to help name products and devise slogans, and I have testified as an expert witness in a number of court cases that wheeled on the wording of a contractual clause or statute.

A few years ago, more than 46,000 Maine citizens signed a petition calling for a July 4, 1988, halt to operations at the Maine Yankee nuclear power plant. Traditionally, such petitions are sent to the state legislature and are then submitted to a statewide vote in the form of ballot referenda. Hoping that the legislature would consider rewording the choice before it reached the voters, the management of Maine Yankee hired me as consulting linguist to analyze the wording of the question that was to appear on the fall ballot:

DO YOU WANT TO LET ANY POWER PLANT
LIKE MAINE YANKEE
OPERATE AFTER JULY 4, 1988,
IF IT MAKES HIGH LEVEL NUCLEAR WASTE?

Whatever my personal and political views regarding nuclear power plants, I felt that I as a caring linguist could apply my skills and experience to help ensure that the question adhered to Maine law mandating that all such referenda be cast in "clear, concise, and direct language." After a great deal of analysis, I concluded and reported that the wording, especially the sections "like Maine Yankee" and "if it makes high level nuclear waste," was ambiguous and the format nontraditional. Here is the gist of my report, the analysis of a professional language scientist:

My handy desk dictionary defines *like*, when used as a preposition, as "having the characteristics of; similar to." In the minds of most people the difference between the phrases "power plants *like* Maine Yankee" and "power plants, *such as* Maine Yankee" is that the first excludes Maine Yankee from the targeted plants and considers only plants with similar characteristics, while the second cites Maine Yankee as one of the group.

This misleading use of the preposition *like* creates two related kinds of confusion: First, if "any power plant" is meant to refer to and include Maine Yankee— as those words are indeed meant to—we are stuck with the rhetorical absurdity of saying that Maine Yankee is like Maine Yankee. Second, it follows that the words "any power plant like Maine Yankee" will imply to most voters that the plant or plants in question are ones similar to, but do not include, Maine Yankee.

To visualize this analysis in concrete, dramatic terms, imagine this scenario: A voter is in favor of keeping the Maine Yankee plant in operation, but that voter does not wish to see additional power plants, plants "like Maine Yankee," built and operating in Maine. This voter could very likely vote "No" in response to the proposed statement because he or she would assume that a "No" vote would stand against the operation of future plants *like* Maine Yankee, but not Maine Yankee itself.

Let's move on to a second flaw in the sentence. We live in an age of great American overspeak in which we are bombarded by repetitive redundancies, such as "free gifts"—even "complimentary free gifts"—and sprays that "kill bugs dead." But all gifts are free by definition, and killing always renders something dead. The ancient Greeks named this kind of rhetorical overkill *pleonasmas*, and the conditional adverb clause in the referendum sentence, "if it makes high level nuclear waste," is a striking example of a pleonasm because nuclear power plants are plants that by definition produce "high level nuclear waste."

Consider this example: If a parent is asked, "Do you want your child to eat eggs that contain cholesterol?" the parent will very likely be led to the conclusion that there exist, or could exist, eggs that are cholesterol free. But all consumable eggs contain cholesterol, and any parent who responds negatively to the question posed will unknowingly be eliminating eggs from his or her child's diet.

The same is true of the proposed referendum statement. Rhetoricians universally agree that the words that appear at the end of a given sentence are the most telling because they make the final impression. In the ballot question, the clause "if it makes high level nuclear waste" comes last and conveys the powerful impression that it is possible to eliminate high level nuclear waste from the operation of nuclear power plants.

Thus, a typical voter might reason: "I want Maine Yankee to continue generating power but without producing high level waste. So I'll vote no and force Maine Yankee to stop making those wastes." Like the parent of the egg-eating child, the voter would not realize that he or she would unalterably be shutting down Maine Yankee.

The format of the referendum is equally problematic. It is a time-honored tradition in debating that the issue to be argued in a given debate is always cast so that the affirmative position seeks to change the status quo and the negative position seeks to maintain the status quo: "The death penalty should be abolished throughout the United States," "Under certain conditions mercy killing should be legal."

There are at least two reasons for this traditional casting of debate topics: First, we don't want to waste people's time by proposing status quo questions, such as "The United States should keep operating under the Constitution." Second, because the affirmative seeks to change the status quo, the affirmative traditionally bears the burden of proof. Yet the wording of the ballot question requires that citizens in favor of the status quo—maintaining a nuclear power plant—vote yes and those for change—shutting down Maine Yankee—vote no. In addition to violating universal debating rules, the illogical formatting of the proposed question runs contrary to the traditions and reverses the intent of Maine's ballot measures.

On May 1, 1987, the *Portland Press-Herald* reported that "the Maine Senate capped an emotional debate by refusing to change the wording of the fall ballot." The vote was 19–16. On November 3, 59 percent of Maine voters responded yes to the referendum question, allowing the Maine Yankee plant to continue operating.

During my involvement in the Maine Yankee case, I received some agitated mail and telephone calls excoriating me for supporting an environment-destroying nuclear plant. My response was that I simply wished to defend the cause of clear language so that citizens could make informed choices about their sources of power.

Two years after the Maine Yankee litigation, I found myself allied with a very different coalition of concerned citizens. In 1990, Thermo Electron Energy Systems, a Massachusetts-based company, sought permission to build a twenty-eight-megawatt, waste-wood-to-energy, $50-million power plant on a 41-acre site in the Pelham Industrial Park, located in the northwest corner of Pelham, New Hampshire. In July of 1990, the Pelham Planning Board voted unanimously to accept the project.

Arguing that the facility represented a health hazard to the region, residents of the neighborhoods adjoining the park who opposed the project formed a group called Safe Environment for Southern New Hampshire. Thermo, they contended, would be burning wood and wood byproducts that could contain arsenic, lead, toxic glues, and other pollutants that would have a deleterious impact on the area. A generator operating twenty-four hours a day for seven days a week, wood-chipping machines, and eighteen-wheeler trucks rumbling to and from the site would, they contended, produce another kind of pollution: noise pollution.

The coalition asked me to testify at a special session of the Pelham Zoning Board of Adjustment in March of 1991. The Board was convening to review the question of whether or not the Thermo application conformed to the wishes stated in the Pelham zoning statute.

My charge was to interpret the language of that statute, which reads in part: "The following uses shall be permitted in the Industrial District: . . . All light industrial and manufacturing uses." The linguistic question in this case revolved around whether Thermo Electron's wood/energy plant conformed to the town of Pelham's zoning law allowing "light industrial and manufacturing uses."

Attorneys for Thermo Electron argued that the word *light* referred only to *industry* and not to *manufacturing*, that the statute permitted light industry and any level of manufacturing in the zoned area.

As a linguist, I observed in my testimony before the Zoning Board that to anyone who is a native or experienced speaker of the English language, the adjective *light* in the phrase "All light industrial and manufacturing uses" clearly refers to and modifies both *industrial* and *manufacturing*.

In the pairing "the old man and woman," for example, the assumption of an experienced speaker of English is that the adjective *old* modifies both *man* and *woman*. If the speaker or writer wishes to detach the second noun from the initial adjective, he or she will always provide some cue, as in "the old man and the young woman."

By analogy, I stated that if the framers of the zoning statute had intended *light* to be joined only with *industrial* and not *manufacturing*, they would have modified *manufacturing* with another word, such as *normal* or *heavy*, as in "light industrial and normal manufacturing uses."

I also noted the illogicality of taking the position that *light* modifies only *industrial* and not *manufacturing*. *The Random House Dictionary of the English Language* (1987) gives as the first meaning of *industry* "the aggregate of manufacturing or technically productive enterprises in a particular field, often named after its principal product: *the automotive industry; the steel industry.*" The third definition is "trade or manufacturing in general."

If *industry* is a specific cluster of manufacturing enterprises, or essentially synonymous with *manufacture*, it makes absolutely no sense to permit only light industry but normal or heavy manufacturing, as the second category would contradict the first. To allow normal or heavy manufacturing but not normal or heavy industry would be an exceedingly strange, even absurd, decision.

In a filed memorandum, attorneys representing Thermo Electron argued that because *industrial* and *manufacturing* were both adjectives defining the word *uses*, *light* applied only to the first word, *industrial*. In the statement "the light green and brown cloth," where *green* and *brown* are clearly adjectives, *light* modifies *green* but not *brown*. Therefore, in "light industrial and manufacturing use," *light* must modify only *industrial* and not *manufacturing*.

I attempted to rebut this line of reasoning by explaining that "industrial use" and "manufacturing use" were essentially noun expressions, no different from *industry* and *manufacture*, so that *light* is really an adjective. I countered with the example of "a very old and wrinkled man," wherein *very* is also an adverb, yet it clearly modifies both the adjectives *old* and *wrinkled*. Even if *light* in the statute is an adverb, it applies to both the adjectives that follow.

It is impossible to assess the impact of my testimony at the Pelham Board meeting that night. I can only report that, by a 3–2 vote, the Zoning Board of Adjustment overturned the earlier decision by the Planning Board to accept the plant. After unsuccessful attempts to reinstate its case, Thermo Electron has abandoned its efforts to erect a waste-wood energy plant in the Pelham area.

In 1992, six school systems and students from those systems brought suit against the State of New Hampshire. The petitioners argued that the way the state finances the operation of its public schools violates the New Hampshire Constitution.

The New Hampshire system of school financing relies almost exclusively on local property taxes. These taxes account for more than 90 percent of all revenue for education, direct state participation less than 8 percent, and federal participation less than 2 percent. Nebraska is the next lowest contributor of state funds, providing 24.5 percent of the local cost of education, more than three times the New Hampshire funding level. Wealth varies considerably among the property-rich and property-poor cities and towns of New Hampshire. As a result of these substantial disparities in property values among school districts, the property tax revenues that can be raised by the districts also vary dramatically.

Petitioners argued that the statutory system does not adequately fund the public schools at a level consistent with Part 2, Article 83, of the New Hampshire Constitution—that the tax structure denies petitioners the equal protection of the law and taxes the citizens of the property-poor towns unreasonably. Here is the article in question:

Knowledge and learning, generally diffused through a community, being essential to the preservation of a free government; and spreading the opportunities and advantages of education through the various parts of the country, being highly conducive to promote this end; it shall be the duty of the legislators and magistrates, in all future periods of this government, to cherish the interest of literature and the sciences . . .

When a judge threw the case out of Merrimack County Superior Court, the plaintiffs' attorneys asked me to review the petition filed in the case and to analyze the wording of Part 2, Article 83, in the state constitution. After examining this material, I agreed to enter the case as an expert witness for the plaintiffs.

My examination of the historical context and the language of the Constitution presented powerful evidence that the framers were clearly imposing a duty on "legislators and magistrates, in all future periods" to spread educational opportunity throughout New Hampshire, in order to preserve the very government that they had just fought a war of independence to create. The New Hampshire Constitution was written by men who were attempting to form and preserve a government that would keep them free from tyranny and oppression. Therefore, the duties set forth in the Constitution were obviously of great significance to the framers, or they would not have enumerated those obligations in such an important document.

When we look at Part 2, Article 83, I argued, we see that this section specifically refers to action that is "essential to the preservation of a free government." *Essential* descends from the Latin *essentia*, the very being of a person or institution (*esse*, "to be"). The sense of "the most important or basic element of anything" is first recorded in English in 1656. A *governor* was in Greek originally a steersman or pilot, and etymologically *government* is designed to steer and pilot the ship of state that carries its citizens. In other words, a government, like a steersman, takes an active role in the direction of the state.

The constitutional fathers recognized that the general diffusion of education (from the Latin *educere*, "to bring out," "to bring up children") throughout the state was crucial to the general diffusion of knowledge and learning throughout the community. The word *duty* comes to us through the Anglo-French *deute,* "moral or legal obligation." To ensure the achievement of their highest goal of preservation (late Latin, "keep from harm, keep alive") of their democratic vision, the framers placed a duty on "the legislators and magistrates, in all future periods of government, to cherish the interest of literature and the sciences."

Given the historical context, and further considering that the article in question describes what is necessary for the continued "preservation of a free government," we must note the specific use of the word *cherish* in its setting. Here the verb (from French *cher,* "dear") means not only "to hold dear," but also "to treat with fostering care, to foster tenderly, to nurse (children, young creatures)" and "to foster, tend, cultivate (plants)," primary meanings recorded in the *Oxford English Dictionary* and well established by the end of the sixteenth century. This is a verb that requires not only action but the passing on of something—in this case the opportunities and advantages of education—from the actor (the state) to the receiver (children). As an indication of the importance attached to this cherishing, the framers mandated this duty in perpetuity, "in all future periods of this government."

Part 2, Article 83, is the only place in the entire state constitution where the word *cherish* appears. Recognizing that knowledge and learning were crucial to the perpetuation of their new and free government, the constitutional framers clearly imposed an active duty of protection, an active duty to keep and to guard, an active duty to cultivate and to nurture education in New Hampshire forevermore.

Words are "the skin of living thought," wrote Supreme Court justice Oliver Wendell Holmes, Jr. As this book goes to press, plaintiffs have appealed to the New Hampshire Supreme Court, and my affidavit is at the center of their argument. I hope that my analysis will make a difference in the way New Hampshire pays for its education. After all, laws are acts of language, and language is a subject about which linguists have something to say.

*O*ys and Joys

*F*or centuries, fair-haired sea rovers from North Germany—Angles, Saxons, and Jutes—habitually cruised about the British coast in beaked Viking ships and attacked cities for booty and a lust for battle. In the middle of the fifth century, around A.D. 449, these Anglo-Saxon plunderers sailed across the North Sea and came to the islands then known as Britannia. They found the countryside pleasant and the people, fighting among themselves, easy to conquer, and so they remained there and took the land for themselves. That is how Anglo-Saxons came to be the ancestors of English and why English is, at its heart, a Germanic language. The hundred most frequently used words in English are all of Anglo-Saxon origin, as are eighty-three of the next hundred. Two women of exceeding importance to my life have helped to bring home to me the continuing influence of the Germanic tongues on our English language.

My mother, Leah Perowoski Lederer, was born in

the United States at the very end of the nineteenth century, after her father, mother, and older brothers and sister had come over here from Vilna, Russia (now Lithuania). Mother's first language was Yiddish, but, like all the other parents in our West Philadelphia neighborhood, she spoke Yiddish as a way of keeping us children from understanding what was being said. If immigrants were going to become Americans, they must speak English—and English only! But in the process of Americanizing, we second-generation American Jews lost part of our heritage. We lost a language handed down from generation to generation and from nation to nation, fraught with incisive idioms, expressions, and sayings that exude a magic and laughter, blended with sober reality.

When Isaac Bashevis Singer was awarded the Nobel Prize for literature in 1978, he remarked in his acceptance speech, "The high honor bestowed upon me is also a recognition of the Yiddish language—a language of exile, without a land, without frontiers, not supported by any government, a language which possesses no words for weapons, ammunition, military exercises, war tactics. There is a quiet humor in Yiddish and a gratitude for every day of life, every crumb of success, each encounter of love. In a figurative way, Yiddish is the wise and humble language of us all, the idiom of a frightened and hopeful humanity."

The word *Yiddish* derives from the German *jüdisch*, "Jewish." The principal parent of Yiddish is High German, the form of German encountered by Jewish settlers from northern France in the eleventh century. Yiddish, a language written in the characters of the Hebrew alphabet and from right to left, has enjoyed borrowing words from Russian, Polish, English, and all the other languages and countries along the routes that Jews have traveled during the past thousand years. Journalist

Charles Rappaport once quipped, "I speak ten languages—all of them Yiddish."

Although Yiddish has been in danger of dying out for hundreds of years, the language is spoken today by millions of people throughout the world—in Russia, Poland, Romania, France, England, Israel, Africa, Latin America, New Zealand, Australia, Canada, and the United States, where, like the bagel, it was leavened on both coasts, in New York and Hollywood. It is spoken even in Transylvania: A beautiful girl awakens in bed to find a vampire at her side. Quickly she holds up a cross. *"Zie gernisht helfen,"* says the vampire, smiling. Translation: "It won't do you any good."

Most of us already speak a fair amount of Yiddish without fully realizing that we do. The five hundred "Yinglish" words that have become part of our everyday conversations include:

cockamamy: mixed-up, ridiculous.

fin: slang for five-dollar bill, from *finf,* the Yiddish word for "five."

gun moll: a double clipping of *gonif's Molly,* Yiddish for "thief's woman."

kibitzer: one who comments, often in the form of unwanted advice, during a game, often cards.

maven: expert.

mazuma: money.

mish-mosh: a reduplication for a mess.

schlep: to drag or haul.

schlock: shoddy, cheaply produced merchandise.

schmeer: the entire deal, the whole package.

schmooze: to converse informally.

schnoz: nose.

yenta: blabbermouth, gossip, woman of low origins.

. . . and so on through the whole *megillah:* long, involved story.

A number of poignant Yiddish words defy easy translation into English:

chutzpah: nerve, unmitigated gall, a quality we admire within ourselves, but never in others. The classic definition of *chutzpah* is the quality demonstrated by the man who killed his mother and father and then threw himself on the mercy of the court because he was an orphan.

mensch: a real authentic human being—a person.

naches: the glow of pleasure-plus-pride that only a child can give to its parents: "This is my son, the *doctor!*"

oy; oy vay; oy vay is mir: literally "Oh, pain," but not so much words as an entire vocabulary. *Oy vay* and *oy* can express any emotion from mild pleasure to vaulting pride, from mild relief to lament through a vale of tears. Albert Einstein's theory of relativity laid the theoretical foundation for the building of the atom bomb. When the great scientist received the news of the mass destruction wrought by the bomb dropped on Hiroshima and Nagasaki, he reacted with two Yiddish words often invoked in such black circumstances: "Oy vay."

tsuris: the gamut of painful emotions—some real, some imagined, some self-inflicted.

Yiddish is especially versatile in describing those poor souls who inhabit the world of the ineffectual, and each is assigned a distinct place in the gallery of pathetic types: *schmo, schemdrick, schnook, schmegge, schlep, schlub, schmuck, putz, klutz, kvetch,* and *nudnick.* Yiddish readily coins new names for new, pitiable personalities: a *nudnick* is a pest; a *phudnick* is a nudnick with a Ph.D. The rich nuances that suffuse this roll call are seen in the timeless distinction between a *schlimeil,* "a clumsy jerk," and a *schlimazel*, "a habitual loser": the schlimeil inevitably trips and spills his hot soup—all over the schlimazel. (And the *nebbish* is the one who has to clean it up.)

Yiddish never apologizes for what it is—the earthy, wise soul of an expressive people who have learned that life is but a mingled yarn, good and ill together. Which reminds me of the *zaftig* ("buxom, well-rounded") blonde who wears an enormous ring to a charity ball. "It happens to be the third most famous diamond in the whole world," she boasts. "The first is the Hope diamond, then comes the Kohinoor, and then comes this one, which is called the Lipschitz."

"What a stone! How lucky you are!"

"Wait, wait," says the lady. "Nothing in life is all mazel ['good luck']. Unfortunately, with this famous Lipschitz diamond comes also the famous Lipschitz curse."

Gasping, the other woman asks, "And what is this famous Lipschitz curse?"

"Lipschitz," sighs the lady.

Then there is the even less famous *Lederer* curse, borne by my wife. Near the end of 1991, I committed an act of public matrimony. My coconspirator was Simone van Egeren, whose last name reveals that she is of Dutch descent. She was born in Rotterdam and came to the United States at the age of three. Throughout my relationship with Simone I've been enjoying saucy Holland days.

Actually, I'm somewhat embarrassed to be such a lover of the English language and married to a Dutch woman. For one thing, we English speakers have used the word *Dutch* in confusing and derogatory ways. Probably no other nationality has come in for so consistent a torrent of verbal abuse from the English as their neighbors across the North Sea, the Dutch. In dozens of compound words and expressions, the Dutch are depicted as cowardly, cheap, or deceitful.

Take the word *Yankee*, which has had its ups and downs during its several-hundred-year history. The Dutch love for cheese was well-known, and *Yankee* was first an ethnic insult that English colonists hurled at Dutch freebooters in early New York. The English fashioned *Yankee* from the Dutch *Jan Kaas*, which literally meant "John Cheese," combining the common Dutch first name *Jan* (pronounced "Yahn") with *Kaas* (the Dutch word for "cheese," the country's national product). Over time, the ethnic slur got blurred into *Yankee*. After a while, the feisty American revolutionaries were given the name by the loyal British. The song "Yankee Doodle" was originally one of derision, sung by British soldiers to mock the poorly clothed colonists. But the colonial army gave the melody new lyrics and adopted it as a robust and proud marching song.

While Simone and I were courting, we invited friends to go out with us for dinner, and they insisted on going "Dutch treat." Simone knew that the phrase was negative—a Dutch treat (or going Dutch) isn't a treat at all because each guest pays his or her own way—but she wondered why. In my search for an answer, I discovered more than sixty disparaging Dutch compounds and expressions in the English language, including:

double Dutch: gibberish; the kind of talk deliberately intended to confuse the listener.

Dutch act (also *to do the Dutch*): suicide.

Dutch auction: one that reverses the order of an ordinary auction; it starts with high bids and regresses to lower ones.

Dutch bargain: a one-sided deal, not a bargain at all.

Dutch comfort: small comfort, if any; typified by the line "Well, it could have been worse."

Dutch courage: the kind of bravery that comes out of a bottle. As far back as 1625, the British poet Edmund Waller wrote, "The Dutch their wine and all their brandy lose, / Disarmed of that from which their courage grows."

Dutch defense: retreat or surrender.

Dutch leave: to be AWOL.

Dutch reckoning: guesswork; a disputed bill.

Dutch uncle: not an uncle at all but an old busybody who reprimands or lectures a young person.

Why have the good people of the Netherlands been made to suffer so in English parlance? Why are the Dutch so in Dutch (meaning "in trouble") in our idioms? Until well after Shakespeare's time, the Dutch were highly regarded in most literary references by British authors. But during the seventeenth century, the two nations became rivals in international commerce, fighting for control of the sea and parts of the New World. For a number of years the Dutch colonial empire loomed as the chief threat to the British, so the disrespectful references began.

Even when the British and Dutch empires ceased their conflicts, the slurs on the Dutch crossed the ocean from the British Isles to the United States. In fact, the Dutch people have been so offended by the prejudice against *Dutch* in the English language over the past three centuries that in 1934 their government ordered its officials to drop the word *Dutch* and use *Netherlands* wherever possible.

Growing up speaking a lot of Dutch at home, Simone felt ambivalently about her native tongue. Although she loved the sound of Dutch, she believed it to be an unglamorous language. "People around the world speak English, Spanish, and French, but almost nobody but the Dutch speaks Dutch," she said.

Simone's heart was warmed when I showed her that Dutch teems from our English tongue. Our *cop*, for example, comes from a Dutch word that means "to seize or catch." *Dote* derives from a Dutch word that signifies "to be silly," the meaning of which we see more clearly in our words *dotage* and *dotty*. *Easel* is built from the Dutch word material that means "little ass," because the artist's stand acts as a small beast of burden. *Filibuster*, borrowed from the Dutch *vrijbuiter*, "freebooter," first meant "pirate, adventurer" in English, a sense retained in the current denotation of *filibuster*: "holding a piece of legislation captive by making long and windy speeches."

Quack, in the sense of bogus doctor, descends from the Dutch compound *quacksalver*, which itself is cobbled from *quack*, "to make a sound like a duck," and *salve*, "ointment," and *-er*, "one who." In days of yore, a quacksalver was a snake oil doctor who traveled about hawking (quacking) all the maladies his unguent or salve could cure.

When the Dutch came to the New World, the figure of St. Nikolaas, their patron saint, was on the first ship. The pronunciation of *St. Nikolaas* became folk etymologized, and the English in New York heard their Dutch neighbors saying *Sinterklaas*. They recognized the Dutch name Klaas and thought they were hearing "Santa Klaas." After the Dutch lost control of Nieuw Amsterdam to the English in the seventeenth century, *Sinterklaas* gradually became anglicized into *Santa Claus* and acquired some of the features of the English Father Christmas.

It is time to cut through the poppycock (from the Dutch *pappekak*, "soft dung") by noting the enormous contributions that the Dutch language has made to British and American English. A partial list of gifts from our friends in the Netherlands includes *barracks, bedspread, boodle, boor, booze, boss, boy, brandy, bully, bulwark, bump-kin, buoy, bush, caboose, coleslaw, cookie, cruise, cruller, cuspidor, date, deck, decoy, dingus, dope, dumb, excise, furlough, gas, gin, golf, groove, halibut, hay, hobble, hop* (plant), *hose* (stockings), *huckster, husk, hustle, jib, kit, knapsack, landscape, loiter, luck, mangle, mart, pickle, pit* (in fruit), *placard, rack, school* (of fish), *scow, skate, sketch, sled, sleigh, sloop, slur, smuggle, snap, snatch, snoop, snort, snow, snuff, splint, spook, spool, stoker, stoop* (porch), *tackle* (fishing), *uproar, waffle, wagon, walrus, wiseacre, yawl.*

The Dutch themselves have not retaliated in kind, and their language is free of meanspirited English treats, English uncles, and English leaves. People who fail to recognize our linguistic debt to the Dutch will soon find themselves in deep trouble—in English.

A Guide to Britspeak, A to Zed

*T*he summer after we were married, Simone and I spent ten smashingly lovely honeymoon days on vacation (what the Brits call on holiday) exploring the southwest of Britain. We took a drive and walk through time from the ancient stone mysteries at Stonehenge and Avebury to the modern glitz of Manchester's Granada Studios—Great Britain's answer to our Universal Studios theme park.

Confident that the island natives spoke our language, we expected few communication problems. We did, however, encounter a number of strange words and locutions that you should know when you visit the U.K. (United Kingdom). To clear the fog and unravel some transatlantic tangles, I offer a selective list of differences between American English and English English. After all, I don't want you to miss the delights of Britain just because of a little thing like a language barrier.

If you choose to rent an automobile in the U.K., with it will come a whole new vocabulary. Be sure to fill it with petrol, not gas. Remember that the trunk is the boot, the hood is the bonnet (what the Brits call a hood is our convertible top), tires are tyres (and they have tracks, not treads), a headlight is a headlamp, the transmission is the gearbox, the windshield is the windscreen, a fender is a wing, and the muffler is a silencer.

Station wagons (*waggons* in Britspell) that speed by you are called estate cars or hatchbacks, trucks are lorries, and streetcars are trams. Most British drivers (motorists) belong to AA—the Automobile Association, of course!

Our buses are their coaches. When a hotel in the British Isles posts a sign proclaiming, "No football coaches allowed," the message is not directed at the Don Shulas and Joe Paternos of the world. "No football coaches allowed" means "No soccer buses permitted."

While you are driving down the motorway (highway) and busily converting kilometers into miles, you must note that, in matters automotive, the Queen's English can be as far apart as the lanes on a dual carriageway (divided highway). A traffic circle a roundabout, an intersection a junction, an overpass a flyover, a circular road around a city a ringway or orbital, a place to pull off the road a lay by, a road shoulder a verge, and a railroad (railway) crossing a level crossing. All the time, you must be sure to stay to the left, not the right! As the joke goes, why did the Siamese twins go to England? Answer: So that the other one could drive.

When you use the subway in London, you should follow signs to the underground (informally, the tube). The American subway turns out to mean an underground passage across a road, not the subterranean train system. When you get on and off the underground, you'll hear a polite voice on the loudspeaker warning you to "mind the gap." That message means "Look out for the space between the train and the platform." As you make your way upward to the streets of London, be aware that *Way out* is not a vestigial hippie exclamation. *Way out* signifies an exit.

If you decide to walk somewhere, you'll have to bear in mind that what a North American calls a sidewalk is an English pavement, while an American pavement is an English roadway. If someone directs you to the Circus, don't head for a big top. Rather, look for a large circle, such as Piccadilly Circus, where several streets converge.

At the end of World War II, Winston Churchill tells us, the Allied leaders nearly came to blows over a single word during their negotiations when diplomats suggested that it was time to "table" an important motion. For the British, *table* meant that the motion should be put on the table for discussion. For the Americans it meant just the opposite—that it should be put on the shelf and dismissed from discussion.

Also at the end of the war, the British government made an urgent request for thousands of bushels of corn. So the U.S. government shipped just what the Brits asked for—corn. What the British officials really wanted was wheat. Had they wanted corn, they would have called it "maize" or specified "Indian corn."

Such confusions serve to illustrate the truth of George Bernard Shaw's pronouncement that "England and America are two countries separated by the same language." Or, as Oscar Wilde put it with equal drollery, "the English really have everything in common with the Americans, except, of course, language." Wilde made this comment when he heard that audiences in New York weren't queuing up to see his plays. They were waiting in line. Wilde would have hoped that the performances went "like a bomb," which in Britspeak means "successfully."

Many of the most beguiling misunderstandings can arise where identical words have different meanings in the two cultures and lingoes. When an American exclaims, "I'm mad about my flat," she is upset about her tire. When a Brit exclaims, "I'm mad about my flat," she is not bemoaning her "puncture." When a Brit rails against "that bloody villain," he is describing the dastard's moral character, not his physical condition. When a Brit points out that you have "a ladder in your hose," the situation is not as bizarre as you might at first think. Quite simply, you have a run in your stocking.

Some of this bilingual confusion can get downright embarrassing: When Brits tell you that they will "come by in the morning and knock you up," they are informing you that they will wake you up with a knock on your door. (Similarly, a "knock up" in tennis means, simply, to hit the ball around.)

When a Brit offers to show you his collection of bloomers, he means his examples of bloopers, or verbal faux pas. When a Brit wants to escort you "to the BM," she is talking about the British Museum. When a Brit volunteers to take you to a solicitor, that's a trip to a general-practice lawyer. When a Brit asks you if you need a rubber, she is trying to make your writing safer. English rubbers are erasers. When a Brit tells you how marvelously "homely" you are, that's a compliment. He means that you are domestic and home-loving. In the U.K. it is quite possible to be both homely and attractive at the same time.

For centuries, the Brits have strenuously objected to every Americanism that they have not deemed standard English—meaning standard British. In his monumental work, *The American Language,* H. L. Mencken informs us that the first British criticism of American English appeared in 1733 and was directed at the Americanism *bluff,* signifying "the bank of a river." Not long after, the Brits made fun of Thomas Jefferson's use of the verb *belittle* and the American "I guess" (instead of "I suppose"), conveniently ignoring the fact that the English poet Geoffrey Chaucer had written in the fourteenth century: "Of twenty yeer of age he was, I gesse."

In the early part of this century, Finley Peter Dunne's Mr. Dooley wryly observed, "When the American people get through with the English language, it will look as if it has been run over by a musical comedy." And as recently as 1974, Morton Cooper sneered meanly that "giving the English language to the Americans is like giving sex to small children; they know it's important, but they don't know what to do with it." A recent message on a London theater (theatre) marquee went so far as to advertise, "American Western Film—English subtitles." A London store sign announced, "English spoken here—American understood."

We Yanks have struck back with the force of numbers. Mark Twain said of British vs. American English: "The property has gone into the hands of a joint stock company, and we own the bulk of the shares." Mencken himself put it this way: "When two-thirds of the people who use a certain language decide to call it a freight train instead of a goods train, the first is correct usage, and the second is a dialect."

With the increasing influence of film, radio, television, and international travel, the two main streams of the English language are rapidly converging like the streets of a circus. Still, there are scores of words, phrases, spellings, and constructions about which Brits and Yanks just don't agree. During a transatlantic telephone conversation, one of my British publishers told me that my book was attracting considerable newspaper coverage and she would be sure to send me the "cuttings." I asked her what she called the sections of plants one gets from gardens. She answered, "Those are clippings, of course." Of course—and not surprising in a land where the beer and Coke are warm and the toast is cold.

Here's a pop quiz that will help you discover how "bilingual" you are. "Answers and Explanations I" repose on page 164.

1. Look over these words and compound words that occur in both Britspeak and American. Then ask yourself what each one means in British English: billion, biscuit, bitter, bob, braces, catapult, chemist, chips, crisp, dinner jacket, full stop, ground floor, hockey, ice, jelly, knickers, lift, M.P., minister, plaster, pocketbook, public school, pudding, spectacles, stone, stuff, sweet, till, tin, torch, vest, waistcoat.

2. What would the average Brit call each of these words and compounds: aisle, bar, bathroom, bobby pin, clothespin, counterclockwise, hardware store, kerosene, napkin, quilt, shrimp, silverware, sled, swimsuit, telephone booth, thumbtack, zero.

3. What is the American equivalent of each of the following Briticisms: advert, banger, bobby, chucker-out, don, draughts, dressing gown, dustbin, fortnight, hoover, plimsolls, porridge, pram, scone, spanner, starter, switchback, takeaway, telly.

4. The *Dictionary of British Pronunciation With American Variants* shows differences in the pronunciation of 28 percent of the words therein. The broad *a* of *ahsk* and *clahss* is probably the most familiar mark of "educated" British speech, even though the flat *a* that most Americans use is actually the older of the two pronunciations. How would a speaker with the so-called standard (or received) British accent pronounce these words?: ate, been, bone, clerk, duty, either, evolution, fear, figure, garage, herb, laboratory, leisure, lieutenant, missile, patriot, privacy, schedule, secretary, suggest, tomato (and potato), vitamin, zebra.

5. The written form of the two languages exhibits such differences in spelling that it is practically impossible to go through a single page without being aware of the writer's nationality. The most obvious divergence is in words that end in -*or* in American but -*our* in Britain— *behaviour, flavour, harbour, honour, labour, odour,* and *vigour*. Perhaps you have noticed the credit that pops up in many British films: "Colour by Technicolor."

How would these words be spelled in British English?: airplane, aluminum, check, defense, fiber, gray, inflection, inquire, jail, jewelry, judgment, maneuver, marvelous, organization, pajamas, plow, program, specialty, spelled, story (floor of a building), tons, vial, whiskey.

6. Some differences exist between British and American usage. In what form is each of the following constructions and idioms likely to appear in British English?: Japan is leading the world in exports; different from; in the hospital; living on Baker Street.

In the *Oxford Dictionary of Slang*, editors John Simpson and John Ayto identify slang as "English with its sleeves rolled up, its shirttails dangling and its shoes covered with mud." One of the hardest-working and most earthy of slangs is that of London's East End cockneys.

The word *cockney* originally meant an odd or misshapen egg. Traditionally, a cockney is anyone born within the sound of Bow Bells, the bells of Bow Church, also called St. Mary-le-Bow Church. By Victorian times, the cockney dialect had spread well beyond the tintinnabulation of those bells.

Rhyming slang was first officially recorded in the mid 19th century. In a series of articles in the *Morning Chronicle* in 1849–50, Henry Mayhew called it "the new style of cadgers' cant, all done on the rhyming principle." Mayhew suggested that cockney slang originated in the language of beggars and thieves and was fabricated to baffle the police.

It is an indirect sort of slang that substitutes a rhyme for the word in mind. Thus, in "Pass the Aristotle," the last word, as you can guess, stands for bottle. In "Be sure to get the brass tacks," *tacks* stand for facts, leading some word sleuths to deduce cockney as the source of the cliché "Let's get down to brass tacks." It's all as plain as the I suppose on your boat race—the nose on your face.

By far the great number of such expressions substitute not a word but a phrase. I'm going down the frog and toad—road. I'm going up the apples and pears—stairs. He's gone into the soup and gravy—Navy. She's gone out for saint and sinner—dinner. She's at the near 'n' far—bar. He's on the off 'n' on—John. "Would ye loik Lilian Gish, Jack the Ripper or Kate and Sidney for Jim Skinner?" translates to "Would you like fish, kipper or steak and kidney for dinner?"

Do you get it now, me briny marlin—darlin'?

The process of substitution does not stop with rhyme. In clipped speech, the actual rhyming word is often omitted. Only the first part of the phrase is spoken, and the rhyme and the word in mind are both assumed. Thus, in "'Ow ye doin', me old china?" "me china" means my friend: china plate—mate. I'll bet you can't hardly Adam it. Adam and Eve—believe.

For those not born within the sound of Bow Bells, here are more examples:

It's a bit peasy in here. Peas in a pot—hot.

We've got some great bargains on our tom. Foolery—jewelry

I like me glass of pig's. Pig's ear—beer.

'Ow about a cup o' Rosy? Rosy Lea—tea.

Some geezer ain't usin' 'is loaf. Of bread—head.

I come for a spot o' tiddly. Wink—drink.

How d'ye like me new whistle? And flute—suit.

I'll pay you back when I get me greens. Green-gages—wages.

Let's have a butcher's at it. Hook—look.

'E's on 'is Pat. Malone—own.

Where'dye get that luverly titfer? Tat—hat.

Sometimes the journey is a long one. "Last night Pat, went out with quite a Richard" means that "Pat went out with quite a woman" (Richard the Third—bird—woman). "Not on yer Nellie!" means "not on your life!" (Nellie Duff—puff—breath of life).

7. Blimey! 'Ere's yer chance to test yer eye and ear for cockney rhyming slang. (The parenthesized words are often omitted in actual cockney speech.) What is each sentence saying in standard English?:

 a. Put some army (and navy) on my beef.
 b. My compliments to the babbling brook.
 c. In 'is 'and 'e 'eld a lady from Bristol.
 d. That's worth a lot o' bees (and honey).
 e. Bring the food to the Cain (and Abel).
 f. 'Ow 'bout a game o' 'orses (and carts)?
 g. D'ye 'ear me, or are ye Mutt and Jeff?
 h. Conan Doyle me some potatoes for kidney punch.
 i. I'm dead on me plates (of meat).
 j. That's one o' me favorite ding dongs.
 k. Ye're a flipping holy friar.
 l. It's 'round the next Johnnie Horner.
 m. 'Ow's the trouble (and strife) and the dustbin lids?
 n. Please pass the Uncle Fred, the stammer (and stutter), and the stand at ease.
 o. If ye drink too many o' them apple fritters, ye'll get elephant's trunk.
 p. 'E's got some long ham (and eggs).

*P*rep School Slanguage

*S*lang is hot and slang is cool. Slang is nifty and slang is wicked. Slang is the bee's knees and the cat's pajamas. Slang is groovy, awesome, bad, the most, the max, and totally tubular.

Those are a dozen ways of saying that, if variety is the spice of life, slang is the spice of language. Slang adds gusto to the feast of words, as long as speakers and writers remember that too much seasoning can kill the taste of any dish. At St. Paul's the New Hampshire boarding school where I have taught English for more than three decades, the table of language is laden with a veritable banquet of slang, and I as an observational linguist have compiled a lexicon of Prepspeak.

Not long ago (it could have been any night), a group of St. Paul's students sat around waiting for a shipment of starch to arrive from a local pizza emporium. When almost an hour had passed beyond the appointed time of delivery, one of the boys called up and asked the store to "bag the za" (meaning "cancel the pizza").

The pizza parlor person asked, "You want me to what the what?"

"Bag the pizza," the boy explained.

After a pause, the voice replied, "We don't bag pizza here. We put it in boxes."

Take five hundred boys and girls who are blessed with an abundance of linguistic exuberance and word-making energy, gather them into a close-knit boarding school community far from a big city, and you can be certain that they will create their own special vocabulary, full of daring metaphors, cryptic abbreviations, surprising semantic shifts, and curious coinages. Because one of the purposes of such parlance, like the thieves' cant to which it is close kin, is to help the group *not* to be understood by the uninitiated, the pizza man, quite naturally, did not comprehend the special usage of *bag the za* in St. Paul's School slang.

Nobody is quite sure where the word *slang* comes from. According to H. L. Mencken, *slang* developed in the eighteenth century (it was first recorded in print in 1756) either from an erroneous past tense of *sling (sling-slang-slung)* or from the word *language* itself through blending and clipping, as in "(thieve)*s'lang*(uage), (beggar)*s'lang*(uage), and (circu)*slang*(uage). Both theories make the point that jargon and slang originate with a particular trade, class, or group. The boundaries between slang, cant, argot, and colloquialisms are wavering, but slang words often emigrate and become adopted and adapted by large cross sections of the general population.

The average prep school student combines the more outré elements of American jive talk, beat lingo, student cant, and regionalisms with a number of terms that are pure preppie. Thus, I have adopted the broad term *slanguage* for this disquisition on the informal speech (seldom the writing) of students (seldom faculty) at St.

Paul's School (with considerable overlap with other schools, both private and public). Most of these words are not to be found in even the most up-to-date dictionaries of American slang.

Slanguage words tend to lead mayfly lives, counting their duration by days instead of decades. For every one that survives there are dozens of crib deaths. Like Shakespeare's poor player, they have their hour upon a school's stage and then are heard no more. But while their birth is more violent and their extinction more rapid than those of standard English speech, all slanguage words are created by a number of time-honored methods of word formation. Analyzing the nature and shape of slanguage words offers us insight into the ways that *all* new words are formed.

CLIPPING. The shearing away of a part of a word so that the remainder comes to stand for the whole is called clipping. Much of prep school slanguage consists simply of the shortening of familiar terms used so often by a homogeneous group that a hint is sufficient to indicate the whole. Brevity is the soul of slang.

Thus, one who attends *prep* (preparatory) *school* is a *preppie* (clipping plus the pet suffix *-ie*). Preppies start life at school as *newbs* ("new boys"; girls are also newbs). Preppies who board live in *dorms*, decorate their rooms with *taps* (tapestries), and look forward to the hours for *interviz* (intervisitation: permission for boys and girls to visit each other's rooms). Preppies start each day by going to *breck* (breakfast) and perhaps *chap* (chapel) for nourishment and nurture. Afterward come classes, whose titles are sometimes clipped—*Am Hist* (American History), *Gee-Trig* and *Calc* (Geometry-Trigonometry and Calculus), *Anthro* (Anthropology), *Eco* (Ecology), and (gasp!) *Hum Per* (Human Personality).

Preppies who get *psyched* (clipping and conversion of "psychology") to *moto* (clipping and affixing of "motivate") and don't *vedge* (vegetate) or *noid* (clipping and conversion of "paranoid") on *exams* will produce good grades to show their *rents* (parents) and look good on their *aps* (college applications). Then all will be *kosh* (kosher). On spring afternoons some preppies go to *lax prac* (lacrosse practice), where they hope to be *jocks* (jockstrap) not *spazzes* (spastics) as their *bods* (bodies) soak up *rays*. If a preppie gets *hammed* (hammered) on alcohol, he or she may experience harsh *vids*. *Vid*, a clipping of "video" or "videre," means something one sees or experiences—almost anything really.

ACRONYMANIA. The most extreme forms of shortening are initialisms and acronyms, in which words are reduced to their initial letters, which may be pronounced individually or strung together as words. Such verbal compacting is bound to occur in a community whose members need to refer to buildings and activities succinctly yet comprehensively. Students often initialize the names of their schools—SPS for "St. Paul's School" and *CD* for "Country Day"—and they relax at the CC (community center) and pick up their mail at the *PO*. Transgressors of school rules may find themselves cowering before the *DC* (Disciplinary Committee) to be *DCed*. PGs are postgraduates—large-muscled jocks whom other schools recruit solely for the purpose of competing against us. PGs have beards. They also have wives and children who come to games to root for them.

The arrival of coeducation at St. Paul's in 1971 inspired the verb *to scope* (a foreclipping and conversion of "telescope") and the derived noun *scoper*, "one who appreciatively ogles the opposite sex." From this process has arisen an unofficial organization named *SCOPERS*, a reverse acronym, or bacronym, for "Students Concentrating On the Palatable Extremities of the Reciprocal Sex." The society is open to both boys and girls.

SHIFTY CONVERSIONS. Because modern English has shed most of its endings that mark the parts of speech, its words are endowed with the happy facility of changing identity with great ease. This ability of words to rail-jump from one grammatical class to another is called function shift or conversion.

As the boundaries between slanguage word classes become blurred, almost any interchange, it seems, is possible: "that guy's a real *grind*" (verb into noun), "they sure serve great *munchies* at our *feeds*" (verbs into nouns), "let's go *pond* a newb" (noun into verb), "she totally spaced; she just didn't *deal*" (transitive verbs into intransitive verbs); "the teacher really *dissed* me on that test" ("wiped me out," prefix into verb), and, most exotically, "I've just been *harshed* and *latered*" ("done in," adjective and adverb into passive verbs).

Very often, several methods are simultaneously at work in the formation of a slanguage word. When a preppie smokes a cigarette, he or she *bogues.* Turn the last name of cigarette-sucking Humphrey Bogart into a lowercase word, convert it to a verb, and then lop off the last syllable. Voilà, *to bogue.*

CURIOUS COMBINATIONS. True to its Germanic heritage, the English language loves to form compounds by welding together two independent words to create a new concept. Among such combinations in the slanguage corpus are:

> **moon-man:** a noun describing a person not like us. We are popular, attractive, and clever. Moon-men

may be intelligent, but they are not popular, attractive, and clever. Moon-women do not exist.

space cadet: a neophyte moon-man.

embryo Joe: a large-brained computer jock; a science-loving moon-man. Easily identified by his flannel shirt buttoned to the neck and the myriad of pencils and pens sticking out of the front shirt pocket.

all-nighter: what is pulled when one stays up all night studying.

wale on: to embarrass or to triumph, as in "I waled on his face."

sesh corner: from *session;* the partying area of a student's room.

Sometimes in English we combine words in such a way that the beginning of one word runs into the end of another. *Smog* (smoke + fog) and *motel* (motor + hotel) are well-known modern examples. Two prep school slanguage terms that mean "sickeningly sloppy" may fit this category. About half of my informants insisted that *scuzz* is a blend of "scum" and "fuzz," while the other half claimed that *scuzz* is a clipping of "disgusting." Similarly, some maintain that *rasty* is a blend of "rancid" and "nasty," while others assert that it is a pure coinage.

FIGURATIVELY SPEAKING. In the slanguage of prep schools the metaphorical substitution for the plain, literal word can be seen in full activity, and it is not surprising that the words with the greatest metaphorical energy concern academic life. Disastrous performances on tests generate two striking linguistic clusters. The first I call the rotisserie metaphor: one doesn't just do poorly on an exam; he or she (in vaguely increasing degrees of heat) gets *smoked, lit, torched, fried, burned, baked, toasted, roasted,* and *sizzled.* Then there is the violent, paramilitary pattern: one gets *bombed, shot down,* or *blown away.*

Note that all the verbs are cast in the passive voice. The preppie is seen as a helpless victim of menacing, uncontrollable forces. (No wonder they noid!) In pale contrast stand a few active verbs, most notably *"to ace a test"* (probably a golfing metaphor). In truth, preppies often perform superbly on examinations, but they don't care to talk about it.

A few other slanguage metaphors are:

cooler: a refrigeration metaphor for the infirmary, where one's social activities are put on ice.

tool: one who is exploited by others; a stooge.

to cruise: a ship or airplane metaphor denoting a social tour of the campus after hours or an illegal visit to another's room.

butter: a student who fawns on others, especially on teachers.

tasty: refers to almost any good thing besides food— Grateful Dead music, high grades, pretty women.

to brick: to noid in the extreme; a clipping of "to s—t bricks," as in "I looked at the first question on the test and totally bricked."

to bag: to drop from one's agenda, as in "bag the za."

In the figures of speech we call synecdoche and metonymy, a part of the whole or something closely associated becomes a designation for the whole, as in "wheels" for "automobile" and "White House" for "U.S. government." Preppies do not watch television;

they watch *the tube,* or they *tube out.* They also play *puck* (ice hockey), *pit,* and *hoop* (the last two being basketball). Such players are called *jocks.* In *jock* an item of sports apparel has been (figuratively) clipped and has come to stand so metonymously for the person that girls can also be jocks.

SEMANTIC ANTICS. Once a word has entered the language, it doesn't just stand still and remain the same forever. Old words often don new meanings to fit new situations, and some words over time acquire more than a hundred different definitions.

In prep school slanguage we discover that the word *lush* now means "easy," as in "a lush course," or, through conversion, "I'm going to lush out this winter and not take a sport"; that a *fog* ("he's a real fog") is not a weather phenomenon but, rather, like the space cadet and moon-man, a person who is out of it; that *score* now means "to get," as in "score me another dessert"; that a *rack* is a bed; and that *jamming* is collective pigging out.

One process of semantic change linguists call emptying. Words that once possessed very real and specific meaning can, with time, become vague and general. In the late sixties in prep schools and elsewhere, everything was *cool* or *nifty,* from the style of a friend's boots to an epic poem. By the mid seventies the vogue words expressing approval were *unbelievable, fabulous,* and *fantastic.* Today the affirmative grunt words on campus include *intense, awesome, jock* (as an adjective), *coping,* and *chill,* be the object an athletic victory or a symphony. The most frequently used negative grunt words are *rude, rasty, lame, harsh, heinous,* and *hurtin':* "After that test, I'm really hurtin' " or, through personification, "This meal is hurtin'."

GLITTERING COINAGES. Few words in English are fashioned from unrelated meaningless elements. The abundance of word-making resources that I have outlined and the cheerful willingness of English to borrow from other languages combine to make outright coinages rare. Nonetheless, the prepspeak mint has turned out an impressive array of pure fabrications:

> **doof** (or *doofus*): one who habitually spaces.
>
> **dweeb:** a nerd; a social incompetent who wears white unalligatored socks and high-water, polyester trousers.
>
> **gomer:** another label for a social reject. Close kin to a nerd and a dweeb.
>
> **frelk:** to cavort wildly. Possibly a blend of "freak" and "frolic."
>
> **yack:** to throw up. Probably related to "yuck."
>
> **snarf:** the act (or non-act) of falling asleep on or in a bed with one's clothes on. One who snarfs is a *snarfer*. The concept of snarfing has become so sophisticated that four degrees have been identified—*fourth-degree snarf*: falling asleep on top of bed with no shoes on; *third-degree snarf*: falling asleep on top of bed with shoes on; *second-degree snarf*: falling asleep under covers with no shoes on; *first-degree snarf*: falling asleep under covers with shoes on.

To understand the true meanings of words and to catch the colorful music of a language, we must hear and see a vocabulary not in isolation but in context. As a demonstration of prep school slang as it is really slung, I offer this monologue written by Anne Fulenwider when she was a student in my tenth-grade English class at St. Paul's:

HEINOUS FIRE INSPECTION VIDS

Hey, dude! We totally motoed on our room to make it the most coping setup. But now I'm completely noiding about fire inspection rules. Dude, there's no way our room'll pass!

Yah, I'm really gonna put my bed so there's a straight line to the door. What if some heinous newb walks in at like 7:30 in the morning and asks some absurdity like how to get to breakfast? I mean she's sure to wake me up with my bed right in front of her, and I just would not be psyched for that. Racking is key in my life, dude.

And what's this "no delays" deal? How can you create a mellow sesh corner without like a wardrobe and bookshelves all around? That's lame!

What's even lamer is how our room would look without any delays. I mean, you'd walk into our room, and everything would be right there, ya know? Dude, what kind of gomer would have their room set up so you could walk in and everything's right there? Suppose you were changing or something and it was interviz and some guy busted you in just a towel or something? Dude, not at all!

Besides, once they get past the beds, people have a perfect view of the whole room—sofa and chair lined up neatly against the wall—and you can't even cover the sofa and chair with taps! Sure, I have a sofa and it's unupholstered, but it's secondhand, like from the Salvation Army or something, and it's the biggest rast show I've ever seen in my life! It has like little brown and puke green vids all over it, so that once the people get into the room, they'll probably yack all over the floor. It just doesn't deal, dude.

Okay, what's the sesh about the walls? Only twenty-five percent covered? That is just lame! I'm just not gonna live surrounded by bright white walls, es-

*pecially when I could have a poster of Jerry Garcia up
there. And it's just uncool that they give you like one
outlet for the* whole *room. Like you're supposed to
turn on the hein overhead fluorescent light. The thing
is just not chill.*

Dude, I think I'd rather just die in the fire.

Throughout history it has been the custom to frown
on slang as a kind of vagabond language that prowls the
outskirts of respectable speech. The cynical Ambrose
Bierce wrote in *The Devil's Dictionary* that "slang is the
speech of him who robs the literary garbage-carts on
their way to the dumps." Back in 1710, Jonathan Swift
railed against the "continual corruption of the English
tongue," especially "the refinement which consists in
pronouncing the first syllable in a word that has many,
and dismissing the rest," as in "mob" (for *mobile vul-
gus*). Other subjects of Swift's scorn were "certain words
invented by some pretty fellows," including *sham, ban-
ter, bubble, bully, shuffling,* and *palming*. Not long after,
in 1755, Dr. Johnson, insisted that words such as *frisky,
gambler,* and *conundrum* "ought not to be admitted to the
English language." Despite the weighty authority of
such purists as Swift and Johnson, all of the words condemned above have achieved solid positions in even the
most dignified discourse.

In fact, slang is nearly as old as language itself. In all
languages at all times, slang expressions have entered
the stream of standard usage to enrich or pollute, depending on one's point of view. But, whereas previously it took decades or even centuries for a slang word
or expression to gain acceptance, today such terms often pass into sturdy use overnight. This accelerated
achievement of status may be explained by our pen-
chant in America to laugh at tradition or by the increasing frankness of all expression. The process may be

spurred by mass communications or the blurring of class lines.

Slang is a powerful stimulant that keeps a language alive and growing. Many of our most valuable and pungent words and expressions began their lives keeping company with thieves, vagrants, addicts, hipsters—and preppies. One day in the not so distant future, everyone may laugh at dweeb newbs who snarf at parties, and pizza chefs will not space when asked to bag the za.

$\mathcal{T}$eaching in Ghettoburg

> $\mathcal{N}$*ine score and fourteen years ago our white forefathers brought forth upon this continent a black race of slaves, deceived in liberty and dedicated to the supposition that all men are created equal and treated equal, except black men.*
>
> —"The Ghettoburg Address"

Thus wrote one of my tenth-grade students in an essay entitled "The Ghettoburg Address" during my sabbatical year of teaching English at Simon Gratz High School, an inner-city (euphemism for all-black) school in North Philadelphia. In 1955 I had graduated from West Philadelphia High School; fourteen years later, I took my one-year leave from St. Paul's School to go home again and return to the school system that had spawned me.

During that school year of 1969–70 I began to discover the political realities of school in the ghetto and to see how the setup produced a lot of built-in failure.

117

Gratz sat on the corner of its boundaries. If you happened to live across the street (in which you might be white or middle class), you didn't go to Gratz. Whether or not gerrymandering aforethought was at work, our student body was 99.44 percent black (we had three Asians and one Caucasian on our rolls) and 95 percent poor, removing the kind of social mix that is a crucial factor in lifting achievement levels. While two other high schools sat underused just outside our territory, Gratz bulged with 4,500 students who were processed in two sequential shifts—7:50 A.M. to 12:05 P.M., then 12:15 P.M. to 4:30 P.M. Our kids were with us at least an hour less than most youngsters in other schools, and they spent their shifts going straight through classes without any breaks for lunch, study hall, or socializing. When two of my "slow" classes came to me each day for sixth and seventh periods (3:10–4:30), many were numbed, hungry, and eager to get out of the building.

Apathy, not violence, was the most formidable opponent to education at Gratz. Our average daily attendance was 68 percent, and once inside the building, the student body collectively cut thousands of classes a week. Only half of our tenth-graders returned to Gratz the next year, and only one in three graduated from the school.

Still, as I recollect in the tranquillity of more than two decades after my experiences at Gratz, I feel some joy. If education means change and the discovery of psychic mobility, I know that some of my students had at least a day of education in my classroom. I know that I touched some of my students and that they touched each other. I remember the faces, often vacant, hostile, and weary of the ritual. But almost every day something beautiful happened to some of the faces, and the heavens, rather than falling, opened. What happened often had to do with language.

I wanted my students to know that language is not a set of "thou shalt"'s out there, but an instinct in here, as natural as breathing and digesting and mating—a part of people, not apart from them, a making of meanings in the brain, a gathering of meanings from the world, an offering of meanings to the world. In the service of this philosophy, the core of my writing program was a weekly journal, ungraded and risk-free, in which each student began not with an exterior assignment but with him or herself. I stressed that bold and sincere thinking, and even sheer quantity, would count more than mechanics. In response there poured forth talent so rich and vast that it made my blood quicken:

> *"I'm all alone in this world," she said.*
> *"Ain't got nobody to share my bed.*
> *Ain't got nobody to hold my hand,*
> *The truth of the matter's I ain't got no man."*
>
> *Big boy opened his mouth and said,*
> *"Trouble with you is you ain't got no head!*
> *If you had a head and used your mind,*
> *You could have me with you all the time."*
>
> *She answered, "Babe, what must I do?"*
> *He said, "Share your bed and your money too."*

> *I remember once when I was stopped by the fuzz for suspicion of snatching some lady's pocketbook. So he took me down to the 39th police station, and it seemed like it was two hours while I was down there, and you talk about somebody being hungry. Man, I was ready to eat the cigarettes in my pocket.*

> *When the freedom, or should I say bush, came out, the pink man did not like this one bit. And he was very*

mad when our females started wearing it. Want to know why? He is angry because some of our women are not spending the money on all that possum fat. VO5 pinkies are mad because they can't go home and tell their families about "that dumb nigger lady," as they would say it, who has bought $10 worth of hair lard.

According to the Coleman report (*Equality of Educational Opportunity*, 1966, based on 600,000 school-age children), the sense of relationship to the environment, what our principal called the student's sense of "fate control," is crucial to his or her ability to learn. What happened to my students' sense of life's promises, I asked myself, when only one in fifteen had a room of their own at home and only one in ten a room where they could go to study? Again and again in their writing my students questioned their place in and control over the universe, as in these haiku poems:

> *Why have I risen*
> *From the bosom of life*
> *Into this world of hatred?*

> *I am lost in a river—*
> *The river of prejudice.*
> *What am I doing here?*

> *The birds sing with beauty.*
> *Blood stains the turning earth.*
> *What does it all mean?*

> *Where is the key to education?*
> *What will I find*
> *When the door is opened?*

> *Why must I hold this gun?*
> *Why must I kill my brother?*
> *Is God alive?*

And this quatrain:

> *Mama's sick.*
> *Daddy's drunk.*
> *Brother's in jail*
> *And I just flunked.*

And this free verse:

> *Thoughts*
> *Running freely*
> *Skipping, hopping,*
> *Never stopping.*
> *Life,*
> *Death,*
> *Heroin, meth.*

I wanted my students to know that Black English is a major dialect spoken by a great number of Americans of African descent, that Black English has a long and rich history that began in Africa when people from many villages were transported to American slave markets, and that many of the distinctive forms of Black English have been identified as residues of West African languages.

All language is dialect, including both Black English and standard English. But Black English is a dialect with a difference. While most other dialects are confined to specific geographical regions, Black English is a way of speaking shared by many black people living throughout the United States. And while the majority of regional dialects are relatively free from social stigma, Black English has been branded as an inferior form of standard English. Yet Black English is a vessel that fully serves the needs of its users. Its grammar is just as elaborate, rule-governed, and internally consistent as that of standard English. It's just a different grammar. The meaning of "He didn't do nothing" is perfectly understood by all Black English speakers and by standard English speakers as well. In "They bad kids" the subject-verb relationship is quite clear, and in "You don' stop messin' wif me, I'm gonna hit upside you head," the *if-then* logic is perfectly evident, even if not stated. "My sister sick" means that she is sick right now but it won't last very long, while "My sister be sick" indicates a continuing, long-term illness. Such a subtle distinction is more easily and concisely communicated in Black English than in standard English. As Ishmael Reed makes clear, the use of Black English indicates neither a lack of education nor an inability to speak in other tongues: "You not gone make me give up Black English. When you ask me to give up Black English you askin me to give up my soul. But for reasons of commerce, transportation, and hassleless mobility in everyday life, I will talk to 411 in the language both the operator and I can understand."

Still, it was only fair to warn my students that in certain contexts someone, perhaps a prospective employer, might make a damaging judgment about a double negative or an *a* before a noun beginning with a vowel, as in "a ink pen." Those who wanted to get a job outside their community would have to think about learning the mainstream, standard dialect and becoming, so to speak, bilingual. At the same time, I asked my students to pray with me for the rapid withering of that so very comforting, so uniquely human myth: *We* talk right and *they* don't. Would anyone want to snuff out such "non-standard" expressions as "I offed him," "I just snapped out," "She runs her mouth too much," and "The boys in our neighborhood throw their eyes up the girls' dresses"?

Such sentences suggest an integral part of my students' writing that constantly delighted me. In the academic life at St. Paul's School we take for granted a convention called "the writing voice" that differs in varying degrees from one's speaking voice, depending on the writer and the task of writing. At Gratz few students employed such an aesthetic distance in their composing.

It is unfortunate that the beautiful oral language of many of my students got clogged up in their pens. But when the style and content were able to traverse that tricky route from mind and spirit to paper, the results were often, as Franz Fanon describes in *The Wretched of the Earth*, "a vigorous style, alive with rhythms, struck through with bursting life; . . . full of color too, bronzed, sunbaked."

As my students found and practiced their voices, they increasingly affirmed their blackness. In celebrating their negritude, in exploring aspects of their consciousness that were being liberated, and in the combative tone of their writing, my students were acting out the history of black literature in the United States and the rearrangement of political relationships during their lifetimes:

BLACK IS BEAUTIFUL

Black is beautiful.
Beautiful is black.
Let's get together.
That's where it's at.

Black is powerful.
Black is sharp.
Everybody's learning
To be proud of their dark.

Black is colorful.
Black is cool.
We're no nigger children.
We're no fools.

Black is being proud.
Black is black.
Let's stick together
'Cause that's where it's at.

I've Got a Name

I've got a name.
Don't call me boy.
I've got a name.
I'm not a walkin' toy.

Try "Mister" or "Sir"
To suit your taste.
But don't call me boy
'Cause you're out of place.

Mother Africa

This is my land.
I've made it so.
With the sweat of my brow
I've helped it grow.

By the laws of man
I should be free.

But the white man's laws
Are as chains to me.

HEY, WHITEY

Back off Whitey,
'Cause Nigger is no longer my name.
Back off Whitey,
'Cause your dog and mine are no longer the same.
Back off Whitey,
'Cause I'm hip to your dehumanizing game.

WHEN SOMEBODY SAYS

When some cracker says,
"You're a good boy,"
You don't know whether to blush
And melt like a stick of butter
Or to just stand there and stink
Like a fresh shit.

My students in the Ghettoburg classroom never let
me get hung up on aesthetic abstractions. Either the
material overlapped with their realities and needs or
they turned off with unsophisticated visibility. They allowed me a few castles in the air, but early in each building project they demanded foundations underneath. In
preparing to study George Orwell's *Animal Farm,* for example, we spent two weeks reading a number of Ethio-
pian and Greek fables. The students wrote their own
fables, taking care to use appropriate animals and appropriate plots to yield a moral that followed from the
story. Then we discussed this question: "If you were a
modern writer of fables, what aspects of contemporary
society would you choose to make a comment on?"
From the discussion to the blackboard went such social

problems as gangs, drugs, violence, racial prejudice, cars, cigarettes, and pollution. Finally, the students fashioned their own fables for our time:

THE ALLIGATOR AND THE FROG

Once upon a time there lived an alligator and a frog. Each lived on the opposite side of each other. One day they were sitting on a rock and the alligator said, "We the alligators are better than you green and all-colored frogs." And the frog said, "We the frogs are better than you scaly punks." And they just kept it up until they challenged one another.

"All right, you little short sissy, we'll see you and your puny gang tomorrow," said Alligator.

"Your challenge is accepted," said Frog hatefully.

The day arrived and the fight was about to begin. After a five-minute prayer they all began to fight. The frogs were hopping all over the alligators with knives and clubs in their feet, while the alligators were biting and snapping at the frogs with their mouths.

And finally the fight ended and the alligators and the frogs realized that all their leaders had been killed along with others. So from that day on everyone took heed of the killing.

Moral: *Gang war—it just don't make no sense.*

When we experienced *Animal Farm* itself, our emphasis was on the uses and abuses of power and the malignant growth of discrimination among the animals. During one lesson, we compared the goals and commandments of the Animal Revolution with those of the Black Panther Party: "Any party member found shooting narcotics will be expelled from the party"; "No party member will use, point, or fire a weapon of any kind unnecessarily or accidentally at anyone."

In our next unit we explored the world of Greek my-thology. We compared the ancient stories with the Black Muslim myth of the creation of white people by Mr. Ya-cub, a malevolent, "big-head" scientist, as told in *The Autobiography of Malcolm X*. We saw that the scientific, empirical truth of a myth is not what is most important. What counts is that it furnishes a transcendent set of explanations for a particular group of people, that it fills their lives with sufficient meaning to make their living and striving worthwhile. The students then created their own gods and myths, and many of the writers cap-tured in mythic form a sense of their own existences:

> *Jason, god of drugs, is a descendent of Linus, god of Laziness. Jason and his followers are very dangerous people. They steal and kill just for money to keep their habit going, and they call to their god Jason to bring them Speed, Monster, and Skag.*
>
> *Jason is an evil god. After his followers have taken the dope, Jason makes them sick and they need another shot. Many of the followers die from O.D.'s.*
>
> *Finally, Zeus promised to overthrow Jason by fire. Zeus conjured up one of his biggest fireballs. It struck Jason and that's where we get Sunday.*

Teaching at Simon Gratz High School was the best course I ever took. I knew that when I visited the ghetto for one year, I would go there to learn all I could. I tried not to delude myself into thinking that I would be sav-ing any minds or souls. Still, it doesn't seem fair that most of the time I was the one doing all the learning.

$\mathcal{H}$appy Media

$\mathcal{O}$ne well-lit July afternoon, Stu, Chris, and Gary go to the St. Paul's School auditorium to set up their video cameras at various angles to and distances from the long steps in front of the hall. Stu mounts his studio camera for a side view, Chris readies his for straight-ahead shots, Gary plants his inside the hall, atop the balcony and looking down the steps, and Al, who has come along to help, prepares to rove the set with his portable rig.

Responding to an announcement at lunch, fifty students and teaching staff assemble for an hour to play out the scene. With calm authority, Doug, the director, explains the concept of the action to the assembled throng and sends them to their places. The cameras start.

On the finished videotape, the students are frolicking—dancing, horseplaying, tossing Frisbees. Suddenly "SUDDENLY" flashes on the screen, and the background music changes from light to ominous. The teachers appear, locked in two rigid lines, their lips set

128

tightly, their grim faces begoggled, their heads be-
decked with hunting hats. Summer school director Phil
Bell, in the role of the czarist general, waves the faculty
forward. They advance inexorably, each one thrusting
forth a tennis racquet.

The students panic and career wildly down the long
steps. The music builds. Dozens of quick cuts: twisted
faces, churning legs, plummeting bodies; several shots
of Doug frozen in a silent scream.

The first line of pedagogues kneels, raises a column
of stringed weapons, and delivers (literally) a volley of
tennis balls at the confused kids. Many victims fall dead
or wounded. A second line rises above the first and,
with deft overhead arcs, bats out another round. More
students hit the hard stone of the steps. Amidst the tu-
mult, Jeff lifts Bev into his arms and mounts the stairs
fearlessly, advancing into the threatening shadow of the
waiting faculty forces. "MY CHILD IS WOUNDED" appears on the screen. Another fuzzy fusillade, and Jeff
and Bev collapse.

Then a tennis ball strikes Carolyn. The impact jars
the baby carriage she has been tending, and the carriage
teeters on a step and careers forward. More cuts as the
camera follows the carriage and the horrified reactions
of the students as the music rises in a grinding cre-
scendo. The forces of tyranny have crushed the inno-
cence of callow frivolity. "STUDY HOURS RESUME."

It has been a typical hour in the life of Mass Media,
one of the courses that make up the St. Paul's summer
school program. Film cognoscenti will recognize the
student project as an exercise in parody derived from
what may be the most archetypal images in international film, the Odessa steps sequence in Sergei Eisen-
stein's 1925 silent classic, *The Battleship Potemkin*.

As you know by now, I am an unrepentant, self-confessed verbivore, a man caught in the web of words. But

I have long felt that language consists of more than just words. I have always viewed my beloved teaching tool, the book, as an audiovisual aid, among the first in history.

Of the medium of print Socrates, in *Phaedrus*, complained, "The discovery of the alphabet will create forgetfulness in the learners' souls, because they will not use their memories. They will trust to the external written characters and not remember of themselves." We now know that the book has enriched our memories and perceptions of the human tragedy and comedy. If, like the book, nonprint media can offer students a broader range of stimuli to which they can respond, they will be more likely to communicate and will tell their stories more richly.

Early in my career as an English teacher at St. Paul's School, I saw that my students lived in a culture that was becoming increasingly involved in television, radio, film, tape, and the computer, and that in these media so many of us are finding much of our information and many of our dreams and modes of living.

The mass media are even putting words in our mouths and minds. In 1984, Minnesota senator and former U.S. vice president Walter Mondale was engaged in a bitter primary race against Colorado senator Gary Hart. In an effort to discredit his rival's policies, Mondale publicly and repeatedly asked, "Where's the beef?" That question may well be the most memorable catchphrase to come out of politics during the tongue-tied 1980s, yet Mr. Mondale was simply lifting "Where's the beef?" from a then-current television commercial for the Wendy's International hamburger chain. In that commercial, three elderly women were shown eyeing a tiny hamburger in a large bun, manufactured by one of Wendy's competitors. While the first two women admire the size of the bun, the third—played by Clara

Peller, who became famous for fifteen minutes (from a statement by pop cultist Andy Warhol)—asks, "Where's the beef?"

In March 1985, Pres. Ronald Reagan told the American Business Conference that "I have only one thing to say to the tax increasers: 'Go ahead—make my day.' " Like Mondale, Reagan was perpetrating a flagrant act of mediaspeak. The president was quoting Clint Eastwood/Dirty Harry Callahan, who, in the 1983 film *Sudden Impact*, pointed a .357 magnum at the small space between some scumbag's eyes. "Go ahead," Harry rasped. "Make my day."

Messrs. Mondale and Reagan are no more mediastruck than the rest of us. As Kurt Vonnegut has observed, "What passes for culture in my head is really a bunch of commercials." Our idioms and catchphrases used to issue from the hum and buzz of everyday, real-life activity. Village blacksmiths knew to heat the irons on their anvils red-hot before hammering them into shape. Otherwise, they would lose the opportunity and would have to fire up the forge all over again. That's why we must "strike while the iron is hot" or there may not be a second chance to "go at it hammer and tongs." One way to seize the moment is to avoid having "too many irons in the fire."

When I assert that a mass media tower of babble is becoming a primary source of English words and expressions, I am absolutely on the level. In this phrase the *level* is a tool used by carpenters and masons to ensure that a frame or surface is precisely horizontal or vertical. May that explanation suit you to a T and get you all squared away. Both *suit you to a T* and *all squared away* are references to the T-square used by draftspersons to make sure that their drawings of right angles and parallel lines are precisely accurate.

Nowadays, pop goes our culture. And as that pop

culture adds snap and crackle to our everyday parlance, our words and expressions are increasingly brought to us courtesy of a new irreality. Television, radio, film, and advertising make us an offer we can't refuse (*The Godfather*), so we come on down ("The Price Is Right") and awaaay we go (Jackie Gleason). I mean cowabunga, dude (*Teenage Mutant Ninja Turtles*, which took it from a greeting exchanged by Buffalo Bob Smith and Chief Thunderthud on the "Howdy Doody" TV show of the 1950s), just when you thought it was safe (slogan for *Jaws*) to think about language, that all-pervasive and persuasive mediaspeak is baaack (*Poltergeist II*). Now it's the real thing (Coca-Cola) and fingerlickin' good (Kentucky Fried Chicken) to the very last drop (Maxwell House coffee). You may shrug "Never mind," but I say "Excuuuse me" and "Isn't that special?" (from "Saturday Night Live" comedians Gilda Radner, Steve Martin, and Dana Carvey).

We are all immersed in a new media environment, a product of forces dramatically converging in our lifetime. By the time he or she is five years old, the typical American student will have spent more hours in front of a television set than he or she will ever spend in a college classroom. By the time that student graduates from high school, he or she will have spent half again as many hours watching television as he or she will have spent in class.

If language is a system through which we deal with reality, I wanted to become familiar with the languages of the new nonprint media in order to help my students catch and crystallize their new realities. Print is certainly a major part of those realities, but it is scarcely the only mass medium to merit careful study. Communication today consists of an orchestration of print and newer technologies, all part of an emerging media ecosystem. In the service of this philosophy, I founded and taught for thirteen years the Mass Media summer school course at St. Paul's.

For six weeks each summer, about two hundred public and parochial high school students from around New Hampshire come to live at St. Paul's, each choosing a major course of study from offerings in mathematics, science, history, foreign language and culture, religion, creative arts, and media. The idyllic setting, the abundance of time, and the motivated and gifted boys and girls who voluntarily forgo the leisures of summer to come and imbibe one another's excellence make for a platonically ideal educational environment. As I try to capture the special life of the summer school, and the Mass Media experience in particular, I feel like a small figure on tiptoe holding out a butterfly net and hoping to snare a few significant and colorful moments before they forever fly away.

Mass Media begins with a fire hydrant. It is the middle of the first week, and the students have embarked on their first field experience with video cameras. Their assignment: to film an inanimate object. The purpose is to explore and develop the potential of early video cameras to "record" the world around them. The kids are nervous, inexperienced, and technologically awestruck. For a while, it seems that the best they can venture is to adjust the focus occasionally. Everyone stands three or four feet from the hydrant and obtains the same static, lifeless shot. A few are bold enough to walk around the hydrant, but none dare approach it.

None, that is, until Melanie gets her hands on the camera. Immediately, she goes for the zoom lens and begins to probe every crack and corner of the hydrant. She pans the chain, tries overhead and low-angle shots, homes in on the artifact's ripples and textures, rack-focuses from one valve to another, and even shoots through the chain links. As thoroughly as Melanie has worked over the hydrant, she has worked over the class. Everyone catches on; everyone is infected with video fever. The students begin to view technology not as an intimidating force, but as potentially creative and liberating force in their lives. Later, while viewing the playback of the class's collective footage, someone says, "I never knew a fire hydrant could be so beautiful."

During the course of the summer, students spend half of each morning learning about the aesthetics of film through a series of short, unconventional films, such as *Begone Dull Care* and *Dream of the Wild Horses*, highly visual experiences that elude literary categorizing and penetrate the consciousness at the deepest levels. The goal here is to open the kids' eyes to the screen as an aesthetic surface, not as just a "window" into a story world of pseudoreality. Then we move on to studying short narratives, such as *An Occurrence at Owl Creek Bridge*, essay films, such as *Why Man Creates*, and documentaries, such as *Nanook of the North*. Finally, we trace the early history of film, from the very first film program publicly presented, the Lumiere brothers' series of short subjects screened at the Grand Café in Paris on December 28, 1895, to a week-long, sequence-by-sequence exploration of Orson Welles's *Citizen Kane*.

Through reading, writing, discussing, reporting, storyboarding, and fieldwork, we want our students to become "cinemate" as well as literate—to enter into the magical conspiracy of electric and electronic light and darkness; to see, feel, and eat film and tape; to participate in the joyous collectivity of film- and video-making.

During the second and third weeks of the summer program, the students' growing cinemacy becomes transformed into reality. Now they are free to experiment with miniprojects, media adventures in which the emphasis is more on the process than the product. The

Ode-SPS sequence by Chris, Stu, and Doug is one such project. Sue, Sheri, and Bev combine to fashion a scratch-and-doodle film, scratching and drawing each frame directly onto a piece of 16-millimeter clear leader to produce a film made without a camera. To the accompaniment of John Denver's "Teacher I Need You" an animated stick-figure student appears on the screen and bewails the mountain of homework confronting him. Lit by a halo scratched onto the film, Saint Paul enters and pities the poor boy, who wakes up the next morning to find his assignments all done.

Joe works in the school radio station producing a tape of "The Joey K Show," a professional blend of news and music that will be played back during a school lunch. Melanie and Gerry experiment with video montage, intercutting sequences of student life with clips from violent war films. Carolyn and Sally create a multimedia advertising campaign of their original product, Jock Sox. Ross, our resident artist, works with super-8 film and makes an exquisite animated film of the Garden of Eden. Chuck and Al play with audio feedback, a process by which music is fed into the back of a television monitor and, with the manipulation of cameras and our production bay, is transmuted directly into abstract video images.

As the students complete their audio-visionary experiments, they decide to join forces in a collective mini-project, a videotape they call "The Great Escape." On the screen, the students are shown staggering under the weight of tremendous work loads and gagging on dining-hall food. They plan and execute an escape from the grounds but are headed off by headmaster Bell, who, stationed at the school gate with whip in hand, lashes them back to the toils of summer school.

After lunch, each project is shown in the common room for all summer school students who care to come.

Most do, and the screenings become exceptionally intimate times, sprinkled with sounds of laughter and surprise at what is happening on the television or film screen. Usually the media students mingle with the others, answering questions and discussing their work. In their projects, the students have fallen easily into the roles that best suit their respective talents, and each person is unremittingly available to help a classmate by toting a camera or handling a microphone. They become bonded into a kinetic example of film critic Pauline Kael's observation: "Filmmaking is the greatest collective art form since the building of medieval cathedrals."

On the door of the AViary, as our suite of audiovisual rooms is called, is a picture of a woman's face with the caption "People Are Media." Nothing in the course illustrates the cojoining of people and machines better than the crowning Mass Media project—the making of a "yeartape," a videotape yearbook of the entire summer school program.

For the yearbook, most mornings are spent shooting footage in the school chapel and in every summer school class; each afternoon a crew goes out to capture sports action; and the cameras mingle with the evening to record dormitory life, square dances, and cookouts. Now it is easy to spot the media students. They are the ones with the strained neck muscles, the ones who look depressed every time something funny or exciting has the temerity to happen when no camera is present to record it, the ones who, it seems, view the world as if through the lens of a camera, the ones who cannot see without first adjusting their horizontal and vertical sync pulses.

The students shoot a total of forty hours of source material, and they log it all. From that forty hours they create a final storyboard consisting of hundreds of cuts and edits. Continuity and transitions begin to accumulate: a triangular beaker in the chemistry lab dissolves into a fishing net from an ecology-class field trip; the camera cuts from a student writing musical notes on a blackboard to a teacher writing mathematical symbols on another board in another classroom; an experiment in constructing pyramids of cardboard cylinders in a calculus class transmogrifies into the building up and tumbling down of human pyramids at one of the cookouts. The teachers in the Ode-SPS Steps sequence raise their tennis racquets—and then the scene cuts to the tennis courts and the beginning of a sport sequence. I watch my students evolve into electronic children who are extending their senses and perfecting their intellectual and emotional circuitry.

A race against the clock begins. As graduation nears, the editing facilities glow day and night. Students and staff begin to live in the AViary, and one learns to step over the slumbering bodies. As one student wrote at the end of the course, "Showing the yeartape was like watching three weeks of sweat and tough work go up on display wide open for comment. The feeling is as big a high as you can ever get. I really can't comment much further because the day is hazy with tears of joy and sadness.

"I got out of Mass Media exactly what I paid," wrote one student. "I paid with lack of sleep, with screaming, quietly discussing, laughing, singing, listening, and loving. I know that you have to go through hell to get to heaven. But if you make it, it ain't like any other place you've ever been or ever will be again."

Two nights from the end, the students ask Ann, a college intern in English, to come to the AViary and sing "The Lake Isle of Innisfree," a song she had previously presented in chapel. They stretch out on the floor, and there is total silence but for Ann's bell-clear voice:

I will arise and go now, and go to Innisfree,
And a small cabin build there, of clay and wattles made:

Nine bean-rows will I have there, a hive for the honey-bee,
And live alone in the bee-loud glade.

The mood is relaxed, intimate, contemplative. Ann finishes, and no one moves or speaks. A deep sadness is felt, and the members of the class become aware of a strange fact: they want to finish this yeartape, but to finish will mean the end of their time together.

Next evening, the last of the session, the class video-tapes the summer school talent show and stays up much of the night editing the raw footage onto the master tape. Finally the credits are done and so is our task. Martha, a college intern in the course, sings to the class; some of the students go out to watch the sunrise; and Gary, the other intern, is awakened by a vapor of baby powder dumped on his head.

The kids ask us to take them downtown for a last breakfast, and together we all sit giggling over our eggs and orange juice. Two hours later we go to graduation, string three monitors around the auditorium, jack the sound into the hall speakers, and show the tape to the other students and their families.

"I still get an incredible feeling every time I think of the yeartape," wrote another student, "because we created that! At sixteen I became a surrogate parent, watching my child grow and mature. That's a corny way to express it, but making something like that has part of you in it."

On the screens, the students see themselves as luminous presences living and moving and having their being in places that have become precious. They will return for a reunion the next June, and once more the yeartape will work its magic upon them, re-creating memories grown dim. Everyone will cry. It is always the best moment of the year.

*L*etters to Lederer

*M*y weekly column, "Looking at Language," began life in June of 1981. From the start of my more-than-decade-long adventures in language columny, my readers have presented graphic evidence that the art of letter writing is alive and well and living in northern New England. Thousands of letters have come as daily gifts that inspire ideas for more columns and books. The word *inspire*, from the Latin, means "to breathe into," and submissions from my readers have breathed life into my mission as a verbivorous teacher.

I also believe that the act of writing breathes life into the writer him or herself. In fact, researchers have recently demonstrated what most writers already know — that setting words to paper makes one feel better. A series of studies concluded that people who wrote about their traumatic experiences produced significantly higher levels of T cells with which to fight viruses and infections, and visited doctors and psychotherapists less frequently than they had before.

My correspondents range in age from centenarians

to elementary-school pupils. Not long ago I received a letter from Emily Minkow, a nine-year-old third-grader at the Pleasant Street School, in Laconia, New Hampshire: "Dear Mr. Lederer: I read your book *Crazy English*. I also like fooling around with words. I drew some pictures of crazy phrases and words."

Attached to Emily's letter were three skillfully executed drawings. The first shows a girl meeting a ghost and saying, "Get a life." In the second drawing another girl finds black envelopes in her postal box, and the caption reads, "Blackmail." The third picture depicts a farmer offering a cow to a boy. The farmer says, "Keep her. She gives good milk," and the boy answers, "OK." The caption reads, "Have a cow."

Children are so alive to the possibilities of language and see words and phrases and life itself in startling, fresh ways. My friend Chester Ryeguild, a quadriplegic, tells the story of a time that a little girl saw him coming down a hallway in his wheelchair and exclaimed, "Look, Mommy. There's a man with round feet!" Mother blushed crimson with embarrassment and tried to silence her daughter. But Chester was not at all offended, simply delighted by the girl's linguistic imagination.

A child looks at his grandmother's varicose veins and wonders why "she has lightning in her legs." Another child gazes at a crescent moon and observes, "The moon is just waking up." A two-and-a-half-year-old looking at the stars dancing across the black night sky says, more wisely than she can know, "Look, Mommy, that's God's big dot-to-dot."

A first-grader explains that because her principal is female, she's really a "princessipal." A six-year-old boy jumps up on a kitchen sink and exclaims, "Look, Mommy and Daddy, I'm sink-ing!" Small children sometimes call a tongue depressor an "ah-stick" and a sliding board a "whee-down."

The poet Carl Sandburg quotes a little boy who had just pulled up a large weed from the soil. When his mother said, "My, you were strong to get that out!" the boy answered, "I sure was. The whole earth had hold of it!"

When I visited classes at the Antrim, New Hampshire, Elementary School, I found that the fourth-graders used their artwork re-creationally to interpret words and phrases:

- "I blue up the balloon": a little girl blowing up a blue balloon.
- "My lips are sealed": a girl with a mammalian seal on her lips.
- "Mom said there is such a thing as a fur tree": a large tree wearing a black fur coat.
- "Dad said to put *dear* at the beginning of the letter": a deer stands at the top of a letter, followed by "Mom."
- "Mommy says, 'When your car breaks down, a toe-truck comes to pick it up' ": a huge toe on wheels pulls an automobile.
- "They were all board at the meeting": boards sitting in a row of seats.

Where has all the wordplay gone? Long time passing. Where has all the word fun gone? Long time ago. Fortunately, most of us do not lose our innocent, fresh-eyed love of and abiding curiosity about language. Day after day, through more than a decade, inquiries about etymology, dialects, bloopers, and puns have gleamed out from my mailbox, and I'm pleased to share some of the brightest gems, these from my Maine and New Hampshire readers.

Every time I receive a question about language from a reader, I say to myself, "I'm glad you asked me that." Often the reason for my reaction is that, in the process of thinking about or researching the query, I learn something about language that I hadn't known before.

DEAR MR. LEDERER: What's up with the adverb up? *Warm up, tune up, ink up, do up, crank up, cook up—there's no end to it!* —H.L.

DEAR H.L.: Thousands of thanks for catching us up on *up*, the ever-present two-letter word that may have more meanings than any other and, at times, no meaning at all.

It's easy to understand *up* when it means skyward or toward the top of a list. And clearly there are crucial differences between *call* and *call up* and *beat* and *beat up*. But I have to wonder why we warm ourselves up, why we speak up, why we shower up, why a topic comes up, and why we crack up at a joke.

Let's face up to it: we're all mixed up about *up*. Usually the little word is totally unnecessary. Why do we light up a cigar, lock up the house, polish up the silverware, and fix up the car when we can more easily and concisely light, lock, polish, and fix them?

At times, verbs with *up* attached mess up our heads and screw up our minds with bewildering versatility. To look up a chimney means one thing, to look up a friend another, to look up a word something else. We can make up a bed, a story, a test, our face, and our mind, and each usage has a completely different meaning.

At other times, *up* verbs are unabashedly ambiguous. When we wind up our watch, we start it; when we wind up a meeting, we stop it. When we hold up our partners in doubles, are we supporting or hindering them?

What bollixes up our language worse than anything else is that *up* can be downright misleading. A house doesn't really burn up; it burns down. We don't really throw up; we throw out and down. We don't pull up a chair; we pull it along. Most of us don't add up a column of figures; we add them down. And why it is, pray tell, that we first chop down a tree, and then we chop it up?

Maybe it's time to give up on the uppity *up.*

DEAR MR. LEDERER: I am enclosing a sonnet I have written and which I thought might amuse you. I have found many people who feel as I do about the lively word gay. *I am sure you have heard from many of them.*

DESECRATION

With homosexuals I have no quarrel:
"Chacun à son goût" is what I always say.
But one thing they have done which is immoral.
They've raped and ravished, ruined the word gay.

It was a lovely, lyrical, laughing word,
A ribbon round a maypole in the spring,
Spoke of lambs gamboling; madrigals were heard,
Lifted low spirits, caused saddened hearts to sing.

They stole the word—it was a thoughtless theft—
And took it for the status it would bring,
Sexed it and used it; now all that is left:
An empty word with an archaic ring.

Dear gay, *with childlike charm, once pure and chaste,*
It breaks my heart to find you so debased.

—B.K.

DEAR B.K.: *Gay* originated from the Old French *gai,* and for many centuries did mean "keenly excited, effervescent, high-spirited." That meaning is evident in a sentence from Louisa May Alcott's *Little Women* (1870), "As Mrs. March would say, what can you do with four gay girls in the house?" and in the label "The Gay Nineties," one that no longer works to name the current decade.

It was not until the second half of the twentieth century that *gay* began traveling the linguistic path of specialization, making the same journey as such words as *chauvinism, segregation, comrade,* and *colored.* Shortly after World War II, homosexual activism popularized the concept of Gay Liberation—and many of my readers have written to complain that a perfectly wonderful word has been lost to general usage.

But as much as you and I may need *gay,* the gay community needs it more—as an emblem of self-esteem, as an emphasis on the cultural and social aspects of homosexuality, and as a weapon of self-defense. Many bewail the transformation of *queer,* but it was the heterosexual constituency that altered that word and made it also a noun. In the same way that African Americans came to insist that *Negro* was a word fraught with too many negative connotations, homosexuals seized upon *gay* as a more acceptable and palatable term than *fag, homo, queen, fruit, pervert,* and—another antique and airy word that had already been transmuted by antihomosexuals—*fairy.*

For those who lament the loss of *gay* to general discourse, I recommend that henceforth they be merry.

DEAR MR. LEDERER: My friends and I at Hopkinton High School were wondering if there is a word for each individual flake in a box of Wheaties. If so, how is that word spelled? —R.A.

DEAR R.A.: Puzzles like these allow people like me to use the tools of linguistics, the scientific study of language, to address the crucial issues that shape our lives. The controversy you raise is whether or not the plural word *Wheaties* has an analogous singular. That is, is there a Wheaty or Wheatie?

One of the loopier aspects of the English language is that it contains many words that exist only in plural form. You can't contract just a single heebie-jeebie, willy, jitter, jimjam, or delirium tremen. No matter how short a period of time you examine among the annals of history, you will never discover an annal. Sift as thoroughly as you can through the debris in a room blown to smithereens; you'll never come upon just one smithereen.

Is *Wheaties* one of those plurals with no corresponding singular? Here the linguist asks if the word *Wheaties* can be significantly distinguished from the other plurals I have listed above. I believe that it can.

When we have a group of physical entities that somewhat resemble each other, such as professors or kites or leaves, those objects usually have both singular and plural descriptors. *Heebie-jeebies, annals,* and *smithereens* are not concepts composed of discrete entities similar to each other in appearance, but a box of Wheaties is clearly made up of individual flakes that look somewhat alike. Just as each item in a Wheaties box is a flake, each flake could be called a *Wheaty* or *Wheatie*.

Now what about the spelling? Is it *Wheaty* or *Wheatie?* To answer this burning question, let's examine the structure of the word. *Wheaties* clearly consists of a root, *Wheat,* and what is known as a "pet suffix," pronounced *ee* and denoting cuteness and affection. We find this pet suffix in such words as *daddy, mommy, kitty, doggy, cutie, nightie,* and *sweetie.* Note the pattern: words with short vowels followed by doubled consonants tend to take -*y* as the spelling for the pet suffix, while words with long vowels tend to take -*ie.* Paying special heed to the word *sweetie* as a near twin in sound, *Wheatie* is my orthographic preference.

* * *

DEAR MR. LEDERER: For some time I have been search-ing for the origin of the phrase waiting with bated breath— *or is it* baited? *So far no luck at the library or with my own collection of books on word and phrase origins. Can you help me in this search? —D.C.*

DEAR D.C.: You are not the only one to experience confusion with *bated* vs. *baited*. A recent headline in our state newspaper proclaimed, "Bath Iron Works Submits Bid With Baited Breath."

By failing to write ". . . With Bated Breath," the edi-tors opened up a real can of worms. In the context of "bated breath," *bated* is a form of *abated* and means "re-duced in force or intensity, restrained." You may have heard about the cat who chewed on some strong-smell-ing cheese, breathed into a mouse hole, and waited with baited breath. Otherwise, it's *bated*.

The *baited/bated* confusion illustrates the difficulties that we English speakers can experience with homo-phones, words that sound alike but have different spell-ings and meanings. How many times have we read about menus guaranteed to "wet your appetite"? If writers would bear (not bare) in mind the knife's-edge metaphor—the menu is the whetstone upon which the knife's edge of the appetite is sharpened—they would always spell the verb correctly.

Olive Tardiff, a reader of mine from Exeter, New Hampshire, once encountered this sign on a bulletin board: "Fur Trees for Sale, $2 and $3." That homopho-nous howler inspired Olive to wax poetic:

> *Oh, woodsman, won't you spare that tree*
> *And save the luxury furs for me?*
>
> *Good mousetrap builders, so they say,*
> *Can scarcely keep the world away,*

And one whose trees bear ocelot
Can sell them, by the carload lot.

Chinchilla would be fine, I think,
But give me trees that drip with mink.

Since money doesn't grow on trees,
I settle for a row of these.

Not long ago another newspaper in my state began a story with a sentence describing a woman whose "voice broke with emotion as she clutched her toe-headed daughter." If I had a toe for a head (perhaps a result of toe-maine poisoning), I'd need a lot of clutching too.

Again etymology is the key to spelling. For centuries, *tow* has been a name for flax or hemp prepared for spinning. A towhead is a person, usually a boy, who has very blond hair, almost flaxen or pale yellow. The little girl in the news story was actually towheaded, not (gasp) toe-headed. Ewe no watt eye mien.

DEAR MR. LEDERER: An expression that I've heard frequently during the past five years is "That's a whole nother ball game." Since nother *isn't a real word, how do you explain the sentence? —J.B.*

DEAR J.B.: The *whole nother* construction has indeed caused head-scratching among verbivores. Here's my theory:

English words often contain prefixes at the beginning of words, like *prewar*, and suffixes at the end of words, like *goodness*. But the rampant usage that you cite contains, in my opinion, the rarest of rare: a printable American infix.

An infix is a syllable or syllables inserted not at the beginning or the end, but inside a word. The Greeks called the process tmesis, from a classical root meaning "cutting." Infixes are fairly common in such languages as Sanskrit, Latin, and Filipino, but almost nonexistent in English. In fact, it may be that only slang can split the atom of an English word.

For emphasis, the British often employ *bloody* as an infix, as in *absobloodylutely*, or *blooming*, as when "Fair Lady" Eliza Doolittle sings, "Oh, so loverly, sitting absobloominglutely still." In the United States, especially in the South, we encounter the likes of "I'll guarangoddamntee it" and the insertion of a vulgar participle, as with *inf——ingcredible*. In the phrase *a whole nother ball game* I believe that *whole* is a printable American infix that has been plunked down in the middle of the word *another*.

DEAR MR. LEDERER: *I am outraged! Who is this Professor A. L. Rowse that he dares to modernize the works of Shakespeare? May all his nibs drop ink blots! Why on earth should he feel it necessary to make Shakespeare's beautiful writing "easier for present-day readers"? If they can't handle the Elizabethan English style, let 'em read comic books.*

I get equally vehement over all the idiotic translations of the Bible. I refuse to even consider any version but the King James. A friend in Papua New Guinea once sent me the New Testament in Pidgin English, which was far more acceptable than some of these "new" Bibles. —B.Y.G.

DEAR B.Y.G.: A. L. Rowse is an Oxford University professor emeritus and a formidable and controversial Shakespearean scholar. In his series *The Contemporary Shakespeare*, Rowse has roused considerable debate by turning the traditional language of the Bard's thirty-seven plays into modern English, smiting the *thou*s, *thee*s, *hast*s, and *spake*s and excising what he calls "superfluous difficulties," such as archaic grammar and unintelligible words. As the *London Telegraph* waggishly proclaimed:

> *How kind of Doctor Rowse*
> *To cut out all those "thees" and "thous."*

Translating centuries-old English literature into modern idiom is nothing new under the sun. Except for a handful of professors and graduate students, most of us who encounter the *Beowulf* poet read him in modern translation, and Geoffrey Chaucer's works have undergone numerous updatings.

But *Beowulf* was written in Anglo-Saxon, which is essentially a foreign language to modern readers, and the Middle English of Chaucer is inaccessible to all but the most scholarly. Shakespeare, on the other hand, speaks to us across four centuries in an eloquent and recognizable tongue. While an intelligent accompanying gloss is generally required, I agree with you that Professor Rowse's "translation" appears to be an act of gratuitous mutilation.

The Bible is another matter. Because it was originally written in Hebrew, Greek, and Aramaic, translation is essential, and the King James Version (1608–11: also known as the Authorized Version) is certainly the best-known and most widely revered English translation. But does that Bible, the language of which is woven into the warp and woof of our collective consciousness, render all other versions invalid? I think not.

Bear in mind that the King James is far from being the earliest English version of the Bible. It was both a new translation and a revision of the first Protestant rendering into English, that of William Tyndale (1525) and completed by Miles Coverdale (1535). It retains 80 percent of the language of the earlier versions and preserves a style that is more archaic than the diction of the time in which it was written.

Another reason for the various revisions of the King James Version is that many of the words that existed in the early seventeenth century are no longer in use or no longer have the same meaning. In Genesis, we read: "And Joseph made haste; for his bowels did yearn upon his brother." Obviously *bowels* possessed a different meaning in Middle and early Modern English: "the center of the emotions." Most readers today are puzzled by the word *naughty* as it appears in this passage in Jeremiah: "One basket had very good figs, even like the figs that are first ripe: and the other basket had very naughty figs, which could not be eaten, they were so bad." The puzzle is solved when we learn that *naught* and *nought* were once simply variant spellings, and *naught* meant "nought-y, or worthless."

Turning to the New Testament, we note that the Holy Ghost is not a ghost in the modern sense but, rather, the Holy Spirit. And, because it has taken on new associations, the word *charity* has been changed to *love* in newer translations of Paul's ringing statement in First Corinthians: "And now abideth faith, hope, and charity, these three: but the greatest of these is charity."

The most widely accepted English translation since the King James Version, among Protestants and many others, is the *Revised Standard Version* (1946–52), recently ecumenized in the *Common Bible* (1973). These new Bibles incorporate material from ancient and medieval manuscripts, especially the Dead Sea Scrolls, which were unknown to the King James translators. At the same time, many readers of these modern editions are astonished to find how much of the original King James language has been preserved therein.

Professor Rowse himself readily admits that "changing Shakespeare is like putting your head in a hornet's nest." I join you in putting the sting on him by asserting that dumbing down the Bard is none of his beeswax. But discoveries of new sources and new concepts in linguistics, anthropology, and archaeology, along with

constant changes in contemporary English idiom, combine to demand ever-newer translations of the Bible.

*KIND SIR: Our f-f-family has a chromosomic f-f-fault, and
to a woman, all souls f-f-find it impossibly f-f-frustrating to
say a word which starts with f, without a humiliating amount
of vocal stumbling.*

*Possibly by this point, Richard (Oh, may I call you Rich-
ard? You truly stand as a grand Sabbath habit in our happy
bungalow), your sharp sight has cast about and found that
which is unusual about this communication. What is awry in
this script? Think, Richard, think! A vital unit is missing!*

*It is truly amazing how many various words you can form
without using this tiny linguistic building block. It won't occur in this work, nor will you find it in my following small
story about four good chums—David, Mary, Dorothy, and
John. Astonishing and astounding, not to say confounding.*

*All four boon pals plan a gala party. David and John opt
for watching football, but Dorothy and Mary will play at punning, or Fictionary or, possibly, musical chairs.*

*Mary says, "I want a small drink. Would you kindly bring
a dry martini for us, David?"*

*"Naturally, my darling. And Dorothy? What may I bring
for you?"*

*"Oh, David, how about a virtuous nonalcoholic nip? Pos-
sibly a glass of good, nourishing milk?" purrs Dot.*

*"I'm with you, Dorothy," says David, as John and Mary
cast knowing looks back and forth.*

*John joins our group. "I'll go for a Scotch mist. Mary
mustn't drink solo."*

*"Oh, thanks, darling John! Now all can avoid caviling
about our bibulous drinking habits," sighs Mary, with grati-
tudinous joy.*

*"It's truly bacchanalianism," murmurs Dorothy puck-
ishly.*

Quickly, to avoid additional fulmination, David says, a bit crustily, "But now—a toast!"

"Skoal!"

"Prosit!"

"Salud!"

"To us!"

Finish

This linguistic task can find a solution in twenty-five additional ways. May I point out an unmistakably tacit finding? A tyro may wish to start with an omission of q or x, or possibly z.

—Yours truly, Mary Edge Merrill, Friendship, Maine

DEAR MARY EDGE MERRILL: Thousands of thanks for your sprightly linguistic circus of words. You brilliantly clown around with words in a way that is not that visible to most who look at what you say.

I'll stop playing your game now and reveal that your story is, of course, "ill at *e*'s," devoid of the most frequently occurring letter in our language. This gimmick has a name: passages that deliberately omit one or more letters of the alphabet are called *lipograms*. The most extensive lipogram in English is the 1939 novel *Gadsby* by Ernest Vincent Wright, which contains fifty thousand words—and not a single letter *e*. In lipogram service, however, no writer in English has ever equaled the achievement of Spanish writer Carlos Ibañez, who in each of his twenty-eight novels banished a single and different letter of the Spanish alphabet.

Alas, though, there are four words in your missive that are afflicted with the offending letter. Those words are *Edge, Merrill, Friendship,* and *Maine.*

Just kidding!

*W*hat's in a Name?

*D*EAR MR. LEDERER: *Upon reading your columns on palindromes, I must say I was personally intrigued. Have you ever wondered if there are people who have first and last names that, when spelled backwards, read the same—names such as mine?*

—*Marc Cram, Topsham, Maine*

DEAR MR. CRAM: First and last names can be self-contained palindromes. The best-known palindromic first names for males are Bob and Otto. Because female first names more commonly end with vowels or are clipped, the distaff list is considerably longer: Ada, Ava, Anna, Eve, Hannah, Lil, Mim, and Nan.

Hannah can also be a last name, as in Daryl Hannah, the willowy star of *Clan of the Cave Bear*, *Roxanne*, and *Steel Magnolias*. Similar in the pattern of its letters is the last name Harrah, as in the famous Reno, Nevada, casino and Toby Harrah, former major league third baseman.

153

The most famous palindromic last names in the news today are sported by tennis sensation Monica Seles (who first attained her number one ranking in the palindromic year of 1991) and former New Hampshire governor and Bush administration chief of staff John Sununu. Mr. Sununu's surname is a near-palindrome, needing to be made possessive, as in the beginning of this sentence; plural, as in "What America needs is more John Sununus"; or contracted, as in "Now Sununu's won."

A search through back issues of *Word Ways: The Journal of Recreational Linguistics* for full first-and-last-name palindromes reveals that Kavon Novak was considered as a stage name for Kim Novak and that real, flesh-and-blood people with palindromic names listed in actual telephone books include Leon Noel, Anna Danna, Nell Allen, Mary Byram, Norabel Lebaron, Neil Lien, Revilo P. Oliver, Oyo O. Oyo, and Burmese premier U Nu and Cambodian premier Lon Nol. Now we can add the name Marc Cram, of Topsham, Maine, to the list.

Close kin to the palindrome is the anagram, a rearrangement of all the letters in a word or statement to make another word or statement. According to *Word Ways*, the most widely used American name in which the last name is an anagram of the first is Gary Gray. Other anagrammatical examples of this genus include Ronald Arnold, Roland Arnold, Eric Rice, Edna Dean, Neal Lane, Dale Deal, Norma Moran, Lewis Wiles, Albert Bartel, Erich Reich, and Romeo Moore.

Lewis Carroll, the pen name of Charles Dodgson and author of the playful *Alice in Wonderland*, displayed an extraordinary talent for this kind of anagram. "Flit on, cheering angel!" was his conversion of the letters in the name Florence Nightingale, and "Wild agitator means well" of William Ewart Gladstone. Followers of Disraeli, another Victorian prime minister, extracted "I lead, sir" from his name.

The name of the most famous of all English writers, William Shakespeare, yields four wonderfully revealing anagrams: "Has Will a peer? I ask me"; "We all make his praise"; "I swear he's like a lamp"; and "Ah, I speak a swell rime."

Now take a look at the letters in the name Noriega. Reverse the first four letters, then the next three, and you come up with "Iron Age," an apt double play that characterizes the unyielding primitiveness of the world's most (in)famous Panamaniac.

The actress Theda Bara did the job herself. Her screen name was a deliberate anagramming and palindromizing of the letters in *Arab death*. If you've ever wondered why the legend of Elvis Presley continues to grow so remarkably years after his death, remember that "lives" is an anagram of Elvis. That's why Elvis lives.

During the 1990–91 crisis and war in the Persian Gulf, Saddam Hussein became what was perhaps the most anagrammed name in history. Some of the most telling rearrangements include: "Hissed, 'Damn USA,'" "Dimness had USA," "He damns Saudis," "Mad hand issues," "Sad human sides," "Mad as his dunes," "U.S. demands his a . . . ," "Mess Saudi hand," "I, uh, mad sadness?" "A mad sun hissed," "I smashed Sudan," and "His end a sad sum." The best palindrome I've seen about the Baghdad Bully was created by writer and wordmeister Clem Wood: "Drat Saddam, a mad dastard."

All of this palindromic and anagrammatical word magic should come as no surprise. After all, an anagram of the word *palindromes* is "Splendor am I!" and the reversal of the word *anagram* is "Margana," which sounds as if it should be somebody's name.

I wish that Ross Perot had been elected president of the United States in 1992. That is not a statement of po-

litical philosophy but, rather, the fond hope of a logologist, a player with words.

Ross Perot is a man who was born to be an anagram
because his name surrenders the most apt anagram in
the political history of our nation—"sore sport." Add
Perot's first initial, *H.,* and you get the almost-as-won-
derful "short poser."

Having criticized Al Gore as "the ozone man,"
George Bush transmogrifies into "He bugs Gore."
Bush, of course, succeeded Ronald Wilson Reagan,
whom some accuse of being an "insane Anglo war-
lord."

Instead of Ross Perot or George Bush, we have as
president William Clinton, whose first and last names
present a daunting challenge to the anagrammarian because they contain three *l*'s, three *i*'s, no *e*'s, and a high
density of consonants. We note the tantalizing words
illicit and *nation* dancing among the letters in *William
Clinton,* but "Illicit man won" lacks one *l* from the original name, "I will calm nation" needs an extra *a* from
somewhere, and "Nation will climb" an extra *b*—and,
alas, Mr. Clinton's middle initial is *J,* for *Jefferson.* Fortunately, we are able to extract from *William Clinton* the
perfect anagrams "No calm till I win" and "Can now
limit ill." Unfortunately for Bill, from *William Jefferson
Clinton* we can unscramble "Jilts nice women. In for
fall."

What's in a name? Plenty, when you start playing
around with the first, middle, and last names of our
American presidents. Here's a forty-two-question quiz
in honor of our forty-two chief executives, from Washington to Bush, the only two to share their first name,
by George, to Clinton, the only president, along with
Washington, whose name ends in *-ton.*

One-sixth of our presidents had different names in
office than the ones with which they were born. Ulysses

S. Grant came into this world as Hiram Ulysses Grant. When his name was mistakenly entered on the West Point register as Ulysses S. Grant, he eagerly embraced the error because he detested the initials H.U.G. and loved having the initials U.S., as in "United States" and "Uncle Sam."

By the time they became president, Stephen Grover Cleveland and John Calvin Coolidge had deleted their first names, while David Dwight Eisenhower simply reversed the order of his first two names. Gerald Rudolph Ford and William Clinton are the adopted names of Leslie Lynch King and William Blyth.

In this forty-two-question quiz (Mr. Clinton is indeed our forty-second president, but only forty-one men have held the office), I use the names by which these men were popularly known when they were president.

All answers to this quiz repose in "Answers and Explanations I."

1. Quick: name four presidents whose last names consist of just four letters.

2. Who is the only twentieth-century president whose last name begins with a vowel?

3. Who are the only two presidents whose last names begin and end with the same letter?

4. What five presidents have last names that are also familiar words when uncapitalized?

5. What eleven presidents have last names that form two complete words when uncapitalized?

6. Who are the only four presidents whose last names contain *oo*?

7. What is the longest uninterrupted sequence of presidents who have double letters somewhere in their first, middle, or last names?

8. What is the longest sequence of presidents whose

last names begin with letters that are in alphabetical (but not touching) order? What is the second-longest string?

9. Who is the only president with a two-syllable last name in which the stress falls on the second syllable? He is also the only president whose last name ends with a vowel.

10. How many presidents have a last name ending in *-son?*

11. When *-son* ends a last name, it usually means "son of." What other presidents have patronymic last names?

12. No president has a last name whose letters occur in alphabetical order, although *Fillmore* comes wonderfully close. Who is the only president whose last name is composed of letters in *reverse* alphabetical order? What is unusual about that sequence?

13. Who are the only three presidents whose last names alternate between consonants and vowels?

14. If we take away the first letter of the word *president,* we get *resident.* This technique is called a beheadment. List the last names of five presidents, each of whose last names can be beheaded to form a new word. Which two can be beheaded a second time?

15. Which two sequential presidents' last names are the farthest away from each other alphabetically?

16. What two presidents were succeeded by a man named Johnson?

17. Who is the only president to have a state named after him?

18. What four presidents have had state capitals named after them?

19. Who is the only president to have the capital of a foreign country named after him?

20. Who is the only president whose last name consists entirely of letters that, when capitalized, remain themselves when turned upside down?

21. What two presidents share the same first- and last-name initials? What second pair of presidents shares first- and last-name initials that are the reverse of the pair you've just named?

22. Who was the only president with a middle name consisting of a single letter?

23. Who is the first president with a first name that is shared by no other president?

24. What president has a first name that is both the first name of a famous cartoon character and the last name of an important religious leader?

25. Who are the only two presidents to serve sequentially and to have the same first name?

26. What is the most popular presidential first name?

27. What president owns the following distinctions?: He changed his first and middle names so that they matched the initials of his country. He is the only president with a first name beginning with a vowel other than *A*.

28. What president's first name became the name of a popular doll?

29. Who is the only president whose first name begins with the same letter as his last name ends?

30. What four presidents have first and last names that are alliterative, that is, beginning with the same letter?

31. Who is the only president who has twice as many letters in his first name as in his last?

32. In what president's last name can you find the first name of an earlier president?

33. In what president's first name appears the last name of a later president?

34. What two presidents' middle names are the last names of earlier presidents?

35. Note the pattern in *Taft:fat*, a description of our three-hundred-pound twenty-seventh president. Complete the pattern of the following sentence by filling in the last name of a president: *To last,*   *retracts a lot.*

36. What two presidents have a last name that, when the letters are reversed, becomes a negative statement to an inferior?

37. Which president's last name is the complete name of a famous cartoon character?

38. Which two presidents have last names that are also the names of a current car model and car company?

39. Other than having been president, what is Ronald Reagan's connection with Grover Cleveland?

40. Who is the first president to be popularly called by his initials?

41. Gerald Ford and George Bush are the only presidents with exactly ten letters in their first and last names. Name four presidents whose first and last names total just nine letters.

Identify the presidential names that generate the following anagrams:

42. a. War on: he gets going. (first and last names)
   b. Loved horse, tree too. (first and last names)
   c. A word with all: I'm fat. (first, middle, and last names)
   d. Eleanor kin, last fond lover. (first, middle, and last names)
   e. He invaded wiser, with God. (first, middle, and last names)
   f. Zing! Joy darken, then fled. (first, middle, and last names)
   g. Hush, nix—criminal odor. (first, middle, and last names)
   h. Old age ran, ran. (first and last names)

$\mathcal{A}$nswers and Explanations I

Phrases *(page 10)*

1. unfinished business **2.** split-second timing **3.** Truth is stranger than fiction. **4.** Put it in writing. **5.** parting of the ways **6.** keeping body and soul together **7.** Blood is thicker than water. **8.** two jumps ahead of the sheriff **9.** right between the eyes **10.** Leave well enough alone. **11.** a drop in the bucket **12.** The buck stops here.

Homophones

The list on page 48 consists of words that form homophones of themselves when the letters in each word are rearranged (anagrammed), as in *break-brake*. Try it and see. The next list consists of words that form homophones of themselves when a letter other than the first or last is deleted, as in *heroine-heroin*.

Triple homophones (explanations for unusual or ambiguous words are provided):

1. adds, ads, adz (cutting tool) **2.** aisle, I'll, isle **3.** ait (island), ate, eight **4.** bald, balled, bawled **5.** beau, bo (hobo), bow **6.** bight (bend in a coast), bite, byte **7.** bird, burd (maiden), burred (characterized by burs) **8.** bole, boll, bowl **9.** born, borne, bourn (stream) **10.** braise, brays, braze (to solder)

11. burro, borough, burrow **12.** bused, bussed, bust **13.** cay (reef or low island), key, quay (one of only two triads in which each word begins with a different letter) **14.** censer (dispenser of incense), censor, sensor **15.** cent, scent, sent **16.** chord, cord, cored **17.** cinque (five), sink, sync (informal for *synchronization*) **18.** cite, sight, site **19.** clamber, clammer, clamor **20.** crews, cruise, cruse (small vessel)

21. dew, do, due **22.** do (in music), doe, dough **23.** does (deer), doughs, doze **24.** earn, erne (sea eagle), urn **25.** ewe, yew, you (a quadruple if one counts the *yoo* in *yoo hoo*) **26.** ewes, use, yews **27.** fane (church), fain (happy), feign **28.** fays (elves, faiths), faze, phase **29.** firs, furs, furze (gorse shrub) **30.** flew, flu, flue

31. for, fore, four **32.** fraise (fortification), frays, phrase **33.** frees, freeze, frieze **34.** gild, gilled, guild **35.** gnu, knew, new (the second triad in which each word begins with a different letter) **36.** gored, gourd, gourde (monetary unit of Haiti) **37.** heal, heel, he'll **38.** hoard, horde, whored **39.** holey (having holes), holy, wholly **40.** idle, idol, idyll

41. knap (to break with a quick blow), nap, nappe (sheet) **42.** knead, kneed, need **43.** knows, no's, nose **44.** lacks, lacs (resinous substances), lax **45.** lay, lea (tract of open ground), lei **46.** lea (alternate pronunciation), lee, li (music

term)   **47.** load, lode, lowed   **48.** lochs, locks, lox
49. mean, mesne (intermediate), mien (demeanor)
50. meat, meet, mete

51. mussed, must, musth (state of frenzy)   **52.** nay, née
(born), neigh   **53.** o, oh, owe   **54.** palate, pallet, pallette (armor plate)   **55.** pare, pair, pear   **56.** peas, pease, pees
57. poor, pore, pour   **58.** praise, prays, preys   **59.** rain,
reign, rein   **60.** raise, rays, raze

61. raiser, razer (one who razes), razor (these last two
clusters contain words of opposite meaning that sound the
same)   **62.** rapped, rapt, wrapped   **63.** read, reed, rede
(counsel)   **64.** road, rode, rowed   **65.** rood (crucifix), rude,
rued   **66.** sac (pouch containing fluid), sack, sacque (short
jacket)   **67.** seas, sees, seize   **68.** sewn, sone (measurement
of sound), sown   **69.** sign, sine, syne (since)   **70.** slew,
slough, slue (to swing around)

71. sol (fluid colloidal system), sole, soul   **72.** sold, soled,
souled (possessing a soul)   **73.** stade (stadium), staid, stayed
74. steal, steel, stele (part of a vascular plant)   **75.** stoop,
stoup (beverage container), stupe (hot, wet cloth)   **76.** tael
(Chinese unit of value), tail, tale   **77.** tea, tee, ti (in music;
Asian tree)   **78.** teas, tease, tees   **79.** their, there, they're
80. to, too, two

81. toad, toed, towed   **82.** vane, vain, vein   **83.** wail,
wale, whale   **84.** ware, wear, where   **85.** way, weigh, whey
86. we, wee, whee!   **87.** whined, wind, wined   **88.** wise,
whys, wyes (Y-shaped objects)

Quadruple homophones: **89.** ai (three-clawed sloth), aye,
eye, I (three different first letters among the four)   **90.** bi (informal for *bisexual),* buy, by, bye   **91.** birr (force, energy,
vigor), brr (expression of cold), bur, burr (Scottish accent)
92. carat (weight of precious stones) caret (mark indicating
an insertion), carrot, karat (purity of gold)   **93.** cense (incense), cents, scents, sense   **94.** heigh (exclamation), hi, hie

(to hasten), high **95.** lays, laze, leas (tracts of open ground), leis **96.** oar, o'er, or, ore **97.** peak, peek, pic (picador's lance) pique **98.** right, rite, wright (worker), write **99.** sew, so, sol (in music), sow **100.** weal (prosperous commonwealth), we'll, wheal (welt), wheel **101.** weald (wooded country), whealed (welted), wheeled, wield.

And the most homophonous champion—**102.** air, are (metric land measure), ere, err, eyre (English itinerant judge), heir (three different first letters)

Punderful Headlines *(page 52)*

1. TV OR NOT TV **2.** SMALL MEDIUM AT LARGE **3.** FARMERS FEAR NO WEEVIL **4.** A SITE FOR SOIREES **5.** OSTRICH IN TIME SAVES NINE

6. MOVIE DEEMED TO HAVE TOO MUCH SAXON VIOLENCE **7.** NY'ERS ARE OFTEN FOUND READING BETWEEN THE LIONS **8.** BAKER INVENTS A FOUR-LOAF CLEAVER **9.** RESIDENTS SUE TRACK FOR INDY SCENT EXPOSURE **10.** CHUNG IN TEAK

11. GREAT BALSA FIRE **12.** IT RAINED DATSUN COGS **13.** SENATOR IS DRAWN AND QUOTED **14.** CHURCH MEMBERS REPAINT AND THIN NO MORE **15.** RESEARCHER DISCOVERS A HAYDN SIKH AFFAIR.

16. WEED 'EM AND REAP **17.** ELIZABETH IS QUEEN OF DENIAL **18.** THE KOALA TEA OF MERCY IS NOT STRAINED **19.** AMERICANS DINE ON THE SOTTED LION **20.** U.S. MEN HAVE A WISH CALLED FONDA.

Britspeak *(page 101)*

1. billion—a million million in Britain, a thousand million in the United States; biscuit—cracker or cookie; bitter—beer;

bob—one shilling, or a small amount of money; braces—suspenders; catapult—slingshot; chemist—druggist; chips—french fried potatoes; crisp—potato chip; dinner jacket—tuxedo; full stop—period; ground floor—first floor; hockey—ice hockey; ice—ice cream; jelly—gelatin dessert; knickers—women's underpants; lift—elevator; M.P.—member of parliament; minister—cabinet member; plaster—Band-Aid; pocketbook—pocket notebook or billfold; public school—private school; pudding—dessert; spectacles—eyeglasses; stone—fourteen lbs.; stuff—unprintable in this respectable book; sweet—dessert; till—cash register; tin—can; torch—flashlight; vest—undershirt; waistcoat—vest

2. aisle—gangway; bar—pub; bathroom—loo or W.C. (water closet); bobby pin—hair grip; clothes pin—clothespeg; counterclockwise—anticlockwise; hardware store—ironmonger; kerosene—paraffin; napkin—serviette; quilt—eiderdown; shrimp—prawn; silverware—cutlery; sled—sledge; swimsuit—swim costume; telephone booth—call booth or kiosk; thumbtack—drawing pin or push-pin; zero—zed.

3. advert—advertisement; banger—sausage; bobby—policeman; chucker-out—bouncer; don—college teacher; draughts—checkers; dressing gown—bathrobe; dustbin—trash can; fortnight—two weeks; hoover—vacuum cleaner; plimsolls—sneakers; porridge—oatmeal; pram—baby carriage; scone—baking-powder biscuit; spanner—wrench; starter—appetizer; switchback—roller coaster; takeaway—takeout; telly—television.

4. ett, bean, bown, clark, dyutee, eyethur, eevohlushun, feah, figger, GArage, herb (with the *h* sounded), labORatory (five syllables), lezhur, leftenant, missyle, pahtriot, prihvacee (short *i*), shedule, SECretry (three syllables), sujjest, tomahto (but potayto), vihtamin (short *i*), zehbra.

5. aeroplane, aluminium, cheque, defence, fibre, grey, inflexion, enquire, gaol, jewellery, judgement, manoeuvre, marvellous, organisation, pyjamas, plough, programme, speciality, spelt, storey, tonnes, phial, whisky.

6. Japan are leading the world in exports; different to; in hospital; living in Baker Street.

7. a. Put some gravy on my beef. **b.** My compliments to the cook. **c.** In his hand he held a pistol. **d.** That's worth a lot of money. **e.** Bring the food to the table.

f. How about a game of darts? **g.** Do you hear me, or are you deaf? **h.** Boil me some potatoes for lunch. **i.** I'm dead on my feet. **j.** That's one of my favorite songs.

k. You're a darned liar. **l.** It's around the next corner. **m.** How are the wife and the kids? **n.** Please pass the bread, the butter and the cheese. **o.** If you drink too many of those bitters, you'll get drunk.

p. He's got some long legs.

What's in a Name? *(page 157)*

1. Polk, Taft, Ford, Bush **2.** Eisenhower, which is also the only presidential last name that contains four syllables **3.** Taft and Nixon **4.** Pierce, Grant, Ford, Bush, Carter, and (in Britain) Hoover **5.** washing/ton, a/dams, a/dams, jack/son, fill/more, john/son, ha/yes, gar/field, ho/over, john/son, nix/on

6. Roosevelt, Coolidge, Hoover, Roosevelt, all twentieth-century presidents, the last three having served sequentially **7.** William McKinley, Theodore Roosevelt, William Taft, Woodrow Wilson, Warren Harding, Calvin Coolidge, Herbert Hoover, Franklin Roosevelt, Harry Truman **8.** Cleveland, McKinley, Roosevelt, Taft, and Wilson; Coolidge, Hoover, Roosevelt, and Truman; also Adams, Jefferson, Madison, Monroe **9.** Monroe **10.** Eight: Jefferson, Madison, Jackson, Harrison, Johnson, Harrison, Wilson, and Johnson

11. In the names Adams, Adams, and McKinley, the *s* and *Mc* are patronymics. **12.** Polk. The letters are within six of each other in the alphabet. Moreover, the name James Knox Polk contains the adjacent letters *j, k, l, m, n, o,* and *p.* **13.** Madison, Tyler, Nixon **14.** a/dams, a/dams, g/rant, h/ayes, t/aft; g/r/ant, h/a/yes **15.** Washington and Adams **16.** Lincoln and Kennedy, both assassinated **17.** Washington, along with the nation's capital, 7 mountains, 8 streams, 10 lakes, 33 counties, 9 colleges, 121 cities and villages, one monument, and at least one famous bridge **18.** Jackson, MS; Jefferson City, MO; Lincoln, NE; and Madison, WI **19.** Monroe—Monrovia, Liberia **20.** Nixon
  21. John Adams and John Quincy Adams; Andrew Jackson and Andrew Johnson. The presidents within each pair share the same first name. **22.** Harry S Truman. The *S* is not an initial and is not followed by a period. **23.** Thomas Jefferson **24.** Calvin Coolidge—Calvin (and Hobbes) and John Calvin **25.** James Madison and James Monroe
  26. James—Madison, Monroe, Polk, Buchanan, Garfield, Carter. Tied for second place are John with four—Adams, Quincy Adams, Tyler, and Kennedy—and William with four—Harrison, McKinley, Taft, and Clinton. **27.** Hiram Ulysses Grant changed his name to Ulysses Simpson Grant. **28.** The teddy bear is named after Theodore Roosevelt, who, while hunting in Mississippi, once spared the life of a bear cub. **29.** Theodore Roosevelt **30.** Woodrow Wilson, Calvin Coolidge, Herbert Hoover, and Ronald Reagan.
  31. Rutherford B. Hayes **32.** Andrew or Lyndon B. Johnson—John **33.** Rutherford B. Hayes—Ford **34.** Ronald Wilson Reagan and William Jefferson Clinton **35.** Like *Taft:fat, To last, Carter retracts a lot* forms a palindromic statement that reads the same forward and backward. *Taft: fat* is an especially appropriate palindrome for the three-hundred-pound president.

36. William and Benjamin Harrison—*No, sirrah*
37. James A. Garfield   **38.** Abraham Lincoln and Gerald R. Ford (Franklin Pierce is another automotive president.) **39.** Reagan played the part of Grover Cleveland Alexander in a film about the pitcher's life.   **40.** Franklin Delano Roosevelt—FDR, coincident with the many alphabetic agencies that were created during his administration

41. John Adams, John Quincy Adams, John Tyler, and James Polk   **42.** a. George Washington   b. Theodore Roosevelt   c. William Howard Taft   d. Franklin Delano Roosevelt e. Dwight David Eisenhower   f. John Fitzgerald Kennedy g. Richard Milhous Nixon   h. Ronald Reagan

II

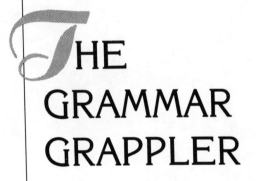

THE
GRAMMAR
GRAPPLER

*L*et the Grammar Games Begin

*I*n the spring of 1988 I received a telephone call from a woman with a charming West Texas drawl. She introduced herself as Sharon Drain, program chairman for the Panhandle Professional Writers Conference, held each summer in Amarillo. "Dr. Lederer, we've read about your bloopers book, and we'd love to have you address our writers' group this August. We'll throw in a modest honorarium—and we'll take you to the Big Texan Steak House, where, if you can eat the seventy-two-ounce steak, you get it free. Then we're all going to go see the musical *Texas,* performed in front of the second-biggest canyon in the U.S. of A., right here in Amarillo."

Not being able to resist Sharon's beguiling pitch and having always wanted to take a tour of Amarillo in August, I made the trip. At the restaurant I didn't even consider ordering and devouring the seventy-two-ounce steak (twenty years ago eating that slab of steak would have been a piece of cake), and, later that evening, I took great delight in the big-as-all-outdoors musical.

171

Even more important, at the conference I met a number of enthusiastic and talented writers and two other program speakers who, quite simply, changed my life.

The first was Robin Rue, the woman who then and there became my literary agent. Ever since, Robin's caring support for my work has ensured that I have been able to write my words about words in books such as this one and to say what I have to say to the universe.

The second speaker was Tom Clark, senior editor of *Writer's Digest*, the national magazine for writers and wannabes. At the Big Texan dinner that evening, Tom invited me to be the *Digest*'s "Grammar Grappler." I accepted and started my grappling in 1989, composing monthly quizzes for more than a quarter of a million writerly readers who are always looking for ways to sharpen their tools of grammar, usage, spelling, and punctuation and to oil the mechanical parts of their craft.

To begin this part of the book, try your hand and mind at a selection of Grammar Grappler games I've designed to test your skills in the mechanics of written English. An additional swatch of spelling and punctuation challenges reposes in a later chapter of this section. Give each quiz your best effort before consulting the extensive "Answers and Explanations II" at the end of this book.

Pluralsy

Are you afflicted with "pluralsy"? Do your eyes glaze over and does your breath quicken whenever you need to pluralize nouns such as *hoof, fish, criterion, Egg McMuffin,* and *mongoose?* If so, you may have the dis-ease.

Almost every noun in English possesses a property called number, which means that it can be either singular or plural. When you were a young and innocent student, you learned how to convert singular nouns to plural nouns, and it all seemed quite easy. To show more than one of something, simply add *s* or *es*, and—presto!—you had your plural. Then, just when you thought it was safe to spell your plurals, along came a myriad of exceptions—borrowings from foreign languages, compounds, and the like.

The following quiz will help you to determine if you are a victim of pluralsy. If you are, "Answers and Explanations II" may provide a bit of a cure.

Write the plural form of these singular nouns:

1. *moose*
2. *bus*
3. *Kennedy*
4. *silo*
5. *wolf*

6. *château*
7. *index*
8. *1990*
9. *runner-up*
10. *mother-in-law*

The Strange Case of English Pronouns

Between you and I, pronouns drive myself crazy, and I'll bet they do yourself too. A brief look at the history of the English language tells us why.

Old English resembled Latin in its dependence on endings, called inflections, to express grammatical relationships. As an example of Old English inflections, consider *stān*, the Old English word for "stone":

Nominative and accusative singular	stān
Genitive singular	stānes
Dative singular	stāne
Nominative and accusative plural	stānas
Genitive plural	stāna
Dative plural	stānum

The form of the English noun has greatly simplified from Old to Modern English. Today, nouns remain the same in the nominative and accusative cases and inflect only for the possessive (genitive) and for the plural. In our streamlined Modern English what was once *stān* appears as *stone, stone's, stones,* and *stones'* —four written forms and two pronunciations.

Pronouns, on the other hand, have retained more of their inflections. The first-person pronoun, for example, can exist as *I, me, mine, my, myself, we, us, our, ours, ourself,* and *ourselves*—eleven written forms and eleven pronunciations. To place the differences between nouns and pronouns in context, note that in the sentences "The teacher greeted the student" and "The student greeted the teacher" the changes in the functions of the nouns *teacher* and *student* are indicated not by form but by word order. In the sentences "I greeted her" and "She greeted me," on the other hand, the first- and third-person pronouns *do* change form as they change location and function. Because pronouns assume so many more shapes than do nouns, these little words drive us crazy.

Ever wonder why so many folks misuse, abuse, and overuse the pronoun *myself?*: "They awarded the plaque to John and myself"; "Priscilla and myself like jelly beans." Red Smith, the late and graceful *New York Times* sportswriter, identified the reason most succinctly: "*Myself* is the foxhole of ignorance where cowards take refuge because they were taught that *me* is vulgar and *I* is egotistical."

The only three contexts in which *myself* should ever appear are as a reflexive pronoun used as an object whose subject is the same, as in "He cut himself shaving," as an intensifier, as in "I myself would never cheat on a test," or in special idioms, such as "I did it all by myself."

Whether or not you have a case of pronoun jitters, choose the correct form of the pronoun in each of the following sentences:

1. Edna and *(she, her)* went to see *Rocky XII.*
2. The guide enticed Paul and *(I, me, myself)* to go bungee jumping.
3. It was *(he, him, himself)* I saw hiding behind the lamppost.
4. This is a perfect day for Don and *(I, me, myself)* to climb Mt. Kearsarge.
5. They had looked forward to *(me, my)* coming and were disappointed when I postponed my visit.
6. I expected to find *(him, his)* working in the garden, but he wasn't anywhere in sight.
7. Uncle Horace invited the whole family—my parents, Florence, and *(I, me, myself)*—to stay the weekend.
8. Should we—Grace, Brad, and *(I, me, myself)*—meet you at McDonald's after the seminar?
9. One of the most important benefits of college is the opportunity to talk to those who know more than *(I, me, myself).*
10. The lawyer told *(we, us)* boys to say nothing about the accident.

To Who It May Concern

In one installment of the "Nancy" comic strip, the frizzy-haired heroine is writing a letter that begins, "To who it may concern . . ." The worried Nancy then crosses out the *who* and changes it to *whome*, and then to *whoom*. With a frustrated "Grrr!" she finally settles on the salutation "Dear you all."

In a "Peanuts" episode we see an open-eyed Charlie Brown in bed thinking, "Sometimes I lie awake at night and ask, 'Is it all worth it?' . . . Then a voice says, 'Who are you talking to?' . . . Then another voice says, 'You mean, "To who are you talking?"' . . . No wonder I lie awake at night!'"

Author Calvin Trillin claims that "*whom* is a word that was invented to make everyone sound like a butler.

Nobody who is not a butler has ever said it out loud without feeling just a little bit weird."

Language guru William Safire wishes to hasten the demise of *whom*. Quoth the maven: "Look: I've never pretended to have a handle on *who-whom*. . . . Let us resolve to follow Safire's Rule on Who-Whom: whenever *whom* sounds correct, recast the sentence."

Nancy, Charlie, Trillin, and Safire aren't the only ones who get edgy about *who* and *whom*. A *Sports Illustrated* cover pictured Cy Young Award candidates Rick Sutcliffe and Dwight Gooden and asked the question "Who Do You Like?" In a Washington, D.C., telephone booth, under the sign "Who Shall I Call First?" some wag retorted "An English Teacher."

When my readers ask me for who the bell tolls, shall I tell them that it tolls for *whom?* In the sentences presented in the preceding paragraph, traditional grammar calls for *whom* as the object of the verbs *like* and *call*. That tradition is breaking down, and *whom* may one day disappear entirely—but not yet, at least not yet in formal writing. When the pronoun is used as a subject or predicate nominative, the form should be *who*. When the pronoun is used as an object—direct, indirect, or of a preposition—the word in formal writing is *whom*. Seems so simple, but it isn't.

We constantly encounter statements like this one in a nationally syndicated television column: "All those critics whom Rivers kept saying picked on her and disparaged her turn out to have been right." The relative pronoun should be *who*, the subject of the verbs *picked* and *disparaged*. "Rivers kept saying" is a throw-in that does not affect the grammar of the main clause. Then there's this sentence from a national sports magazine: "He said 'Pete Rose' when asked whom he would most like to be if he could be any player in baseball history." Alas, the verb *be* takes a predicate nominative; hence, the pronoun form should be *who*.

A teaser on the sports page of a Boston newspaper announces, "Picking 24th, Celtics have to take what's available—and whom may that be? Some predictions. Page 66." Thinking that *whom* is a sign of superior grammar and breeding, a semiliterate snob in *A Thurber Carnival* asks, "Whom do you think you are, anyways?" Demonstrating its skittishness about the *who-whom* confusion, a Connecticut newspaper hedges its bets with this sentence: "Mr. Beeston said he was asked to step down, although it was not known exactly who or whom asked him." We'll bet on *who*, the subject of the verb *asked* in the noun clause "who asked him."

More than fifty years ago, Prof. Arthur H. Weston composed this ditty:

It's hard to devise an appropriate doom
For those who say who *when they ought to say* whom.
But it's even more hard to decide what to do
With those who say whom *when they ought to say* who.

Do you say *who* when you ought to say *whom*, and *whom* when you ought to say *who*? Find out by choosing the correct pronoun form in each of the sentences below and then checking "Answers and Explanations II":

1. (*Who, whom*) do you think was killed in more movies—Jason or Freddy Krueger?

2. We don't know (*who, whom*) to trust.

3. There goes the lineman (*who, whom*) the coach believes is the team's most valuable player.

4. I'll pledge my support to (*whoever, whomever*) promises to protect the environment.

5. We all wondered about (*who, whom*) the intruders were.

Tense Times With Verbs

The fourth most popular film of the summer of 1989 was *Honey, I Shrunk the Kids*, a title that threatens, in one swell foop, to erase centuries of development of those strong, irregular verbs whose internal vowels inflect so mellifluously. In a speech he delivered in the U.S.S.R., Pres. Ronald Reagan said, "Our efforts have slayed a few dragons." A national wire service sports story informed readers that boxer Mike Tyson "bored in under Green's best weapon, his left jab." Another sports report began, "The Chicago Bulls did the major bartering and the Washington Bullets shedded half their frontcourt." When interviewed right after booting a long field goal that won the 1991 National Football Conference championship, New York Giants kicker Matt Bahr said, "It really hasn't sank—or is it sunk?—in yet."

Shrunk, slayed, bored, shredded, and *sank* are five examples of the verbal potholes into which even professional writers stumble when they form the past tenses of certain verbs. Let's take a historical (not "an historical") look at the problem:

English verbs are traditionally divided into two great classes, according to the ways they form their past tense and past participle. Strong, irregular verbs are so called because they have within them the capacity to change tense without recourse to an ending. Such verbs usually travel into the past by way of a change in a vowel and form their past participles by another vowel shift and, in many cases, adding *-n* or *-en: begin-began-begun; write-wrote-written*. Weak, irregular verbs exhibit a pattern in which the vowel doesn't change, but *-d*, *-ed*, or *-t* is affixed to form the past tense and past participle: *walk-walked-walked; bend-bent-bent*.

To complicate the picture, some verbs undergo both a change of vowel sound and an adding of *-d* or *-t: lose-lost-lost; teach-taught-taught*. Others don't change at all: *set-set-set; put-put-put*.

The history of the English language is marked by the progressive winning out of the weak, regular form over the strong, irregular. Thus, the old English *helpan-healp-holpen* has become *help-helped-helped*, and, except in the most poetic of settings, *crowed* has supplanted *crew* as the past tense of the verb *to crow*. In fact, nearly a third of the irregular forms in Old English died out during the Middle English period. As a result, the following past tenses of Old English verbs look bizarre to us today: *ache-oke, climb-clomb, shave-shove, step-stope*.

Over time, we have come to accept the weak, regular verb sequence as the normal pattern so that all new verbs that enter the English language are invariably conjugated by simply adding *-ed* or *-d*, as in *radio-radioed, televise-televised*. The problem we have inherited, then, is that the weak, regular pattern has become the norm while many strong, irregular verbs of the *shrink-shrank-shrunk* pattern remain prominent in our language.

Now it's time for an in-tense quiz. Here are an unlucky thirteen troublesome verbs whose past tenses can make you tense. Write down the past-tense form of each verb and then consult "Answers and Explanations II":

1. *baby-sit*	**7.** *light*
2. *bore*	**8.** *shine*
3. *dive*	**9.** *sneak*
4. *fly*	**10.** *swim*
5. *hang*	**11.** *tread*
6. *kneel*	**12.** *wake*

13. *weave*

Verbs That Lie in Wait

In an address to the U.S. Senate in which he stated his case for vetoing a highway bill, Pres. Ronald Reagan paraphrased an old Scottish ballad by saying, "I am wounded but not slain. Lie me down to rest a while so I can rise and fight again."

In a "Hagar the Horrible" comic strip, the portly Viking and his trusty sidekick Eddie are walking along a road past four signs that read: "Death and Demons," "Lay Ahead," "If You Don't Turn Back . . . ," "You'll Lose Your Head."

Before we mercilessly lay blame on the president and Hagar for blurring the boundaries between *lie* and *lay*, we should note that these two verbs may be the most frequently confused pair in the English language. Here's the problem: *Lie* is a strong, irregular verb that conjugates *lie-lay-lain*. *Lay* is a weak, regular verb that conjugates *lay-laid-laid*. Because *lay* is both the present tense of *to lay* and the past tense of *to lie* and because the weak, regular verb pattern has become dominant in English, many speakers and writers use *lay*, as in "I like to lay in my hammock" (quite a trick!), when they should use *lie*.

The most useful way to sort out *lie* and *lay* is to bear in mind that *lie* is an intransitive verb that means "to repose," while *lay* is a transitive verb that means "to put." *Lay* always takes an object, *lie* never. Something must be laid, and nothing can be lied. Or try visualizing this cartoon: Two hens are pictured side by side in their nests. One is sitting upright, and she is labeled LAYING; the other is flat on her back and labeled LYING. In another bestial cartoon, a man says to his dog, "Lay down!" and the dog rolls over on its back. Then the master says, "Speak!"—and the dog says, "It's *lie*."

Now it's time to lay your knowledge on the line. In each sentence below provide the proper form of *lie* or *lay:*

1. The workers are _____ linoleum in the kitchen.
2. I'm tired and would like to _____ down.
3. Now I _____ me down to sleep.
4. We found a man _____ in a ditch.

5. She had just _____ down to rest when the telephone rang.

6. For months he _____ in a deep coma.

7. I see that you have finally _____ your cards on the table.

8. She _____ the work aside for a few days.

9. The book is _____ on the oak table in the study.

10. For three days, the book has _____ on the shelf.

The Difference a Word Makes

One summer I picked up a discount coupon for Benson's Animal Park in southern New Hampshire. One crucial sentence in the document read: "This coupon is good for $2.00 off the regular admission price for each member of your family."

I was puzzled about the exact meaning of the offer. Was Benson's promising me a $2.00 discount for all members of my family whom I brought to the park, or did I need a coupon for each member? Just in case the second meaning prevailed, I snatched up coupons for each of us, but when I stepped up to the Benson's ticket office, I found that I needed only one coupon for everybody. "This coupon is good for $2.00 off the regular admission price for all members of your family" would have avoided confusion.

Once inside the animal park, I saw this sign in the sea lions' area: *Please Do Not Throw Anything in the Pool.* "How bizarre," I thought. "Why would anybody think that I could or would want to toss around a sea lion?" *Please Do Not Throw Anything into the Pool* would have been clearer.

To discover how a slight difference in wording can make a vast difference in meaning, examine each pair of sentences and choose the one that answers the question correctly:

1. Which baseball player has wings?
   a. The batter flew out to left field.
   b. The batter flied out to left field.
2. Which judge would you prefer?
   a. At the trial the judge was completely uninterested.
   b. At the trial the judge was completely disinterested.
3. Which students received a special exemption?
   a. The draft board excepted all students.
   b. The draft board accepted all students.
4. Which pair had met previously?
   a. We were formally introduced.
   b. We were formerly introduced.
5. Which Pat is a girl?
   a. Pat was smarter than the boys in the class.
   b. Pat was smarter than the other boys in the class.
6. Which request would parents be more likely to make to their children?
   a. Bring the stray dog home.
   b. Take the stray dog home.
7. Which runner put her foot down?
   a. She hoped to reach the finish line.
   b. She hopped to reach the finish line.
8. Which dog is definitely not a bloodhound?
   a. The dog smelled badly.
   b. The dog smelled bad.
9. Which Hood was careless?
   a. In tight situations, Robin Hood tended to loose arrows.
   b. In tight situations, Robin Hood tended to lose arrows.
10. Which newspapers are dishonest?
    a. The newspapers lied about the back room of the casino.

    b. The newspapers lay about the back room of the bar.

11. Which person can see the sky?
    a. The camper lay prone on the grass.
    b. The camper lay supine on the grass.

12. Which child is afflicted with a defect?
    a. Mother went shopping with her toe-headed son.
    b. Mother went shopping with her tow-headed son.

13. Which caveman liked the company of others?
    a. Ug found a club.
    b. Ug founded a club.

14. Which John is a thespian?
    a. John acted as an old man.
    b. John acted like an old man.

15. Which speaker is smarter?
    a. In the room were four geniuses beside me.
    b. In the room were four geniuses besides me.

16. Which twosome is playing doubles?
    a. Ellen complemented Frank's tennis game.
    b. Ellen complimented Frank's tennis game.

17. Which is the greater compliment?
    a. I know you're superior.
    b. I know your superior.

18. Which leader is more resourceful?
    a. The mayor adapted her predecessor's policies.
    b. The mayor adopted her predecessor's policies.

19. Which town probably has the stronger school system?
    a. I admire the town's principles.
    b. I admire the town's principals.

20. Which student will receive the higher grade?
    a. His answers were all most accurate.

    b. His answers were almost accurate.
21. In which case is Phil cashing in on his father's power?
    a. Phil flaunts his father's authority.
    b. Phil flouts his father's authority.
22. Which person is more skeptical?
    a. She is an incredible reader.
    b. She is an incredulous reader.
23. Which invitation is more dangerous?
    a. I invite you to desert.
    b. I invite you to dessert.
24. Which structure got bombed?
    a. The soldiers raised a fort.
    b. The soldiers razed a fort.
25. Which statement has a sock in it?
    a. It's darned good.
    b. It's darned well.
26. Which marriage is stronger?
    a. My wife likes golf better than I.
    b. My wife likes golf better than me.
27. Which man could be called a Romeo?
    a. He spent a lot of time repelling women.
    b. He spent a lot of time repulsing women.
28. Which speaker is more likely to be a magician?
    a. She embellished her talk with a series of allusions.
    b. She embellished her talk with a series of illusions.
29. In which situation should you be careful about lighting a match?
    a. In the room stood a tank of inflammable gas.
    b. In the room stood a tank of nonflammable gas.
30. Which person was not invited to the party?
    a. They left me out of the party.
    b. They let me out of the party.

31. Which boy is angry at his sisters?
    a. He called his sisters names.
    b. He called his sisters' names.
32. Which is worse for the Democratic Party?
    a. Democrats who are seen as weak will not be elected.
    b. Democrats, who are seen as weak, will not be elected.
33. Which private is more nervous?
    a. Shaking with fear, the major reprimanded the private.
    b. Shaking with fear, the private was reprimanded by the major.
34. Which finder is a prisoner?
    a. Locked in a cell, he discovered the jewels.
    b. He discovered the jewels locked in a cell.
35. Which statement definitely contains two people?
    a. Mary implied that she was unhappy with the job.
    b. Mary inferred that she was unhappy with the job.

A Comedy of Errors

Language errors can slither into all sorts of territory—books, newspapers, magazines, advertisements, student essays, church notes, radio and television broadcasts—everywhere. Alas, the grammar gremlins can also show their mischievous faces in our beloved comic strips, which afford us no comic relief from the boo-boos and bloopers, fluffs and flubs, and goofs and gaffes that plague the printed page. Because words within comic strip panels and cartoons are usually hand-lettered, errors in usage can't be written off as mere typos. I do wonder if these not-so-comic goofs and gaffes affect the way our young people read and write.

Here are fifty quotations from various strips that appear, or have appeared, in my local newspaper. Identify the breach of formal English that afflicts each item. Look for atrocities in spelling, punctuation, sentence structure, and word choice.

1. Sir Rodney sweats profusely as he looks at a sign that reads "Arena Today/Slaughter At It's Best." —*The Wizard of Id*

2. Mr. Dithers to Mrs. Dithers: "Look at the money we save each year by using less and less candles on your cake." —*Blondie*

3. Bouncing a basketball off Linus's head, Lucy shouts, "I'm gonna try out for the girl's basketball team." —*Peanuts*

4. Senator: "It is indeed true that on one occasion I did refer to our reception person as a quote, *fabulous babe,* unquote." —*Shoe*

5. "Well, for the third millenium in a row, no Las Vegas night." —*Porterfield*

6. Lawyer to peasant lying on the pavement: "If you crawl ten feet further, I'll make a few bucks for both of us." —*The Wizard of Id*

7. "The great astronomer Carl Sagan scans the heavens . . . taking in the enormity of the universe . . ." —*Bloom County*

8. Zonker: "I think Hadyn's sonatas suffered from incredibly amateurish construction." —*Doonesbury*

9. "Neither the Lord nor myself need any more grocery coupons." —*The Wizard of Id*

10. "The great thing about a garden hose is that it lays there all coiled up in the grass, silent, motionless, just like a snake. But when you step on it . . . it doesn't bite." —*Bizarro*

11. Peppermint Patty: "Not quite the same with you and I, ma'am?" —*Peanuts*

12. King: "All for one and one for all! We are no different than any other team!" —*The Wizard of Id*

13. Garfield: "I think I'll write a book this week. They say everyone has a good book in them." —*Garfield*

14. Voice on television: "And, since using Blockade, I haven't seen any more fleas on Buster . . . and there's none on his dog neither." —*Shoe*

15. "I couldn't help but notice that everyone at the firm had a receeding hairline. Is it stress?" —*Bizarro*

16. Little brother fish to his piscine sister: "Your blind date's here, and it's one of those kind with the eyes bugged way out!" —*The Far Side*

17. "Would you recommend red or white wine to compliment 'mystery meat'?" —*Shoe*

18. "No, but I could aggravate the heck out of him." —*Shoe*

19. Nancy to Sluggo: "We have two classes coming in here for the movie. . . . Can I sit in your lap?" —*Nancy*

20. "Things aren't exactly as they were before! Any more unexpected changes and I may just get nauseous!!" —*Bloom County*

21. Peasant pointing at a speaker's stand: "What's the podium for?" Government official: "That's where the King works out." —*The Wizard of Id*

22. "I'm sorry about this, Mr. Pellaitt, but our genealogy search revealed that your family tree was attacked by beetles, rotted and fell over into the street." —*Bizarro*

23. "So this is just more evidence that the corporate paper shufflers in control of America's great creative mediums are a bumbling bunch of boneheads." —*Bloom County*

24. Sarge: "Beetle, go put up this target. The General is anxious to do some rifle practice." —*Beetle Bailey*

25. Nancy: "I don't know whether to attatch a Christmas card or an apology." —*Nancy*

26. Boss: "Miss Binkley, how do you get out of this intercom without me seeing you?" —*Porterfield*

27. "To whither doest thou go, dear pilgrim?"
—*Bloom County*
28. Garfield to Jon: "Finished with thine breakfast, knave?" —*Garfield*
29. Postman: "I'll play it safe this morning and wait in the Woodleys' yard until Bumstead is gone."
—*Blondie*
30. Nancy walks past various signs in a clothing store: "Women's Fashions," "Misses' Fashions," "Junior's Fashions." —*Nancy*
31. "That is, it's designed to insure that, once and for all, our successors clean up their act." —*Shoe*
32. "Oh. I thought you were effecting an English accent." —*Miss Peach*
33. "Splendid. I, Cutter John, . . . new arrival to this wilderness called Bloom County, now finds himself hurtling toward oblivion." —*Bloom County*
34. Snoopy typing "Cooking Hints": "When mixing dog food in a bowl, the water can either be put in first or added last." —*Peanuts*
35. "I have a simple rule for hunting, son . . . Only shoot what you're gonna eat." —*Shoe*
36. Coach to kids: "The reason we never win is because you never get the ball in the basket . . . which, after all, is the whole idea of the game." —*Miss Peach*
37. In one of his fantasies, Calvin stares out from a spaceship at a barren planetscape and says, "What strange chemicals must compose this alien soil! Crossing a rift, the rocks abruptly change color." —*Calvin and Hobbes*
38. B.D. and Boopsie have a reunion after B.D.'s 242 days as a soldier in Desert Shield and Desert Storm. They look at each other and simultaneously exclaim, "It was hardest on me." —*Doonesbury*
39. Mom receives four red roses for Mother's Day. "Roses! They're lovely," she exclaims.

"Four red ones to symbolize Mike, Liz, April, and I," explains her husband. "And one beautiful yellow one to represent you!" —*For Better or for Worse*

40. Eddie says, "O wise man! Say somethin' wise to me!" The wise guy answers, "Carpe Dium." —*Hagar the Horrible*

41. Zonker asks Doonesbury, "How goes the Muzak wars today?" —*Doonesbury*

42. Nancy sighs, "I wish I was better looking."

"Don't worry about it," Sluggo counsels. "Maybe you're one of those people who's beautiful on the inside." —*Nancy*

43. Cookie: "Daddy just had a pizza delivered."

Alexander: "Great! Dad orders more toppings than anyone in the world."

Cookie: "Well, this time I think he outdid himself."

Alexander: "Why do you say that?"

The two children stare as Dagwood comes into the room directing two pizza men lugging a huge vat labeled "Pizzaria." —*Blondie*

44. When a friend asks her, "Of which political party are you a member, Rose?" Rose replies, "The 'I agree with whomever is speaking' party!" —*Rose is Rose*

45. As her young son jerks and yowls in her arms, Mom says to her brother, "I thought you'd sit around with us for awhile and relax!" —*For Better or for Worse*

46. When Winky tells Missy, "I just seen a asternut on T.V.," Mother corrects him, saying, "I *saw* an astronaught, Winky." —*The Ryatts*

47. As little Marvin is making out his Christmas list, his dog remarks, "Kind of waited 'till the last minute, didn't you?" —*Marvin*

48. Peppermint Patti says to Charlie Brown, "I've developed another new philosophy. Remember, it used to be, 'Who cares?' Now it's, 'What do I care?' " —*Peanuts*

49. Zonker announces on the radio, "Moreover, a

faculty panel of deconstructionists have reconfigured the rhetorical components." —*Doonesbury*

50. A pack of dogs are driving down the street in a big car. Suddenly, one of the canines, with a rope around his neck, flies out of the car. The caption explains: "Careening through the neighborhood with reckless abandon, none of them suspected that Tuffy was still tied up."

Usage and Abusage

How strong is your grasp of English grammar, usage, spelling, and punctuation? To help you find out, here's a passage marred by more than thirty goofs that are frequently found in print. How many can you catch and correct?

SAD DAY IN THE CLASSROOM

"I sincerely feel like you students should have passed the test," lamented the teacher who obviously felt badly about the whole affair. Each student in the class refused to except the fact that they had failed, but the teacher was one of those pedagogues who was a tough grader.

Jack was an obvious choice as class spokesman, although he would of gone along with whomever else was chosen. Mary's situation was different than Jack. Her class standing was more effected by the grade because she had answered less questions correctly. Trying hard to answer rationally, the reply Mary offered was "This test is harder and longer then any I have taken. Can you tell us what the test was about and your purpose in giving it?"

The teacher answered, "If I was in you're place, I too would be upset." The class was impressed by the teacher trying to explain his position so clearly, nevertheless, it seemed to them that, in their opinion, the teacher should not have taken points off for spelling. An extremely nit-picking approach.

Neither Mary or the other members of the class was in a position to disagree strongly with the teacher, although they could not help but scarcely feel that they knew more about fairness than him.

Now that everyone had lain their cards on the table, the teacher preceded to explain how important it was to be experienced and how much the students lacked it. "Please do not imply," he added, "that it is all together easy to insure fairness on tests."

*C*onan
the Grammarian

*T*he owner of a small zoo lost two of his prize animal attractions in a fire. To order another pair, he wrote a letter to a zoological supply company: "Dear Sirs: Please send me two mongooses."

That didn't sound quite right, so he began again with "Dear Sirs: Please send me two mongeese."

Still not sure of this plural, he pulled the letter out of the typewriter and made this third attempt: "Dear Sirs: Please send me a mongoose. And, while you're at it, please send me another mongoose."

Many people throughout our land are like the zoo owner, unsure about their "grammar" and fearful of public embarrassment. In my role as the monthly Grammar Grappler for *Writer's Digest*, as a language commentator on National Public Radio, and as a writer of books, columns, and articles about words and phrases, I am often asked to make Solomonic judgments about matters "grammatical." But, to clear up a term, the questions usually pertain to usage, not grammar.

192

Scholars of language define *grammar* as a set of rules that reflect how a language is actually used. All human beings do, in fact, speak and write in accord with the structure and patterns of their native tongue. In a broad sense, there is no such thing as ungrammatical English; "bad grammar" is a contradiction in terms. Everyone who speaks must use grammar, although some uses are more unconventional than others. "Him and me ain't got no money" and "Irregardless of our warning, he laid down on the railroad tracks" are perfectly grammatical because many fluent speakers of English speak and even write such sentences. But these statements do violate the rules of standard English usage, a set of conventions accepted by the well-educated and by knowledgeable grammarians.

Often a yawning chasm stretches between the so-called rules of usage and the English language in action. A clear instance of this gulf is the use of a preposition to end a sentence. The rule banishing terminal prepositions from educated discourse was invented by the late-seventeenth-century British critic and poet John Dryden, who reasoned that *preposito* in Latin means something that "comes before" and that prepositions in Latin never appear at the end of a sentence. Dryden even went so far as to reedit his own works in order to remove the offending construction. Prescriptive grammarians have been preaching the dogma ever since.

Unfortunately, Dryden neglected to consider two crucial points. First, the rules of Latin don't always apply to English. There exist vast differences between the two languages in their manner of connecting verbs and prepositions. Latin is a language of cases, English a language of word order. In Latin, it is physically impossible for a preposition to appear at the end of a sentence. Second, the greatest writers in English, before and after the time of Dryden, have freely ended sentences with prepositions. Why? Because the construction is a natural and graceful part of our English idiom. Here are a few examples from the masters:

- "Fly to others that we know not of." —William Shakespeare
- "We are such stuff / As dreams are made on." —William Shakespeare
- "Houses are built to live in, not to look on." —Francis Bacon
- "What a fine conformity would it starch us all into." —John Milton
- ". . . soil good to be born on, good to live on, good to die for and to be buried in." —James Russell Lowell
- "All words are pegs to hang ideas on." —Henry Ward Beecher

The final preposition is one of the glories of the English language. If we shackle its idioms and muffle its music with false rules, we diminish the power of our language. If we rewrite the quotations above to conform to Dryden's edict, the natural beauty of our prose and verse is forced to bow before a stiff mandarin code of structure. "Fly to others of whom we know not"; "All words are pegs upon which to hang ideas"—now the statements are artificial—people simply don't talk like that—and, in most cases, wordier.

The most widely circulated tale of the terminal preposition involves Sir Winston Churchill, one of the greatest of all English prose stylists. As the story goes, a Whitehall editor had the audacity to "correct" a proof of Churchill's memoirs by revising a sentence that ended with the outlawed preposition. Sir Winston hurled back at the proofreader a memorable rebuttal: "This is the kind of impertinence up with which I will not put!"

A variation on this story concerns a newspaper columnist who responded snappily to the accusation that he was uncouthly violating the terminal-preposition "rule": "What do you take me for? A chap who doesn't know how to make full use of all the easy variety the English language is capable of? Don't you know that ending a sentence with a preposition is an idiom many famous writers are very fond of? They realize it's a colloquialism a skillful writer can do a great deal with. Certainly it's a linguistic device you ought to read about."

For the punster there's the setup joke about the prisoner who asked a female guard to marry him on the condition that she help him escape. He used a preposition to end a sentence with.

Then there's the one about the little boy who has just gone to bed when his father comes into the room carrying a book about Australia. Surprised, the boy asks, "What did you bring that book that I wanted to be read to out of from about Down Under up for?"

Now that's a sentence out of which you can get a lot.

My favorite of all terminal-preposition stories involves a boy attending public school and one attending private school who happen to be sitting next to each other in an airplane. To be friendly, the public schooler turns to the preppie and asks, "What school are you at?"

The private schooler looks down his aquiline nose at the public school student and comments, "I happen to attend an institution at which we are taught to know better than to conclude sentences with prepositions."

The boy at public school pauses for a moment and then says: "All right, then. What school are you at, dingbat!"

Joining the preposition rule in the rogues' gallery of usage enormities is the split infinitive. "Many years ago, when I was a junior in Thornton Academy in Saco, Maine, I was instructed never, under pain of sin, to split an infinitive," wrote one of my column readers. Note the expression *under pain of sin*. It speaks of the priestly power of the English teacher to interpret the verbal nature of the universe and to bring down from some kind of Mount Sinai commandments for the moral and ethical use of the Word.

A split infinitive ("to better understand," "to always disagree") occurs when an adverb or adverbial construction is placed between *to* and a verb. In a famous *New Yorker* cartoon, we see Captain Bligh sailing away from the *Bounty* in a rowboat and shouting, "So, Mr. Christian! You propose to unceremoniously cast me adrift?" The caption beneath the drawing reads: "The crew can no longer tolerate Captain Bligh's ruthless splitting of infinitives."

When infinitives are cleft, some schoolmarms, regardless of sex or actual profession, become exercised, even though no reputable authority on usage, either in England or in the United States, bans the split infinitive. Good writers—Philip Sidney, John Donne, Samuel Pepys, Samuel Johnson, Lord Byron, George Eliot, Matthew Arnold, Thomas Hardy, Benjamin Franklin, Abraham Lincoln, Oliver Wendell Holmes, and Henry James, to name a dozen out of thousands—have been splitting infinitives ever since the early fourteenth century, long before science learned how to split the atom. The only explosions that occur when infinitives are split issue from Robert Lowth, an Anglican bishop and self-appointed grammarian who made up the "rule" in 1762, and from those whom Henry W. Fowler, in his dictionary of *Modern English Usage*, describes as people who "betray by their practice that their aversion to the split infinitive springs not from instinctive good taste, but from the tame acceptance of the misinterpreted opinions of others."

Like Winston Churchill, George Bernard Shaw and James Thurber had been stylistically hassled by certain know-it-alls once too often. Shaw struck back in a letter to the *Times* of London: "There is a busybody on your staff who devotes a lot of time to chasing split infinitives. . . . I call for the immediate dismissal of this pedant. It is of no consequence whether he decides to go quickly or to quickly go or quickly to go. The important thing is that he should go at once." With typical precision and concision, Thurber wrote to a meddlesome editor, "When I split an infinitive, it is going to damn well stay split!"

Many so-called rules of English grammar are founded on models in the classical languages. But there is no precedent in these languages for condemning the split infinitive because in Greek and Latin (and all the other romance languages) the infinitive is a single word that is impossible to sever. Many of our best writers—Wycliffe, Browne, Coleridge, Emily Brontë, Browning, Arnold, and Cather among them—do indeed occasionally split infinitives. Thus, when I suggest to my readers that they relax about splitting infinitives, I am not, to slightly paraphrase "Star Trek," telling them to boldly go where no one else has gone before. Several studies of modern literary and journalistic writing reveal that a majority of newspaper and magazine editors would accept a sentence using the words "to instantly trace" and that the infinitive is cleft in 19.8 percent of all instances where an adverb appears.

Rather than quoting instances from the old masters, I'll offer a new master, M. Scott Peck, a highly respected psychotherapist. Doctor Peck's books have sold millions of copies not only because of the passion and compassion of his approach to psychology and spirituality, but because of his fresh and original writing. Yet the road through Dr. Peck's best-selling book, *The Road Less Traveled* (Touchstone), is strewn with split infinitives, of which the following are but a few:

- "While it is true that one's capacity to truly listen may improve gradually with practice, it never becomes an effortless process."
- "To willingly confront a problem early, before we are forced to confront it by circumstances, means to put aside something pleasant or less painful for something more painful."
- "And in any case, it is the responsibility of a competent therapist to carefully and sometimes gradually discern those few patients who should not be led into psychoanalytic work."

Try rewriting these statements to unsplit the split constructions. In the first, "truly to listen" sounds unnatural to my ears and "capacity to listen truly may improve" produces a squinting modifier, where it is not clear what verb *truly* is modifying. In the second example, "willingly to confront" and "to confront willingly" are less natural than "to willingly confront." The third example is a close call. Dr. Peck makes the reader wait quite a while before getting from the *to* to the verb, yet that very wait reflects the patient, thoughtful essence of "to carefully and sometimes gradually discern."

Why is the alleged syntactical sin of splitting infinitives committed with such frequency? Primarily because in modern English adjectives and adverbs are usually placed directly before the words they modify, as in "She successfully completed the course." The same people who thunder against adverbs plunked down in the middle of infinitives remain strangely silent about other split expressions: "She has successfully completed the course." (split verb phrase) "She boasted of successfully completing the course." (split prepositional phrase) "It is better to have loved and lost than never to have loved at all." (infinitive split by helping verb). We hear no objections to such sentences because in English it is perfectly natural to place adverbial modifiers before verbs, including infinitive verbs.

I do not advocate that you go about splitting infinitives promiscuously and artlessly. But there is no point in mangling a sentence just to avoid a split infinitive. Good writers occasionally employ the construction to gain emphasis, to attain the most natural and effective word order, and to avoid ambiguity. How would you gracefully rewrite these sentences from recent newspapers?: "By a 5–4 majority, the court voted to permit states to severely restrict women's rights to choose." "It took 33 seasons for Kansas to get back to number one. It took the Jayhawks one game to almost blow it." "The Red Sox shut out the Yankees 6–0 yesterday to all but clinch the American League East division title." And this last one, written by word maven William Safire: "Thus, to spell it *champing at the bit* when most people would say *chomping at the bit* is to slavishly follow outdated dictionary preferences." In my view and to my ear, you wouldn't want to revise these constructions; they are already clear and readable.

It is indeed acceptable practice to sometimes split an infinitive. If infinitive-splitting makes available just the shade of meaning you desire or if avoiding the separation creates a confusing ambiguity or patent artificiality, you are entitled to happily go ahead and split!

The usage controversy that has attracted the most attention from the press is the *like/as* debate. A generation ago, the airwaves were filled with a little jingle that twanged, "Winston tastes good like a cigarette should." English teachers and other word-watchers raised such a fuss about the use of *like* in the song that the publicity was worth millions to the Winston people. So the cigarette hucksters came back with a second campaign: "What do you want—good grammar or good taste?"

My answer to that question is that the use of *like* in the Winston commercial is both good grammar (more accurately, good usage) *and* in good taste.

Among prescriptive grammarians, the prevailing rule is that we may use *like* or *as* as a preposition joining a noun—"cleans like a white tornado," "blind as a bat"—but we must not use *like* as a conjunction that introduces an adverb clause: The son-of-Winston commercial slogan "Nobody can do it like McDonald's can" is unacceptable because the sentence doesn't sound good like a conjunction should.

Even princes have been royally reprimanded for violating this admonition. Back in the nineteenth century the poet laureate Alfred, Lord Tennyson told the linguist F. J. Furnivall, "It's a modern vulgarism that I have seen grow up within the last thirty years; and when Prince Albert used it in my drawing room, I pulled him up for it, in the presence of the Queen, and told him he never ought to use it again."

Tennyson's adamance about the "rule" is preserved by the panel for the *Harper Dictionary of Contemporary Usage* (1975, 1985). These 166 distinguished language experts condemned the use of *like* as a conjunction 72–28 percent in casual speech and 88–12 percent in writing.

Cheeky as it may appear, I take issue with the lineup of linguistic luminaries, ranging from Isaac Asimov to William Zinsser. Any open-minded, open-eared observer of the living English language cannot fail to notice that tens of everyday expressions employ *like* as a subordinating conjunction. Fill in the following blanks: "He tells it _____ it is"; "She ate _____ there was no tomorrow"; "If you knew Suzie _____ I know Suzie . . ."; "They make the food here just _____ my mother used to." And what about "Winston tastes good _____ a cigarette should" and "Nobody can do it _____ McDonald's can"? I am confident that, despite the fact that each blank kicks off an adverb clause, most native English speakers would naturally supply *like*. If I'm wrong, then I guess I don't know my *as* from a hole in the ground.

Hopefully, this discussion has stimulated your thinking about usage rules. And if the structure of the last sentence sets your grammatical sensibilities on edge, you are not alone.

Since the seventeenth century, *hopefully* has been employed with the meaning "in a hopeful manner," as in Robert Louis Stevenson's aphorism "To travel hopefully is better than to arrive." But during the last three decades in the United States *hopefully* has donned new clothes. Now we can scarcely get through a day without meeting statements like "Hopefully, the changes taking place in Eastern Europe will make a safer world for our children" and "Her first day on the job will hopefully not be her last."

Something has happened to *hopefully* in such sentences. First, the adverb has acquired a new meaning, roughly "it is to be hoped." Second, *hopefully* now applies to situations (as in the two examples above) rather than only to people. Third, rather than modifying a specific verb (such as *travel* in Stevenson's pronouncement), the adverb now modifies the entire sentence.

This highly fashionable (some would say *pandemic*) use of *hopefully* has provoked a ringing call to arms among self-appointed protectors of the English language. The honor of being the first to cry out against the dangers of using *hopefully* as a floating adverb seems to belong to Wilson Follett, in *Modern American Usage*

(1966): "The special badness of *hopefully* is not alone that it strains *-ly* to the breaking point, but that it appeals to speakers and writers who do not think about what they are saying and pick up vogue words by reflex action."

Many linguistic traffic cops have followed Follett's lead and issued tickets and fines to all violators who use *hopefully* as a dangling adverb. Printed on these citations are the words "Abandon *hopefully* all ye who enter here." Confronted with the sentence "Hopefully, the war will soon be ended," 76 percent of the Harper usage panel responded with outbursts such as: "This is simply barbarism. What does *hopefully* modify? Does a war hope?" "I have fought this for some years, will fight it till I die. It is barbaric, illiterate, offensive, damnable, and inexcusable." "I have sworn eternal war on this adverb." "Chalk squeaking on a blackboard is to be preferred to this usage." "On my back door there is a sign with large letters which reads: THE WORD 'HOPE-FULLY' MUST NOT BE MISUSED ON THESE PREMISES. VIOLATORS WILL BE HUMILIATED." "The most horrible usage of our time."

Well, well. Let's now take a deep breath and, as we have been doing, examine structure and actual use. That *hopefully* has taken on a new meaning in no way disqualifies it from respectful consideration. Almost all English nouns, verbs, and modifiers have acquired meanings that they did not possess at birth. *Silly* once meant "blessed" and *awful* "full of awe," while such words as *knight*, once "a boy," and *governor*, once a "steersman or pilot," have come up in the world. Look what has happened recently to such words as *hip*, *energy*, and *grass*. When words like *hopefully* stop sparking off new meanings, our language, and probably we ourselves, will have died. The fact is that, except for a few die-hard dictionaries, all contemporary lexicons accept "it is hoped" as a primary meaning of the adverb *hopefully*.

Now go back four paragraphs. Did you wince at my use of *first, second,* and *third* to kick off each sentence? That would be odd indeed; almost every speaker of English uses these adverbs as introducers. And what about these sentences: "Mercifully, the war will soon be ended"; "Apparently, the war will soon be ended"; "Fortunately, the war will soon be ended"; "Surely, the war will soon be ended." Few English speakers would criticize the architecture of such sentences, yet each begins with an adverb that modifies the entire main clause. Why among all so-called floating adverbs in our language—*apparently, evidently, first (second, third,* and so on), *fortunately, happily, however, luckily, mercifully, nevertheless, obviously, presumably, primarily, surely, thankfully, therefore, thus,* and umpteen other unexceptional expressions—should *hopefully* be singled out as being "barbaric, illiterate, offensive, damnable, and inexcusable"?

Finally (note how *finally* modifies the rest of this sentence as a perfectly acceptable floating adverb), when a new word knocks at the door of our language, we must ask, "Is it a useful addition?" I believe that the new-age *hopefully* has entered English because it does indeed fill a need of those who use the language. In these secular times, we no longer say with ease "God willing." Instead (another floating adverb), we turn to *hopefully* because it avoids the wordiness and weak passivity of "it is to be hoped that" and sidesteps, especially in writing, the egotistical intrusiveness of "I hope." As Richard Crichton puts it, "No one cares if *I* hope the war is over."

Joining *hopefully* in the list of most vilified usages that I hear about most frequently from my readers is the sentence "I feel badly." Syndicated columnist Michael Gartner, whose work on etymology I consider to be among the best in popular linguistics, states the classic view: "Avoid the expression 'I feel badly.' Use 'I feel bad.' *Feel*, as you'd know if you had had Miss Hall in seventh grade, is a linking or, if you'll pardon the expression, copulative verb. These verbs take the adjectival form of modifiers *(bad)*, not the adverbial form *(badly)*. Ask the offended why they object to "I feel badly," and the voices will slip into the tonal groove that the explanation has worn for itself: "If you feel badly, then your fingertips must have been cut off."

Again we confront the triumph of mandarin decree over reality, of mummified code over usage that actually inhales and exhales—another passionate effort by the absolutists to protect the language from the very people who speak it. In English, the form of a word does not necessarily determine its part of speech. It is context, not morphology, that determines part of speech. That a word such as *badly* ends with *-ly* does not make it an immutable adverb modifying an action verb. Although a great many adverbs do indeed wag *-ly* tails, more than a hundred adjectives do, too:

beastly, beggarly, bodily, brotherly, bubbly, bully, burly, chilly, comely, costly, courtly, cowardly, crackly, creepy-crawly, crinkly, crumbly, cuddly, curly, daily, dastardly, daughterly, deadly, deathly, drizzly, early, earthly, easterly, elderly, fatherly, fleshly, friendly, frilly, gangly, gentlemanly, ghastly, ghostly, giggly, gnarly, godly, goodly, gravelly, grisly, gristly, grizzly, heavenly, hilly, holy, homely, hourly, jolly, kindly, lawyerly, leisurely, likely, lively, lonely, lovely, lowly.

That list is from just the first half of the alphabet. Clearly (yet another unattached adverb), I could go on and on. So I will:

manly, mannerly, masterly, matronly, mealy, measly, miserly, monthly, motherly, niggardly, nightly, northerly, oily, only, orderly, pearly, pimply, portly, prickly, priestly, princely, quarterly, roly-poly, scaly, scholarly, scraggly, shapely, sickly, silly, sisterly, slatternly, slovenly, smily, sniffly, southerly, spindly, sprightly, squirrely, stately, steely, straggly, surly, timely, tingly, ugly, ungainly, unmannerly, unruly, unseemly, unsightly, weekly, westerly, whirly, wiggly, wily, wobbly, womanly, wooly, worldly, writerly, yearly.

But, say the tsk-tskers, even if "I feel badly" is supported by structural precedent, doesn't the pairing of *bad* and *badly* as predicate adjectives create an unnecessary doubling up? Methinks not. Just as there are clear and important differences between the adjectives *sick* ("sick at this time") and *sickly* ("chronically sick") and *kind* ("kind at this moment") and *kindly* ("habitually kind"), a distinction between "I feel bad," meaning "I feel ill," and "I feel badly," meaning "I regret," "I'm sorry," is gradually gaining currency in our speech and writing. In English, we have long used "I feel well" and "I feel good" to signal the difference between "I feel healthy" and "I feel happy." Is it not then natural that speakers and writers should want to distinguish between physical and mental ill-being as well as physical and mental well-being? Such a change pulls up a shade, opens a window in the house of language, and lets the sunshine of a new nuance in.

By now you must be thinking that I am a flaming permissivist who adopts as a household pet any new use that crawls out of the language wordwork. But if you have read the preceding chapter, you know that this is not true and that I continue to fight the good fight to maintain precise differences between the likes of *less* and *fewer* and *I, me,* and *myself.* These are useful distinctions to which the majority of educated speakers and writers continue to adhere. Words are ideas fraught with particular recognitions and energies that enlarge and quicken life. Blur shades of meaning in language and you blur shades of thinking.

For many years I have been vice president of

SPELL—Society for the Preservation of English Language and Literature. Founded in 1984, SPELL is an international corps of word-watchers dedicated to the proper use and usage of the mother tongue. In the service of this lofty goal, SPELL each year confers Dunce Cap Awards on perpetrators of especially egregious errors in usage, spelling, and punctuation inflicted on the public's sensibilities. I have been the judge for that contest, a contest that nobody wants to win.

At the end of 1988, I placed the Dunce Cap on the collective heads of ad writers for Dunkin' Donuts, a company that boasts of its products' freshness. Throughout the year, Dunkin' Donuts ran a radio and television commercial explaining that "the problem with supermarket doughnuts is there's no telling how long they've been laying there."

I laid the responsibility upon all advertisers to make the proper choices between *lie,* an intransitive verb that means "to repose," and *lay,* a transitive verb that means "to place." One lies in a hammock and lays a book on a table. A hen on its back is lying. A hen on its stomach may be laying. *Lie* never takes an object, *lay* almost always does. Something must be laid, and nothing can be lied. As one who is all for a SPELL of good English, I dunked Dunkin' Donuts for laying a grammatical egg, however fresh that egg may have been. And I am pleased to report that so many puzzled and outraged listeners and viewers responded to the commercial with letters and telephone calls that Dunkin' Donuts recast the sales pitch and replaced *laying* with *lying*. Who knows? If this trend continues, the company may one day change its name to Dunking Doughnuts.

In addition to confusable word pairs, I do not suffer gladly sentences that are riddled with structural flaws. I cringe when I hear or read dangling and misplaced modifiers, such as "Yoko Ono will talk about her husband, John Lennon, who was killed in an interview with Barbara Walters" and "Plunging a thousand feet, we saw Yosemite Falls." Was it in an interview with Barbara Walters that John Lennon was killed? Did we plummet as we gazed at the falls? Shoddily built sentences like these can only confuse, as well as amuse, listeners and readers.

What I advise my readers to do is to carefully choose their usage crusades, to avoid knee-jerk reactions and knee-bending obeisance to long-ago edicts dispensed in long-ago English classes, to present rationales that generate more light than heat, and to ask why language does what it does. Many well-meaning people concerned about the state of the English language react with horror against any noun that has turned into a verb. But part of the genius of English is words can rail-jump from one part of speech to another with no apparent change in form. We can say "Let's wallpaper the room this morning" instead of the more cumbersome "Let's put wallpaper on the walls of the room this morning."

Folks used to get huffy and puffy about the verbs *to contact* and *to process*, but who today minds? What exactly is wrong with "Tom Hanks will host 'Saturday Night Live' this week"? Is "Tom Hanks will be the host of 'Saturday Night Live' this week" demonstrably superior? I am convinced that the converted verbs *to parent*, *to party*, and *to total* are wonderful additions to the language. On the other hand, I do wonder if *to finalize* adds anything that *to complete* or *to finish* hasn't already supplied, and I fail to see what *to author* accomplishes that *to write* doesn't. Ultimately, what I want to avoid are blanket judgments about all noun-into-verb shifts. That's because all generalizations are bad.

The hotly debated status of the word *unique* offers us a unique opportunity to explore the issue of stability versus change. Until recently, *unique* did not possess a comparative or superlative form; something either was unique, "one of a kind," or it wasn't. Nowadays we hear and see *unique* compared *(more, most)*, intensified *(very, quite)*, or qualified *(rather, somewhat)*. President Reagan praised the United Way as "a very unique opportunity to serve our local communities," and Illinois governor James Thompson called a particular case "the most unique and difficult" one that had ever come before him. Clearly, *unique* is taking on a second meaning of "unusual" to stand alongside the older meaning, "unequaled," and this upstart meaning threatens to swallow up the older one, as evidenced by the following product announcements (which are real; I did not make them up): "They are so unique, we only made a few of them" and "It's so unique, it's almost one of a kind."

When asked to respond to phrases like *a rather unique apartment* and *a most unique reaction*, the Harper usage panel condemned the relativity of *unique* 89–11 percent in writing and 76–24 percent in speaking. Among the sharpest criticisms were "No, it's dumb"; "This comes from the weakening of a great and useful word. Or perhaps I should say a 'most divine' word and 'most perfect'!"; "What corpse is ever 'a trifle dead'?"

But, say most linguists, change in language need not be equated with corruption or decay. English is alive and well and living in our voices, pens, and word processors, and that means all of us, not just the language experts. If vox populi decrees that *unique* means "unusual" as well as "unequaled," we should listen to that vox with the utmost respect.

But what about etymology? Isn't it clear that *unique* is constructed from the Latin *unus*, meaning "one"? Yes, it is, but the etymology of a word does not necessarily fix its meaning forever. Anyone with a knowledge of Latin perceives that the etymons in *manuscript* and *man-*

ufacture signify "hand-written" and "hand-made." Yet only the most superannuated of traditionalists would object to the phrases "a typed manuscript" and "automated manufacture." Obviously the old meaning of *manu*, "hand," has been weakened and superseded. Playing the numbers game, we find that the *tri* in *trivial*, *quar* in *quarantine*, *quint* in *quintessence*, *sept* in *September*, *oct* in *October*, *nov* in *November*, and *dec* in *December* and *decimate* no longer denote "three," "four," "five," "seven," "eight," "nine," and "ten." Why then must the *unus* in *unique* mean "one"?

But isn't *unique* an absolute adjective that will not tolerate comparison, intensification, or qualification? Here we enter a philosophical brier patch that challenges us to define what, if anything, is absolutely absolute in language. Examine these real-life sentences: "Her treatment of the civil rights movement is still the most complete on the subject." "The corpse was very dead." "Fear of spiders is nearly universal." "God is our most perfect creator." William Shakespeare used "most excellent," Thomas Gray wrote, "Full many a gem of purest ray serene, / The dark unfathomed caves of ocean bear," and our own constitution begins with the intent "to form a more perfect union." In each of these statements, a so-called absolute adjective is modified by an adverb or intensified by an inflection, yet each is perfectly acceptable in modern English.

Despite such reasoning, I feel very badly when I see *unique* dying on the language vine. When I witness *unusual* gobbling up *unique*, I see, much in the manner of George Orwell's Newspeak, a precious window darkening in the house of language. *Unique* is a unique word. We have no other adjective that easily and concisely conveys the sense of "one of a kind." Because we already possess modifiers like *unusual* and *distinctive*, there is no reason why *unique* should be wordnapped into their territory. If something is indeed quite unusual and almost one of a kind, I prefer that speakers and writers say "quite unusual." Sure, I know that I may be waging a losing battle, that *unique* may have already fallen before the onslaught of *unusual*. But I shall publicly bewail the devaluing and the loss of a wonderful word. If and when *unique* is completely emptied of its uniqueness, that change will have been tested against the disapproval of people like me and the language will be the better for the give and the take.

Oh, yes. If, throughout this chapter, you have been wondering about whether the zoo owner should have written *mongooses* or *mongeese*, the answer is *mongooses*. *Goose*, from the Old English *gos*, and *mongoose*, from the Hindi *magus*, are etymologically unrelated. While the plural of *goose* is *geese*, the preferred plural of *mongoose* is *mongooses*. Like most native or experienced users of the English language, the fellow got it right the first time.

$\mathcal{G}$rappling
with Questions

$\mathcal{M}$ary and John are two writers who live in Podunk, New Hampshire, a town so small that they are the only two writers who live there. Mary is the best writer in the United States, but she is not the best writer in Podunk, New Hampshire. How can this be true?

The answer is that Mary is the *better* writer in Podunk, New Hampshire. Because Mary and John are the only two writers residing in that town, the comparative, not the superlative, form of the adjective is preferable.

You don't have to be that picky and meticulous to have an abiding interest in the mechanics of English. I know because a great many of the letters that I receive from readers of my column, "Looking at Language," pose questions about grammar, usage, spelling, and punctuation. Here are some of the more provocative inquiries from my northern New England readers:

DEAR MR. LEDERER: While making a sign to hang in front of a friend's house, I ran into a problem. The family's

211

212 • ADVENTURES OF A VERBIVORE

name is Bass. Which is the proper way to print their name: 1. The Bass' 2. The Bass's 3. The Basses 4. The Basses'. — C.M.M.

DEAR C.M.M.: About fifteen years ago, my son brought home from his junior high school woodshop class a handsomely carved sign that read "The Lederer's." My boy had worked so hard and so craftily on the project that I knew I would damage him by pointing out that "The Lederer's" managed to violate the rules of both case and number. So I kept silent, and the sign still adorns our housefront, hung out as some kind of orthographic hair shirt.

We see placards like this all over town—"The Smith's," "The Gump's," and even (sigh) "The Jone's." They are distressing signs of our times. Which Smith? we are entitled to ask. What is it that the Smith possesses? And who, pray tell, is Jone? It's high time that the usage of plural names be cleared up and that a blow be struck against the nationwide conspiracy of shop teachers and sign-painters dedicated to perpetrating and perpetuating apostrophe catastrophe throughout our land.

These signs are designed for domiciles that hold families. Thus, your first two choices—"The Bass' " and "The Bass's"—violate the principle of number because they are singular, not plural. "The Basses" and "The Basses' " are both acceptable, but because it is simpler and because you want to announce who lives in the house rather than that they own the place, I prefer "The Basses."

DEAR MR. LEDERER: What is your opinion of the word ain't? *—W.S.*

DEAR W.S.: Baseball announcer Dizzy Dean, the great St. Louis Cardinals pitcher, was infamous for his idiosyncratic relationship with language. When an offended interviewer exclaimed, "Mr. Dean, don't you know the King's English?" Dizzy shot back, "Sure I do, and so's the queen." On another occasion when Dean was accused of slaughtering the King's English, he retorted, "A lot of people who don't say *ain't* ain't eating."

Then there's the one about the farmer who mortgaged his place in order to give his daughter a college education. At her graduation, the daughter confessed, "Dad, I'm sorry, but I have to tell you that I ain't a virgin anymore." The old man wrung his hands, hung his head in shame, shed rueful tears, and replied, "To think that after all our sacrifices you still say *ain't!*"

A number of readers have asked me if *ain't* is a word. Of course, it's a word, one employed by millions of English speakers around the world. But it is also a word guaranteed to raise supercilious eyebrows and evoke mean sneers in educated company. That's a shame.

Examine the following quotations and fill in the missing items: "We're pretty good cardplayers, _____ we?" "I'm a pretty good cardplayer, _____ I?" Chances are that you wrote *aren't* in each blank, but in the second statement *aren't* produces a disagreement in number between the verb *are* and the singular subject, *I.*

Once we English speakers had a solution to this "aren't I?" problem. *Ain't* was a legitimate and respectable contraction for "am not," but it gradually fell into disrepute as it came to be used indiscriminately with first-, second-, and third-person pronouns, singular and plural.

As an all-purpose replacement for "am not," "is not," and "are not," *ain't* is a useful and logical word that merits our respectful consideration. Perhaps it is time to reach back into our linguistic past and restore "ain't I?" to respectability as a contraction of "am I not?"—although I would lobby for "a'n't I?" because there a'n't any *i* in "am not." I'll even go with the tongue-tying "amn't I?" as preferable to "aren't I?" But, if the truth be told, I a'n't too hopeful that my idea will catch on.

DEAR MR. LEDERER: Is there such a word as preventative? *I think it is* preventive, *and yet the other word is used often. In fact,* preventative *is on the back cover of* WCBB Pulse, *describing a program for educational television. Please tell me that I am right and they are wrong. It would make my day. —S.W.*

DEAR S.W.: In many horror films, malignant monsters, from giant insects to blobs of glop, writhe about. Unfortunately, such grotesque mutations are not limited to science fiction; they are constantly spawning in our language.

For some obscure reason, we English speakers seem possessed by a desire to use a bloated form of certain words when a more compact form will do. These elongated versions are called "unnecessary doublets" and should be avoided.

The most ubiquitous of these linguistic freaks are the unlocked Ness monsters, distinguished by their ugly and distracting tails. Among the varieties sighted are *beautifulness, carefulness, cruelness, greediness, proudness,* and *thirstiness.*

To avoid the affectation of gratuitous syllabification, use *analysis,* not *analyzation; brilliance,* not *brilliancy; spayed,* not *spayded; skittish,* not *skitterish; compulsory,* not *compulsorary; connote,* not *connotate; heartrending,* not *heartrendering; mischievous,* not *mischievious; empathic,* not *empathetic; combative,* not *combatative; accompanist,* not *accompanyist; regardless,* not *irregardless; grievous,* not *grievious; desalination,* not *desalinization; archetypal,* not *archetypical;* and, in most instances, *sewage,* not *sewerage,* and *to orient,* not *to orientate.*

True, *preventative* does repose in many English and American dictionaries, but *preventive*, especially as an adjective, is generally viewed as the preferred form. That's why the impeccable Henry W. Fowler, in *Modern English Usage*, remarks that *"preventative* is a needless lengthening of an established word, due to oversight and caprice."* That's why former cabinet member Margaret Heckler once cautioned that "aspirin is not a substitute for other preventive therapies for heart attack." And that's why *preventative* sounds monstrous to your sensitive ear.

DEAR MR. LEDERER: As I stand in the checkout line at the supermarket looking at the newsrags and wondering if a seventy-two-year-old woman really has become pregnant, I confront a truly vexing dilemma. No, it's not whether I will be charged thirty-three or thirty-four cents for the three-for-a-dollar Jell-O packages.

The question I muse over is: Shouldn't "8 Items or Less" properly be "8 Items or Fewer"? My background has taught me that less *applies to volume and* fewer *to countable items.*

I must move forward now, even though the woman behind me appears not to agree with my interpretation of a six-pack as but one item in the "8 Items or Less" line. —M.W.M.

DEAR M.W.M.: The plague of plaques reading "8 Items or Less" should indeed be avoided like the plague and should read "8 Items or Fewer." But with those ubiquitous supermarket signs and with a major publisher having put out a children's book titled *Ten Items or Less,* when will we ever learn?

Less means "not so much" and refers to amount or quantity. *Fewer* means "not so many" and refers to number, things that are countable: "less food" but "fewer items"; "less nutrition" but (no matter what those over-the-hill jocks say on the Miller Lite commercials) "fewer calories."

I don't know how authentically pregnant the seventy-two-year-old woman was, but I firmly believe that a six-pack should count as a single item in the "8 Items or Fewer" checkout line.

DEAR MR. LEDERER: I am an old nut (nearly eighty!) about limericks. You probably remember this oldie:

> *I went to the duchess for tea.*
> *It was just as I feared it would be.*
> *Her rumblings abdominal*
> *Were simply phenomenal,*
> *And everyone thought it was me!*

Having had a grandmother who was a very strict grammarian, I have been bothered by the grammar of the last line. So I have made up a new version:

> *I went to the duchess for pie.*
> *While there, I thought I would die.*
> *Her rumblings abdominal*
> *Were simply phenomenal.*
> *And everyone thought it was I!*

Isn't that better? —R.K.G.

DEAR R.K.G.: The rivalry between "It is me" and "It is I" has provoked a long-running debate among word mavens. Supporters of "It is I" contend that forms of the verb *to be,* such as *is* and *was,* should unfailingly be followed by pronouns cast in the nominative case, *I* in this instance. Those in the corner of "It is me" counter with the argument that noun and adjective cases in English have disappeared and that pronoun case has become so weakened that the force of word order now overrides the force of case.

The "It's me" gang also tells the joke about the man who appears at the Pearly Gates and is asked by St. Peter, "Who goes there?"

"It is I," announces the man.

"Oh, no," moans St. Peter. "Not another one of those English teachers."

We shout, "Two, four, six, eight, who [not whom] do we appreciate?" because the *who* occurs in the subject part of the sentence, where the nominative case is most prevalent. By the same logic, the placement of a pronoun in the object part of the sentence has caused "It is me" and "It is us" to become increasingly acceptable as standard usage among even the most educated speakers. Walt Kelly's immortal Pogo once proclaimed, "We have met the enemy and he is us!" Those who would prefer "We have met the enemy and he is we!" are the same tin-eared folks who wish that Sammy Davis, Jr., would have sung "I Gotta Be I" and that a certain chain of stores would change its name to Toys R We.

Here are two hallowed literary passages that illustrate the power of word order over pronoun case. The first is from the closing scene of Shakespeare's *Macbeth:*

> *Lay on, Macduff,*
> *And damned be him that first cries, "Hold, enough!"*

The second example is from Percy Shelley's "Ode to the West Wind":

> *Be thou, Spirit, fierce,*
> *My spirit! Be thou me, impetuous one!*

To my ear both passages are triumphs of poetry over grammar.

Final thought: The primary purpose of language is communication. Robert Pooley has justly defined good grammar as "that language which creates the least discomfort among the largest number of participants." If you are trying to communicate with a purist who will be offended by "It's me," use "It is I."

DEAR MR. LEDERER: Why don't we simply spell words the way they sound? —S.H.

DEAR S.H.: "Forskor and sevn yeerz agoe our faadherz braut forth on dhis kontinent a nue naeshun, konseevd in liberti, and dedikated to the propozishun dhat aul men are kreeaeted eekwal."

You've just read the first sentence of Abraham Lincoln's Gettysburg Address recast in the simplified spelling system proposed by Godfrey Dewey. Dr. Dewey is not the only man of goodwill who has proposed a significant overhaul of our "system" of English spelling. Way back in 1200, the Augustinian monk Orm developed a phonetic spelling system, and in succeeding centuries Orm's lead was followed by such luminaries as Benjamin Franklin, Theodore Roosevelt, George Bernard Shaw, and Upton Sinclair.

In *The Devil's Dictionary*, Ambrose Bierce defines orthography as "the science of spelling by the eye instead of the ear. Advocated with more heat than light by the outmates of every asylum for the insane." "English spelling," declares linguist Mario Pei, "is the world's most awesome mess," while Edward Rondthaler, the inventor of the Soundspel System, labels spelling "a sort of graphic stutter we've tolerated for generations."

Nowhere is the chasm that stretches between phonology (the way we say words) and orthography (the way we spell them) better illustrated than in this anonymously written ditty about the demonic letter combination *-ough:*

> *The wind was rough*
> *And cold and blough.*

She kept her hands
Inside her mough.

It chilled her through.
Her nose turned blough.
But still the squall
The faster flough.

And even though
There was no snough,
The weather was
A cruel fough.

It shook each bough,
And she saw hough
The animals froze—
Each cough and sough.

It made her cough.
Pray, do not scough.
She coughed until
Her hat blew ough.

If the road to language heaven is paved with good intentions, why haven't we Americans responded to the succession of well-intentioned spelling reforms proposed by linguists, clerics, writers, statesmen, and presidents? Because, as in most matters linguistic, simplified spelling is no simple matter.

For one thing, spelling reform would plunder the richness of homophones in the English language. *Rain, rein,* and *reign* were once pronounced differently, but time has made them sound alike. *Knight* was a logical spelling in Chaucer's day, when the *k, n,* and *gh* were distinctly sounded. Today its pronunciation matches that of *night.* In Milton's time, *colonel* was spoken with all three syllables. Now it sounds the same as *kernel.*

Thus, the seemingly bizarre spellings that the reformers would excise are actually an aid to differentiation in writing. Think, for example, of the chaos that would be wrought by spelling the antonyms *raise* and *raze* identically.

So-called simplified spelling turns out to be a snare and a delusion of false simplicity. Instituting such reforms would generate a "big bang" effect, blowing apart words that are currently related. Like the builders of the Tower of Babel, lexical neighbors such as *nature* and *natural* would, as *naechur* and *nachurul*, be divorced and dispersed to separate parts of the dictionary. The same fate would be visited upon conversion pairs such as *record* (noun) and *record* (verb) and *progress* (noun) and *progress* (verb), and our streamlined pattern of noun and verb endings would grow needlessly complex. *Cats* and *dogs* would be transmuted into *kats* and *daugz*, *walks* and *runs* into *waulks* and *runz*, and *Pat's* and *Ted's* into *Pat's* and *Ted'z*.

Such transformations raise the specter of losing the rich etymological history that current spelling generally preserves. We cannot deny that *siekaalogee*, *Wenzdae*, and *troosoe* are accurate visualizations of the sounds they represent. But do we really want to banish the Greekness from *psychology* (from the Greek goddess Psyche), the Scandinavianness from *Wednesday* (from the Norse god Woden), and the romantic Frenchness from *trousseau*?

English is the most hospitable and democratic language that has ever existed. It has welcomed into its vocabulary words from tens of other languages and dialects, far and near, ancient and modern. As Carl Sandburg once observed, "The English language hasn't got where it is by being pure." Purifying our spelling system would obscure our long history of exuberant borrowing.

A perhaps more telling fret in the armor of simplified spelling is that even its most ardent adherents acknowledge that many words, such as *shejl* and *skejl,* are pronounced differently in the United Kingdom and the United States, necessitating divergent spellings of the same words. Moreover, when we acknowledge the existence of Irish English, Scottish English, Welsh English, Australian English, West Indian English, and all the other world Englishes, we must wonder up with how many variant spellings we must put.

Compounding the problem is that pronunciation varies widely in different parts of the same country, a reality that leads us to ask this crucial question: If we are going to embrace an exact phonetic representation of pronunciation, *whose* pronunciation is to be represented? For many Londoners, the *raen* in *Spaen* falls *maenlee* on the *plaen,* but for Eliza Doolittle and many of her cockney and Australian cousins the *rine* in *Spine* falls *minelee* on the *pline.* How will reformers decide which spellings shall prevail?

In the Middle Atlantic States, whence I hail, *cot* and *caught* are sounded distinctly as *kaat* and *kaut.* In New Hampshire, where I now live, I often hear *kaat* for both words. Not far to my south, many Bostonians say *kaut* for both words. I say *gurl,* in Brooklyn they say *goil* (as in the charmingly reversed "The *oil* bought some *earl*"), and farther south and west they say *gal* and *gurel.* Because our present system of spelling is as much hieroglyphic as it is phonetic, speakers of English can gaze upon *rain, Spain, mainly, plane, cot, caught,* and *girl* and pronounce the words in their own richly diverse ways.

Even if our spelling were altered by edict, a feat that has never been accomplished in a predominantly literate country, pronunciation would continue to change. As Samuel Johnson said long ago, "Sounds are too volatile and subtle for legal restraints; to enchain syllables, and to lash the wind, are equally undertakings of pride." No surprise, then, that the good doctor went on to point out that spelling reformers would be taking "that for a model which is changing while they apply it." The phoneticizing process of spelling reform would itself have to be reformed every fifty or hundred years.

As with so many other issues, Mark Twain said it best: "Simplified spelling is all right, but, like chastity, you can carry it too far."

DEAR MR. LEDERER: How many exceptions are there to the "i before e" spelling rule? —C.E.D.

DEAR C.E.D.: At the William Cullen Bryant School, in West Philadelphia, my seventh-grade English teacher, Mrs. Huckins, had blue hair, wore wire-rimmed glasses and a paisley smock, and kept an avocado seed in a glass vase on the radiator. I wish that everyone could have a Mrs. Huckins in language arts, for she was the light-bearing mentor who wrought order from orthographic chaos, the lawgiver who taught me the basic spelling rules: how to drop the *y* and add *ie* in words such as *babies* and *studied,* how to double the final consonant in words such as *stopping* and *occurrence,* and, of course, "*i* before *e,* except after *c.*" Alas, though, as I gradually attained the age of the sere and yellow leaf, I came to realize that the last formula did not really work. Granted that an occasional exception may prove a rule, but this rule, honored as much in the breach as in the observance, has so many exceptions that the exceptions bury the rule.

To begin with, the most famous of all spelling jingles has a small amendment tacked on:

> *I* before *e,*
> Except after *c,*
> Unless sounded as *a,*
> As in *neighbor* and *weigh.*

The last two lines suggest aberrations such as *beige, deign, eight, feign, feint, geisha, heinous, heir, inveigh, inveigle, lei, neigh, neighbor, reign, rein, reindeer, skein, sleigh, their, veil, vein, weigh,* and *weight.* That makes twenty-three exceptions to the *i*-before-*e* dictum already.

Another batch of mutants consists of words in which both the *e* and the *i* are sounded: *absenteeism, agreeing, albeit, atheist, being, contemporaneity, decreeing, dyeing, fleeing, freeing, guaranteeing, pedigreeing, plebeian, reimburse, reincarnate, reinfect, reinforce, reinstate, reintegrate, reinterpret, reinvent, reinvest, reissue, reiterate, seeing, simultaneity, spontaneity, teeing,* and *treeing.* This raises the subtotal of exceptions to fifty-two, one for each week of the year.

Now it doesn't take a genius to realize that the *i*-before-*e* rule doesn't work for the names of many people and places: "Eugene *O'Neill* and Dwight *Eisenhower* drank thirty-five-degree-*Fahrenheit Budweiser* and *Rheingold* in *Anaheim* and *Leicester.*" We could add a long scroll of names to the cluster, such as *Stein* and *Weiss,* but we'll be lenient and count all *ei* personal names as one exception and all *ei* place names as another, bumping the subtotal of rule-flouters up to fifty-four.

"Cut the orthographic obfuscation, Lederer," I can hear you thinking. "Your last two categories of *i*-before-*e* violations verge on the bogus."

Very well. Here are thirty-four breaches of the observance that do not involve names, separately pronounced vowels, or a long *a* sound: *caffeine, codeine, counterfeit, eiderdown, either, feisty, foreign, forfeit, heifer, heigh ho, height, heist, herein, kaleidoscope, keister, leisure, neither, nonpareil, obeisance, onomatopoeia, protein, reveille, seismograph, seize, sheikh, sleight, sovereign, stein, surfeit, therein, weimaraner, weir, weird,* and *wherein.*

Having accumulated eighty-eight exceptions to a spelling rule that appears to have been made to be broken, let us now attack the amendment "except after *c.*" This little disclaimer works perfectly well for words such as *receive* and *ceiling*, but what about those in which *c* is followed by *ie*?: *agencies, ancient, aristocracies, autocracies, chancier, concierge, conscience, contingencies, currencies, democracies, emergencies, exigencies, fallacies, fancied, financier, glacier, mercies, omniscient, policies, science, society, species, sufficient,* and *tendencies.*

Now have a look at three more words of this type: *deficiencies, efficiencies,* and *proficiencies.* Note that these are all double plays, each shattering the rule twice in adjacent syllables. But we shall remain lenient and count each as only a single violation, bringing the subtotal to 115.

In the same category, if we are to move upward and outward, we shall have to consult a genius, like Albert *Einstein.* Einstein would point out that his surname is another double violation, but, having already counted all personal names as a single exception, we shall not add his. We do note, however, that an Einstein might spout arcane, abstruse words such as *beidellite, corporeity, cuneiform, deice, deictic, deionize, eidolon, femineity, gaseity, greige, hermaphrodeity, heterogeneity, homogeneity, leifite, leister, leitmotif, meiosis, mythopoeic, peiramater, reify, reive, rheic, seity, sulphureity, weibullite, xanthoproteic, zein,* and *zeitgeist* (another double). These handy, everyday words raise our subtotal of exceptions to 143, just one away from proving that the most renowned of all spelling aphorisms is grossly misleading.

So we ask, is there one more common exception that will bring the count to a satisfying dozen dozen? For the answer we'll have to consult the *Deity.*

DEAR MR. LEDERER: Which is the correct usage of the comma in a series: "The flag was red, white and blue" or "The flag was red, white, and blue"? —S.P.

DEAR S.P.: Thanks for asking this important, controversial, and provocative question. In the sentence I just
wrote, my newspaper editors would excise the second
comma, the one that appears before *and*, because newspapers (and some magazines) omit the final comma in a
series to conserve space and enhance readability.

But in more formal writing, such as essays, business
letters, and literary works like this book, the "serial" or
"series" comma is ordinarily retained before the conjunction that joins the last item in a sequence of three or
more words or phrases—"hither, thither, and yon"; "of
the people, by the people, and for the people." I stoutly
defend the use of the serial comma because I have found
that in many sentences the comma before the conjunction is an aid to clarity and emphasis. Consider these
examples:

"For dinner, the Girl Scouts ate steak, onions and ice
cream."

"For dinner, the Girl Scouts ate steak, onions, and
ice cream."

"We believe in freedom, justice and equality."

"We believe in freedom, justice, and equality."

The first sentence sounds as if the Scouts devoured
a yucky concoction of onions and (urp!) ice cream. The
serial comma in the second sentence avoids such gastro-
nomic ambiguity. In the third sentence, the rhythm of
the series sounds jerky to the ear, while the serial
comma in the fourth helps the final term, *equality*, to
ring out as loudly as the others.

So don't be commatose. Use your comma sense and
press into service the serial comma.

*DEAR MR. LEDERER: The pet peeves that stream in
from your readers bother me. I share much of the linguistic
training that your contributors have been privileged to receive,
and the "abuses" that they cite grate on my nerves also. But*

when I feel such annoyance, I consider it more my problem than the speaker's. It is sad that I should be so trained that I am unable to listen to perfectly comprehensible and generally smooth English without being irked by slight differences between the speaker's idiolect and my own. Languages are, after all, living things, and our English language would be completely incomprehensible to Chaucer, let alone the author of Beowulf. What is "good grammar" now was at one time bad grammar that was eventually accepted by die-hard purists.
—R.J.

DEAR R.J.: Your graceful, learned, and compassionate letter raises a crucial question about language and usage. Who makes the rules and whence do the rules come?

I fully agree with your view that the history of any living language is the history of constant change. One has only to try reading *Piers Plowman* without a full gloss to see how much our English language has evolved over the centuries in its spelling, vocabulary, and word order. You are also right that there are no sacrosanct, immutable language forms that are eternally "good." Standard practices may become nonstandard, while nonstandard ones may become standard. Chaucer's Griselda hurled six negatives at her husband in one sentence. Shakespeare's Antony decried "the most unkindest cut of all," and *right* as an adverb (as in "right good" and "right soon"), which is now frowned upon, was common in Elizabethan English. In the eighteenth century, gentlefolk used "he don't" and "you was," and nobody lifted an eyebrow.

And language continues to evolve even today, as we hear the pronunciation of *often* drift from "of-fin" to "of-tin" and note the disappearance of the pronoun object *whom* and the subjunctive mood in verbs.

But although there are no frozen, eternally sacred language forms, a collection of usage conventions does

exist at any given moment. Among educated people today (even if not yesterday or, perhaps, tomorrow) "he
don't" and "you was" simply will not do. Why? Because such expressions are bound to interfere with the
basic purpose of language—communication.

In Lynn Johnston's delightful comic strip "For Better
or for Worse," Michael, sitting at the family dinner table, exclaims, "Hah! A couple more hours of Driver's
Ed, man—an' then I go for the big one. I am gonna totally ace that driving test! I am doing so good, you
wouldn't believe it!"

" 'You are doing so 'well,' " Mike's mother corrects.

"Uh?"

" 'Doing so good' is bad grammar. You should say,
'I'm doing so well.' It doesn't matter how much you
know or what you can do. If your language is incorrect,
you sound poorly educated."

"No wonder I can't wait to blow outa here," muses
Mike.

If clarity were the only requisite of good English, you
might well ask why "I am doing so good" and "you
was" are not just as effective as "I am doing so well"
and "you were," or why "If clarity was" wouldn't be
just as acceptable as the way this sentence starts. But as
much as I admire your idealism, the fact is that language does more than convey ideas: it also conveys im-
pressions. Language is part of our behavior, just like
our manners, habits of dress, and general conduct. We
jump into dungarees and an old T-shirt before dashing
off to a hayride, but we don't wear such an outfit to
most churches. We don a tuxedo or long gown for a formal dance but not for workaday occasions. Dining at
home, we may pick up a chop with our fingers, but at
most restaurants we use a knife and fork.

So it is with language. When we are among educated
people we must employ the standard prestige dialect.

Using nonstandard expressions and structures is like saying, "Good morning, Joseph" to your best friend or "How's it hangin', Frankie?" to your clergyman. The most important function of language is communication. Inappropriate diction crackles static through any message you are trying to put across.

*T*he Glamor of Grammar

*B*elieve it or not, *grammar* and *glamor* are historically the same word. Back in the eighteenth century one of the meanings of *grammar* was "magic, enchantment"; the Scots let the *r* slip into an *l*, and lo, came forth *glamor*. In the popular mind, however, grammar is anything but glamorous. Whatever magic resides in the subject is felt to be a sort of black magic, a mysterious caldron bubbling with creepy, crawly creatures.

I have long been convinced that the study of grammar need not be an arcane, hermetically sealed exercise. Each year my students and I explore the structure of English, from the parts of speech to phrases and clauses, ultimately applying our knowledge to usage, punctuation, and sentence creation.

"Every self-respecting mechanic," said John Dewey, "will call the parts of an automobile by their right names because that is the way to distinguish them." Thus it is with the writer. If Alexander Pope is correct in asserting that "true ease in writing comes from art, not chance," a naming of the grammatical parts will reduce the chance and enhance the art, even if those names are one day forgotten. And if students are grinding their stylistic gears, we teachers need a common language to communicate these problems: "John, you should use the possessive form before the gerund"; "Mary, try combining these two sentences by using an appositive"; "Your style is repetitive, George. Try varying your sentence openings with introductory adverbs, phrases, and clauses."

Ultimately, though, I believe that, in the words of structuralist Paul Roberts, "The best reason for studying grammar is that grammar is interesting." Grammar may not be glamorous in any glittery, Hollywood sense, but grammar can indeed be very interesting, even enchanting.

That enchantment can even include having fun—yes, fun!—with grammar and usage. Take the study of subject-verb combinations that we term clauses. What do you call a clause that comes every Christmas? A renoun clause named Santa Clause. What do you call Santa Clause's wife? A relative clause. What do you call his elves? Subordinate clauses.

One of the popular items that circulate through the network of folk xerography is a perverse set of rules along the lines of "Thimk," "We Never Make Misteaks," and "Plan Ahe . . ." (and then the space runs out)—injunctions that call attention to the very mistakes they seek to enjoin. English teachers and journalists have been passing around a list of self-contradictory rules of usage for more than a century, and I've been collecting and creating them for almost half of one. Now I can offer you one of the largest accumulations gathered into a single space. I call them "Fifty Rules for Writing Good." Whatever you think of these slightly cracked nuggets of rhetorical wisdom, just remember that all generalizations are bad.

1. Each pronoun should agree with their antecedent.
2. Between you and I, case is important.
3. A writer must be sure to avoid using sexist pronouns in his writing.
4. Verbs has to agree with their subjects.
5. Don't be a person whom people realize confuses *who* and *whom.*
6. Never use no double negatives.
7. Never use a preposition to end a sentence with. That is something up with which your readers will not put.
8. When writing, participles must not be dangled.
9. Be careful to never, under any circumstances, split infinitives.
10. Hopefully, you won't float your adverbs.
11. A writer must not shift your point of view.
12. Lay down and die before using a transitive verb without an object.
13. Join clauses good, like a conjunction should.
14. The passive voice should be avoided.
15. About sentence fragments.
16. Don't verb nouns.
17. In letters themes reports and ad copy use commas to separate items in a series.
18. Don't use commas, that aren't necessary.
19. "Don't overuse 'quotation marks.' "
20. Parenthetical remarks (however relevant) are (if the truth be told) superfluous.
21. Contractions won't, don't, and can't help your writing voice.
22. Don't write run-on sentences they are hard to read.
23. Don't forget to use end punctuation
24. Its important to use apostrophe's in the right places.
25. Don't abbrev.

26. Don't overuse exclamation marks!!!
27. Resist Unnecessary Capitalization.
28. Avoid mispellings.
29. Check to see if you any words out.
30. One-word sentences? Never.
31. Avoid annoying, affected, and awkward alliteration, always.
32. Never, ever use repetitive redundancies.
33. The bottom line is to bag trendy locutions that sound flaky.
34. By observing the distinctions between adjectives and adverbs, you will treat your readers real good.
35. Parallel structure will help you in writing more effective sentences and to express yourself more gracefully.
36. In my own personal opinion at this point of time, I think that authors, when they are writing, should not get into the habit of making use of too many unnecessary words that they don't really need.
37. Foreign words and phrases are the reader's bête noire and are not apropos.
38. Who needs rhetorical questions?
39. Always go in search for the correct idiom.
40. Do not cast statements in the negative form.
41. And don't start sentences with conjunctions.
42. Avoid mixed metaphors. They will kindle a flood of confusion in your readers.
43. Eliminate quotations. As Ralph Waldo Emerson said, "I hate quotations. Tell me what you know."
44. Analogies in writing are like feathers on a snake.
45. Go around the barn at high noon to avoid colloquialisms.
46. Be more or less specific.
47. If I've told you once, I've told you a thousand

times, exaggeration is a billion times worse than understatement, which is always best.

48. Never use a big word when you can utilize a diminutive word.
49. Profanity sucks.
50. Last but not least, even if you have to bend over backwards, avoid clichés like the plague.

After my St. Paul's School scholars complete their study of descriptive English grammar, I frequently assign them the writing of a "supersentence"—a single sentence containing one example of each of the four phrases and three subordinate clauses that are identified in English grammar. These are: prepositional phrase, participial phrase, gerund phrase, and infinitive phrase and adverb clause, adjective clause, and noun clause. These units may occur in any order in the assigned sentence.

One afternoon, while grading a batch of supersentences, I decided to try writing one myself, using the fewest words possible. (If you, dear reader, are a grammar jock, I invite you to try this feat before reading this narrative any further.) An hour of intense industry produced the following:

> [1]*When people* [2]*who swing want* [3]*to see* [4]*what's happening, they try* [5]*attending parties* [6]*given* [7]*by hipsters.*
> (sixteen words)*

---

*The numbers indicate the beginning of each phrase and subordinate clause—(1) adverb clause: "When people who swing want to see what's happening" modifies the verb *try* in the main clause; (2) adjective clause: "who swing" modifies the noun *people;* (3) infinitive phrase: "to see what's happening" acts as the direct object of the verb *want;* (4) noun clause: "what's happening" acts as the object of the infinitive *to see;* (5) gerund phrase: "attending parties given by hipsters" acts as the direct object of the verb *try;* (6) participial phrase: "given by hipsters" modifies the noun *parties;* (7) prepositional phrase: "by hipsters" modifies the passive participial *given.* In subsequent sentences I shall provide numbers but leave the reader to identify the structures, which will appear in varying orders, so as to avoid cluttering these pages with labyrinthine explanations like this one.

I proudly presented my sixteen-word concoction to my departmental colleagues and to my students, who saw and were amazed. A few days later, I was summoned by an emissary from a tenth-grade English class that met a few rooms down the hall from my section, and there on the chalkboard was inscribed:

> Fred, [1]wanting [2]to win [3]by [4]playing hard, practiced more [5]than I, [6]who knew [7]he stank. (fifteen words)

Among the triumphantly glowing faces in that alien classroom was that of Bruce Monrad, the finest young linguist in our school at that time. Bruce, it turned out, was the author of the fifteen-word supersentence, a creation that contains not only an elliptical adverb clause of comparison, *than I [practiced]*, and a hidden noun clause, *[that] he stank,* but compacts the four phrases into the subordinate part of the sentence and the three clauses into the main part.

Not to be outdone, I labored mightily for the next few days and came up with:

> [1]Stung [2]by [3]what happened, Lederer began [4]trying [5]to write better [6]than Monrad, [7]who fainted. (fourteen words)

The next morning, I marched into the rival classroom and confidently wrote my new sentence on the blackboard, only to be instantly one-upped by young Monrad, who stepped forward and inscribed:

> [1]Helping [2]win [3]by [4]scoring more [5]than I, [6]who thought [7]he stank, Fred overcame. (thirteen words)

Here Bruce's brilliant excision of one word is accomplished in his second phrase, the infinitive, in which he lifts out the *to:* "Helping [to] win by scoring . . ."

Now I was growing desperate. Word of the contest had spread throughout the school community. How could I ever again face my colleagues and my students if I were to be defeated by a mere stripling? The whole affair was beginning to give lie to William Cobbett's crabbed pronouncement: "The study of grammar is dry. It engages not the passions." Resolving not to give up, in, or out, I closeted myself for the entire weekend. Finally, "Eureka!" flew from my lips as I emerged with this compacted supersentence:

> [1]*Helping* [2]*win* [3]*by* [4]*overcoming* [5]*what threatened,*
> *Lederer,* [6]*who persisted* [7]*when challenged, triumphed.*
> (twelve words)

In addition to being eminently readable, my fabrication is characterized by two clever strokes: a clause within a phrase within a phrase within a phrase within a phrase in the first five words, and the distillation of the adverb clause into a two-word cluster, "when [he was] challenged," one word shorter than its predecessor, "more than I." Not only are all the structures as concise as they can possibly be, but, with the exception of the subject, *Lederer*, all nouns, adjectives, and adverbs are now replaced by phrases and clauses. O frabjous day! Calooh! Callay!, I chortled in my joy. This sentence was traveling at the speed of light. It could become no smaller. Or so I thought.

On Monday morning, I strutted into Bruce's classroom and hubristically engraved my "ultimate" concatenation on the enemy's board, delivering a learned lecture proving that we had reached the end of the road supersentencewise. As I wheeled to leave, Bruce giggled, "Not so fast, Mr. Lederer." He explained that he too had discovered the formula for the two-word adverb clause and that, moreover, he had been able to replace *all* nouns, adjectives, and adverbs with phrases and clauses. He then chalked up:

> [1]*Whoever rebels,* [2]*daring* [3]*oppose* [4]*by* [5]*fighting* [6]*when opposed,* [7]*which overcomes, conquers.* (eleven words!)

While reaching the theoretical limit for supersentences, Bruce's creation is rather gawky, with the adjective clause, "which overcomes," flapping loosely as a dangling modifier. Still, I have never been able to improve on the lad's effort, and I invite readers to submit more graceful and coherent supersentences of eleven words. Like two kids choosing sides for a baseball game, Bruce and I ran our hands up the bat until there wasn't any wood left. Actually, though, we both won. When the game of grammar is played with a sense of humor and enjoyment, everyone can be a winner.

A Compound Subject

*T*his chapter is the most technical and schematic in the book, and you won't hurt my feelings if you skip it. But if you are familiar with the parts of speech in English and will stay with this discussion for a few more pages, you can share one of the greatest adventures of my life in language.

Since the dawn of English, speakers and writers of the mother tongue, true to the Germanic roots of their language, have created words by joining together two or more independent meaning-bearing elements, called morphemes, to form compounds. As any page of Anglo-Saxon literature illustrates, compound words were abundant in Old English, a language that sought to express new ideas not by borrowing from foreign tongues but by combining whole words already in the vocabulary. Thus, in the Beowulf poem the ocean is the *sea-path*, *whale-road*, or *swan-road*. A ship is a *sea-wood* and a harp a *pleasure-wood*. A warrior is called a *shield-bearer*, his sword a *battle-friend*, and war a *battle-play*. This compound-making enthusiasm has continued unabated into the modern era.

English compounds are astonishingly versatile creatures that can assume any grammatical function: noun *(earthquake)*, pronoun *(herself)*, adjective *(color-blind)*, adverb *(sometimes)*, verb *(dry-clean)*, preposition *(without)*, and conjunction *(whenever)*. Moreover, almost any combination of the parts of speech may be used to form a compound, although some are more common than others. Using the four major parts of speech, the Noun-Adjective-Adverb-Verb matrix that follows illustrates the diversity of compound formations in English:

	Noun	Adjective	Adverb	Verb
Noun	spaceship	homesick	flashback	godsend
Adj.	madman	bittersweet	blackout	freeload
Adv.	upshot	evergreen	henceforth	underplay
Verb	scarecrow	fail-safe	tumbledown	hearsay

Independent word elements may marry in such ingenious ways that the part of speech of a compound may be different from that of either of its components, as in the last two entries above: *tumble* (verb) + *down* (adverb) = *tumbledown* (adjective); *hear* (verb) + *say* (verb) = *hearsay* (noun or adjective). This happy state of affairs raises the question, can the third dimension of the four-by-four matrix be filled out so that each of the sixteen types functions as a noun, adjective, adverb, and verb, yielding a total of sixty-four entries and demonstrating that the potentialities of compounding in the English language have been fully realized grammatically? Here is my response to that enticing question, in the form of a four-by-four-by-four matrix:

	Noun-Noun	Noun-Adj.	Noun-Adv.	Noun-Verb
Noun	spaceship	bootblack	flashback	godsend
Adj.	shipshape	homesick	head-on	handmade
Adv.	sidesaddle	knee-deep	hands down	shell-shocked
Verb	tiptoe	court-martial	zero in	handpick

	Adj.-Noun	Adj.-Adj.	Adj.-Adv.	Adj.-Verb
Noun	madman	deaf-mute	blackout	slowpoke
Adj.	commonplace	bittersweet	straightforward	rough-hewn
Adv.	barefoot	northeast	moreover	roughshod
Verb	blackball	high-low	black in	freeload

	Adv.-Noun	Adv.-Adj.	Adv.-Adv.	Adv.-Verb
Noun	upshot	evergreen	whereabouts	downpour
Adj.	offhand	overdue	never-never	income
Adv.	overboard	outright	henceforth	overmatched
Verb	outlaw	outsmart	fast-forward	underplay

	Verb-Noun	Verb-Adj.	Verb-Adv.	Verb-Verb
Noun	scarecrow	speakeasy	diehard	hearsay
Adj.	breakneck	fail-safe	tumbledown	slapdash
Adv.	makeshift	punch-drunk	worn out	straddle mount
Verb	pickpocket	blow-dry	give up	make believe*

I worked on this verbal Rubik's Cube for about thirty hours over the course of two days, and the last three components I was finally able to insert were *high-low, blow-dry,* and *fast-forward,* all recent but solidly entrenched compounds in English. One who leads first

---

*Even this matrix does not cover all the possible grammatical alliances. Additional combinations include *into* (adverb + adverb = preposition), *whenever* (adverb + adverb = conjunction), *overalls* (preposition + adjective = noun), *he-man* (pronoun + noun = noun), *each other* (pronoun + adjective = pronoun), *himself* (pronoun + noun = pronoun), *whoever* (pronoun + adverb = pronoun), and triple plays, such as *ne'er-do-well* and *well-to-do.*

Within the matrix *shell-shocked* (noun + verb = adverb), *overmatched* (adverb + verb = adverb), *punch-drunk* (verb + adjective = adverb), and *worn out* (verb + adverb = adverb) can function adverbially in sentences like "He staggered from the ring shell-shocked, overmatched, punch-drunk, and worn out."

the high and then the low of a two-card suit in bridge *high-lows*. Two football linemen who block a defensive player high and low are *high-lowing*. One who blows his or her hair dry *blow-dries* it. One who presses the cue button on a tape or video player *fast-forwards*.

The shiny newness of compounds such as *high-low*, *blow-dry*, and *fast-forward* (the only examples I could think of for their respective slots) indicates the experimental vigor of twentieth-century English. Somehow there has grown up over time a collective consciousness among English speakers, who, it seems, would not be satisfied until the language evolved to the point where all sixty-four slots in the matrix could be filled.

Once upon an eon, so the story goes, a troop of monkeys inhabited a cluster of islands set in an emerald sea. Came a moment in time when one of the monkeys discovered how to use a thorn to pry open a nut. Another monkey, observing this new prowess, also learned how to manipulate a thorn. Then another monkey, and another.

When one hundred monkeys on that island had mastered the thorn-prying skill, a kind of critical mass was achieved. As if a spark leapt from island to island to inflame the tinder of a new idea into birth, instantly every monkey in that archipelago knew how to unlock nuts with thorns.

How did our chattering troop of English speakers, going about our business on island Earth, learn to pry open all the grammatical possibilities of compounds? What bound us together to paint all the possible colors and to join in functional symmetry the myriad components of that monumental and elaborate cube? Was the achievement mere coincidence or blind luck, or was it somehow programmed into the microchips of our brains?

*E*nd Games

*B*efore I go, I'd like to share (not only would I like to, but I'm going to do it right here) five additional Grammar Grappler games, these particular challenges focusing on spelling and punctuation. Give each your best shot and restrain yourself as long as you can from peeking at the answers and explanations offered in the next chapter.

The Ultimate Spelling Quiz

One night when Joel Chandler Harris, creator of the Uncle Remus tales, was at his editorial desk, an old-time reporter looked over and asked, "Say, Joel, how do you spell the word *graphic*? With one *f* or two *f*'s?"

"Well," replied Harris in his gentle drawl, "if you're going to use any *f*'s, you might as well go the limit."

We may smile at the naïveté of the reporter's question, yet who among us has not stumbled into the potholes and booby traps that dot the terrain of English spelling? If we try to spell words by the way they sound, we will surely misspell most of them. But who among us is gifted with such vastness of visual memory that we can spell words solely by the eye?

During my thirty years as a high school English teacher, I have compiled a list of the hundred words that my students have most consistently misspelled. My strong hunch is that many of the same words are among the spelling demons that you most fear and loathe.

Here is the list. Look it over and think about it carefully. Then circle each word that you find to be spelled incorrectly and compare your total with the one given in the next chapter:

1. *accommodate*
2. *achieve*
3. *aggressive*
4. *all right*
5. *arctic*
6. *asinine*
7. *assassination*
8. *athlete*
9. *background*
10. *balloon*
11. *banana*
12. *basically*
13. *bastion*
14. *battalion*
15. *benefit*
16. *broccoli*
17. *business*
18. *calendar*
19. *category*
20. *ceiling*
21. *cemetery*
22. *character*
23. *coliseum*
24. *commitment*
25. *complexion*
26. *controversy*
27. *curiosity*
28. *definitely*
29. *description*
30. *despair*
31. *develop*
32. *dilemma*
33. *disappoint*
34. *dissipate*
35. *ecstasy*
36. *embarrass*
37. *environment*
38. *etiquette*
39. *exhilarated*
40. *existence*
41. *fluorescent*
42. *forgo*
43. *forty*
44. *gauge*
45. *grammar*
46. *harass*

47. *hypocrisy*
48. *imitate*
49. *immediately*
50. *independent*
51. *ingenious*
52. *innate*
53. *inoculate*
54. *judgment*
55. *liaison*
56. *liquefy*
57. *marshmallow*
58. *mayonnaise*
59. *metaphor*
60. *millennium*
61. *minuscule*
62. *mischievous*
63. *missile*
64. *misspell*
65. *moccasin*
66. *noticeable*
67. *occasion*
68. *occurrence*
69. *parallel*
70. *pastime*
71. *perseverance*
72. *pharaoh*
73. *pizzeria*
74. *poinsettia*
75. *precede*
76. *prejudice*
77. *privilege*
78. *proceed*
79. *professor*
80. *publicly*
81. *quandary*
82. *receive*
83. *recommend*
84. *renown*
85. *repetition*
86. *restaurateur*
87. *rhythm*
88. *sacrilegious*
89. *sentence*
90. *separate*
91. *silhouette*
92. *sophomore*
93. *souvenir*
94. *subtly*
95. *supersede*
96. *surprise*
97. *threshold*
98. *tragedy*
99. *truly*
100. *unnecessary*

Mark Your Words

If there were no punctuation marks a teacher once said to his students you would soon feel the need of inventing some after thinking over the statement the class agreed with him they realized that punctuation is important often just as important as the words themselves in getting meaning across to readers when we talk we do more than put our thoughts into words because words alone cannot express our thoughts exactly we raise and lower our voice and pause for varying lengths of time to indicate exactly what our words mean the pauses and voice changes which we use without much conscious thought work with the words to make our meanings clear when we write rather than speak we need punctuation marks to serve our readers in the same way that pauses and voice changes serve our listeners in short the primary purpose of punctuation is to make reading easier by now it must be clear to you how difficult reading can be without punctuation

To take an inventory of your control of the marks from commas to semicolons, from quotation marks to parentheses, see how accurately you can punctuate the following sentences. Do not add periods to make new sentences:

1. The Bible which is the central book in religious thought speaks of three virtues faith hope and charity and says the greatest of these is charity

2. Did James travel all the way to Concord New Hampshire to look for the Joneses first edition copy of the story The Tell-Tale Heart he asked

3. Did Julie really declare I refuse to make my bed and I shall never again wash dishes vacuum rugs or water plants asked Jenny

4. Although the school is again warning Mary its warned her many times before the brave wonderfully coordinated young woman wants to try out for the boys football team

5. Roosevelt brilliantly exploited the political situation by bringing together five have not entities the South which had lived for years in a state of chronic depression Roosevelt was to characterize it as the countrys number one economic problem the Roman Catholics

who still formed a minority group in many parts of the country and blacks particularly those settled in the urban communities the Jews and the labor unions (from Brooks Lewis and Warren American Literature The Makers and the Making)

Apostrophe Catastrophes

Of all marks of punctuation the most off-putting is the apostrophe, so much so that people put apostrophes off when they should be putting them on paper and often put them on when they should be putting them off. Indeed, the dread diseases of apostrophlation (gratuitous apostrophes) and apostrophy (the atrophy of proper apostrophes) are sweeping across our land. In an effort to halt the spread of these plagues, I herewith present its (not it's) symptoms, a quiz, and, in the answers and explanations that are coming up, a prescription for its cure.

First, some symptoms:

* A lavish television production repeatedly advertised the play it was presenting as "Charles Dicken's *Nicholas Nickleby*. If Dicken were alive today, he'd be turning over in his grave.
* Teachers at Bellamy High School, in Chicopee, Massachusetts, received $25 from the Midas Muffler Company for spotting and reporting an apostrophe catastrophe on a large roadside billboard that read "It Pay's to Midasize."
* The erudite Harvard Club of Boston was crimson-faced to discover that one of its lavatories was labeled "Mens' Room."
* A full-page Bloomingdale's advertisement in the *New York Times* praised "the seasonless silks of Oscar de la Renta: parlor dressing at it's most pampered."

- Several stores in my town display signs that say, "Boy's Clothes" and "Men's Clothes." Why, I ask, is one sign singular possessive and the other plural possessive? In our municipal parking lots I read, "Vehicles Will Be Towed at Owner's Expense." If *Vehicles* is cast in the plural, shouldn't the penultimate word be *Owners'*?
- In the French market in New Orleans I saw signs that announced "Pear's" and (gasp!) "Peach'es."
- In the early 1990s, supermarket shelves were stocked with a Nabisco product labeled "Teddy Grahams Bearwich's," a double apostrophe catastrophe.
- In a weekly swap-sell guide published in Maine appeared this grisly (not grizzly or gristly) ad: "Wanted: guitar for college student to learn to play, classical nonelectric, also piano to replace daughters lost in fire." Ah, the difference a lost apostrophe makes.
- And then there are the ubiquitous house signs, such as "The Snaggle's" and "The Gump's," that I've talked about in an earlier letters section.

The following quiz will help you to determine if you suffer from apostrophlation or apostrophy. Insert apostrophes or apostrophes and s's, where needed, into each of the items below:

1. the womans car
2. Gus mother
3. Jesus parables
4. Achilles wrath
5. the babies diapers
6. anyones guess
7. its paw
8. the 1990s
9. knows her ABCs
10. doesnt

Punctuation Teasers

Punctuation is not just a code of courtesy to readers. Punctuation also affects the *meanings* of messages in crucial ways. A period in the right place in a classified ad would have converted an astonishing piece of furniture into an ordinary item: "FOR SALE: A quilted high chair that can be made into a table, a pottie chair, a rocking horse, refrigerator, spring coat size 8, and fur collar."

To the Netherlands Chamber of Deputies was brought a motion "for the naturalization of Nathalie Bouwmeester, widow of Peter Bouwmeester and eighteen men." A grave deputy arose to inquire whether it was in accord with public morals to grant naturalization to a woman who had buried nineteen husbands.

Officials soon discovered a clerical error in the drafting of the motion. A comma separating the appositive "widow of Peter Bouwmeester" from "eighteen men" had been omitted. The motion thus amended, naturalization was voted and granted to Nathalie Bouwmeester, and also to the eighteen men.

Oscar Wilde was once asked by his editor what he had accomplished that day. "I moved a comma," answered the droll writer. Clearly, the choice of whether to punctuate or not to punctuate or where to place a comma does make a difference. Read the six sentences below and then punctuate each statement in such a way that its meaning is radically altered:

1. A clever dog knows its master.
2. Call me fool if you wish.
3. Woman without her man is nothing.
4. I saw a man eating lobster.
5. Mary Jane and I went to see the latest Mel Gibson movie.

6. The butler stood at the door and called the guests names.

Now have a look at six apparently confusing sentences. If you provide the proper punctuation, each statement will make complete sense:

7. Other than that one thought he was not there.
8. Ann Boleyn kept her head up defiantly an hour after she was beheaded.
9. *Every lady in this land*
   Hath twenty nails upon each hand
   Five and twenty on hand and feet
   And this is true without deceit.
10. There should be more space between ham and and and and and eggs. (spoken to a sign painter)
11. That that is is that that is not is not is not that it it is.
12. Mary where John had had had had had had had had had had had the teacher's approval Mary would have been correct.

*A*nswers and Explanations II

Pluralsy *(page 172)*

1. *Goose,* from the Old English *gos,* and *moose,* from Algonquian, are etymologically unrelated. While the plural of *goose* is *geese,* inflecting from the inside as do many Old English nouns, the preferred plural of *moose* is *moose.*

2. *Buses* and *busses* are both acceptable, as are *gases* and *gasses,* but the first of each pair is more commonly used.

3. Proper nouns ending in *y* almost never change to *ies*—*Kennedys, Murphys, Marys*—with the exception of mountain ranges—*the Alleghenies, the Smokies.* Nouns ending in *y* preceded by a vowel retain the *y,* as in *donkeys* and *trays.* A major exception is *money:* monies and *moneys* are equally acceptable.

4. Nouns ending in a consonant plus *o* are troublemakers. Some add *es* and some add only *s: echoes, tomatoes, heroes;* but *radios, photos, silos.* Some *o*-ending words have two acceptable plural forms—*mosquitos* or *mosquitoes, tornados* or *tornadoes.* Musical terms take only *s*—*sopranos, altos, banjos, solos.*

5. Nouns ending in *f* or *fe* are like *o* words in their capacity to befuddle, and again there are three categories:

Nouns ending in *f* or *fe* that are native to English usually change ending to *ves* to form the plural—*halves, knives, wolves.* Nouns adopted from French or Norse retain the *f*—*beliefs, chiefs, reefs.* Some words in this cluster have two acceptable plural forms—*scarfs* or *scarves, hoofs* or *hooves, wharfs* or *wharves.*

6 and 7. Plurals of English nouns that come from foreign languages may be formed in three ways—as they are in the original language: *criteria, crises, châteaux;* as English plurals: *encyclopedias, lexicons, asylums;* as both: *symposia* or *symposiums, formulae* or *formulas, indices* or *indexes.*

8. To form the plurals of numbers, letters, and words used as words, add either *s* or *'s.* Modern style prefers the simple *s*—*1990s*—unless a misreading could result—"four *i*'s and four *s*'s in *Mississippi.*"

9 and 10. Compound words usually form their plurals by adding an *s*—*airplanes, get-togethers, high schools.* But note two exceptions to this rule:

A few noun-adverb compounds add *s* to the noun—*runners-up, hangers-on;* and some semilegal compounds add *s* to the noun—*bills of sale, attorneys general* (also *attorney generals*), *mothers-in-law.* Where the plural of *Egg McMuffin*—is it *Egg McMuffins* or *Eggs McMuffin?*—fits into this scheme has not been officially determined.

The Strange Case of English Pronouns *(page 173)*

1. *She* is part of the compound subject of the verb *went.*

2. *Me* is part of the compound direct object of the verb *enticed.*

3. *It* is an expletive, a dummy subject, and *he* is the real subject of the main clause. In formal writing, purists still consider "it was he" superior to "it was him."

4. *Me* is part of the compound object of the preposition *for*.

5. As the object of the preposition *to, coming* is a gerund, an *-ing* form of a verb that functions as a noun. Pronouns preceding gerunds assume the possessive form, in this case *my*.

6. Here *him* is the object of the infinitive *to find*, and *working* is not a gerund but a participle.

7. The appositives stand in apposition with *family* and should agree in case. Because *family* is a direct object of the verb *invited*, the pronoun form should be *me*.

8. Here the appositives should agree with the subject *we*. Hence, *I*.

9. *I* kicks off an adverbial clause of comparison and is the subject of the understood verb *do*.

10. Because *boys* is the direct object of the verb *told*, the pronoun appositive should be cast as *us*.

To Who It May Concern *(page 175)*

1. *Who* is the subject of the passive verb *was killed*. The clause "do you think" has no effect on the grammar of the main clause.

2. *Whom* is the object of the infinitive *to trust*.

3. *Who* is the subject of the verb *is*. Again, the clause "the coach believes" has no effect on the grammar of the main clause.

4. The entire noun clause, *"whoever* promises to protect the environment," is the object of the preposition *to*, but every clause must have a subject, and *whoever* is the subject of the verb *promises*.

5. The noun clause *"who* the intruders were" is the object of the preposition *about.* Within the noun clause *who* functions as a predicate nominative.

Tense Times With Verbs *(page 177)*

1. The strong, irregular past-tense form *baby-sat,* as an extension of *sit-sat,* and the weak, regular *baby-sitted* are competing for ascendency. *Baby-sat* seems to be winning.

2. Here meaning determines form. When *bore* means "to make a hole" or "to move steadily ahead," the past tense is *bore.* When *bore* means "to make weary by being uninteresting," the past tense is *bored.*

3. Either the regular *dived* or the irregular *dove* is acceptable.

4. *Flew,* unless you're speaking or writing about a baseball game. Then it's *flied,* as in "The batter flied out to left field."

5. *Hung* or *hanged.* Many a purist would insist that pictures are hung and criminals are hanged, and most judges do sentence with this sentence: "You shall be hanged by the neck until dead."

6. *Knelt* or *kneeled.* Many verbs in English change a long *e* sound in the present-tense form to a short *e* and add a *t* or *d* sound to form the past tense—*sleep-slept, flee-fled.* In almost all such verbs, the short *e* past-tense form is required. There are, however, three common verbs that may form the past tense by adding *-ed* or by shortening the *e* and adding *t*— *kneeled* or *knelt, dreamed* or *dreamt,* and *leaped* or *leapt.*

7. *Lighted* or *lit.* Ernest Hemingway's "A Clean, Well-Lit Place" would have been just as bright.

8. Again meaning determines form. If the verb is intransitive and means "to radiate," the past-tense form is *shone,* as in "The sun shone all day long." If the verb is transitive and means "to polish," the form is *shined*, as in "In the Army, I shined my shoes every day."

9. *Sneaked* or *snuck*, although some purists and dictionaries label *snuck* as "colloquial" or "substandard." It isn't.

10. As is the case with *shrink-shrank-shrunk*, *swam* is preferable to *swum* in the past tense, with *swum* reserved for the past participle.

11. *Trod* or *treaded*, but the form for swimming is always "She treaded water."

12. *Wake* and its close kin *awake* are two verbs still in ferment. The past-tense *woke* and *awoke* are now more usual than *waked* and *awaked* —"I woke up to the sound of a roaring train." In American English, *woken* and *awoken* and, less commonly, *wakened* and *awakened* are all used for the past participle.

13. Generally *wove* and *weaved* are interchangeable. Many speakers and writers tend to use "He wove a rug" and, when the act of weaving is immaterial, "Her car weaved its way through traffic."

Verbs That Lie in Wait *(page 179)*

1. laying **2.** lie **3.** lay **4.** lying **5.** lain **6.** lay **7.** laid **8.** laid **9.** lying **10.** lain

The Difference a Word Makes *(page 181)*

1. a **2.** b **3.** a **4.** b **5.** a **6.** b **7.** b **8.** a **9.** b **10.** a **11.** b **12.** a **13.** b **14.** a **15.** b **16.** a **17.** a **18.** a **19.** b **20.** a **21.** a **22.** b **23.** a **24.** b **25.** b **26.** a **27.** a **28.** b **29.** a **30.** a **31.** a **32.** b **33.** b **34.** a **35.** b

A Comedy of Errors *(page 185)*

1. Sir Rodney might be sweating because he realizes that his creator has messed up the sign, which should read: "... Slaughter At **Its** Best." *It's* is a contraction, not a possessive pronoun.

2. *Less* means "not so much" and refers to amount and quantity. *Fewer* means "not so many" and refers to number, things that are countable, such as the candles on a cake. "... By using **fewer** and **fewer** candles on your cake" is preferable.

3. Lucy is perpetrating an apostrophe catastrophe. She is trying out for the **girls'** (or **girls**) basketball team, because more than one girl plays on the squad.

4. Even a senator should know that one ends a quotation with **end quote**, not *unquote*.

5. Millennium, not *millenium*. The percentage of instances in which this word is misspelled makes *millennium* very probably the most misspelled word in the English language.

6. Larsen E. Pettifogger should be urging his client to crawl ten feet **farther**, not further. *Farther* indicates concrete, physical distance and means "at a greater distance," while *further* describes abstract distance and means "more, to a greater extent."

7. It is the **enormousness** of the universe that excites Carl Sagan. *Enormousness* and *enormity* both denote largeness, but *enormity* is reserved for the idea of wickedness and *enormousness* for objects and concepts involving great size.

8. If Franz Joseph **Haydn** were alive today, he would be turning over in his grave in the presence of this spello.

9. I, not *myself*. The suspicious-looking *need* is actually correct because it agrees with the nearer pronoun.

10. A hose **lies** ("reposes") there, not lays there. In

"Bloom County," Opus exclaimed, "Those butchers! Come in . . . lay down," and even the know-it-all Calvin, of "Calvin and Hobbes," messed up this verb pair when he said, "If the rest of you lay low, we can take turns going to school, and no one will be the wiser."

11. In "with you and I," the pronouns are both objects of the preposition *with*. Thus, *I* should be **me**.

12. The "Wizard of Id" king is not much of a wizard of idiom here. Standard English speakers use **different from** before a noun or noun expression, not *different than*. After all, nobody would say, "A differs than B."

13. To avoid the disagreement between the singular *everyone* and the plural *them* and the sexism of *him* used to stand for all people, the fat cat could have declared, "Everyone has a good book in him or her." Even better would have been "We each have a good book in us."

14. A rare double boo-boo. Most obvious is the double negative "none . . . neither," which is a no-no. Less obvious is "there's none." Because the announcer is talking about the fleas collectively and not individually, I would argue that the correct form is "there **are** none."

15. A hairline is **receding**, not *receeding*.

16. To keep demonstrative pronouns and nouns in agreement, standard English speakers say, **that kind** or **those kinds**.

17. The speaker really wants a wine that will **complement** ("complete") the mystery meat, assuming that the wine can't exclaim, "Hey, great meat!"

18. Puristically, it's **annoy**, not *aggravate*. *Annoy* means "to irritate," *aggravate* "to make worse."

19. Of course Nancy can sit *on* Sluggo's lap, but she should have asked, "**May** I sit on your lap?"

20. If you say to a language pundit, "I'm nauseous today," he or she may shoot back, "How honest of you to admit it." Brandishing the model *poisonous/poisoned*, purists maintain that *nauseous* means "causing nausea," while **nauseated** means "experiencing nausea."

21. The Id peasant is actually pointing to a **lectern**, not a podium. We stand on a small, portable platform called a podium (from a Greek root for "foot"), but we rest our notes on and speak from an item of furniture called a lectern (from a Latin root for "read").

22. The study of ancestry is **genealogy**, not geneology.

23. **Media** (Latin singular -*um*, plural -*a*) is the standard form of *medium*. Mediums are practitioners who claim to communicate with the dead.

24. Puristically, General Halftrack (who, in the panel, has a smile on his face) is **eager**, not anxious, to take rifle practice. Both *eager* and *anxious* mean "desiring to do something," but underlying *anxious* is a hint of apprehension.

25. The verb is spelled **attach**, not *attatch*.

26. A possessive pronoun, **my**, is required before the gerund object *seeing*.

27. *To whither* occupies a prominent place in the files of the Department of Redundancy Department. Because **whither** means "to where," *to whither* is repetitive, known in the language business as a pleonasm. *Whither* is much like *whence*, which means "from where."

Also, the verb in the panel should be **dost** or **doth**, not *doest*.

28. Garfield is having trouble with another archaic-sounding word—*thine*, which means "yours." The fat cat should have said "**thy** breakfast," as *thy* means "your." Alas, we can't always have archaic and eat it too.

29. The Woodley family consists of more than one Woodley, so the plural possessive form is "the **Woodleys'** yard." In the same comic strip I've also seen a panel that reads, "It's really time to leave for the O'Reilly's party."

30. More apostrophe catastrophe. While *Women's* and *Misses'* are plural possessives, *Junior's* is a singular possessive. **Juniors'** is what was meant.

31. The senator is using fowl language here. *Insure* means "to provide or procure insurance for." **Ensure**, the better word here, means "to make certain."

32. Rather than effecting ("bringing about") an English accent, the Peachy kid is **affecting** ("pretending to have") that manner of speech.

33. Both a subject-verb miscegenation and a jarring shift from the first to the third person have sent this sentence hurtling toward oblivion. Vastly more proper would have been "I, Cutter John . . . now **find myself.**"

34. Snoopy has typed a dangling modifier because the introductory phrase, "When mixing dog food in a bowl," doesn't modify anything in the main clause. Better would have been "When mixing dog food in a bowl, **you** may put in the water first or add it last."

35. The *only* is misplaced here and seems to suggest that the young hunter should only shoot what he is going to eat, not stab or cage it. Clearer would have been "**Shoot only** what you're gonna eat."

36. "The reason . . . is because" is both redundant, because *because* is embedded in *reason*, and structurally shoddy. The *is* should be followed by a noun clause, "**that** you never get the ball in the basket."

37. Little Calvin is dangling his participle in public. Calvin, not the rocks, is crossing the rift. The most graceful revision of the second sentence is "As I cross the rift, I note that the rocks change color."

38. Because B.D. and Boopsie are the only two people in the car, they should use the comparative, not the superlative, form of the adjective and exclaim, even in the heat of passion, "It was **harder** on me."

39. Because the infinitive *to symbolize* is followed by four objects, the sentence should read, "Four red roses to symbolize Mike, Liz, April, and **me**."

40. *Carpe diem* is the Latin expression that means "seize the day." (The *O* in "O wise man" is perfectly correct.)

41. Because *the Muzak wars* is a plural subject, Zonker should ask, "How **go** the Muzak wars today?"

42. Another example of double trouble: Although it is probably unrealistic to ask someone Nancy's age to employ the subjunctive mood, the proper usage for conditions contrary to fact following the verb *to wish* is "I wish I **were** better looking."

It is also a bit much to ask Sluggo to have control of "one of those people," one of the most difficult constructions to master. Because the adjective clause modifies *people*, the sentence should read, "Maybe you're one of those people who are beautiful on the inside."

43. Yet another two-time loser: Alexander's first comment contains an illogical comparison. Because Dagwood can't do something more than he himself can do it, he orders "more toppings than anyone **else** in the world."

Second, the vat of toppings comes from the **PIZZERIA**.

44. "I agree with **whoever** is speaking." *Whoever* is the subject of the verb *is*. The entire noun clause, "whoever is speaking," is the object of the preposition *with*.

45. "For **a while**." *Awhile* is an adverb, as in "Can you stay awhile?" *A while* is the article *a* and the noun *while*, which is used as the object of a preposition.

46. The roots of **astronaut** literally mean "star sailor." Here the corrector herself (or at least her letterer) needs correction.

47. *'Till* is an outré version of *till*. *Till* is not a shortened form of *until*: *till* is actually the older word, dating back to at least the ninth century. In writing for publication, use *till*, rather than *'til*.

48. Commas should appear after clauses such as "s/he said" and "s/he asked" and before quoted statements. In most other settings, including the two in this strip, commas before quotations are gratuitous.

49. Despite the plural noun in the prepositional phrase, the noun *panel* should take a singular verb, **has reconfigured**.

50. Puristically, the joyriding canines are **careering** through the neighborhood. The primary meaning of *careen* is "to cause (a boat) to lean over on one side," while that of the verb *career* is "to go at top speed, in a headlong manner."

Usage and Abusage *(page 190)*

"I sincerely feel **that** [*like* is usually a preposition and, in this case, awkwardly introduces the noun clause; *as if* is also acceptable] you students should have passed the test," lamented the teacher, [comma before restrictive clause] who obviously felt badly [in this context, *badly* is acceptable as a predicate adjective] about the whole affair. Each student in the class refused to **accept** the fact that **he or she** [*each* requires a singular pronoun] had failed, but the teacher was one of those pedagogues **who were tough graders.** [The adjective clause modifies *pedagogues*, not *one*.]

Jack was an obvious choice as class spokesman, although he would **have** gone along with **whoever** [*whoever* is the subject of the passive verb "was chosen"] else was chosen. Mary's situation was different **from Jack's** [*different from* before nouns; illogical comparison]. Her class standing was more **affected** by the grade because she had answered **fewer** [*fewer* for countable entities] questions correctly. Trying hard to answer rationally, Mary **replied,** [dangling participle]

"This test is harder and longer than any **other** [illogical comparison] I have taken. Can you tell us what the test was about and **why you gave it** [faulty parallelism]?"

The teacher answered, "If I **were** [subjunctive; condition contrary to fact] in **your** place, I too would be upset." The class was impressed by the **teacher's** [possessive noun before gerund object] trying to explain his position so clearly. **Nevertheless** [comma splice], it seemed to them that ["in their opinion" is redundant] the teacher should not have taken points off for spelling, **an** extremely nit-picking approach [sentence fragment].

Neither Mary **nor** the other members of the class **were** [with *nor* the verb must agree with the nearer subject] in a position to disagree strongly with the teacher, although they could not help but [*scarcely* generates a double negative] feel that they knew more about fairness than **he** [subject of understood verb *did*].

Now that everyone had **laid his or her** [*everyone* is a singular pronoun] cards on the table, the teacher **proceeded** to explain how important **experience is** and how much the students lacked **that experience** [vague pronoun reference]. "Please do not **infer**," he added, "that it is **altogether** easy to **ensure** fairness on tests."

The Ultimate Spelling Quiz *(page 241)*

The total is zero. That's right: all of the words in the list are spelled correctly. If you happened to circle some of the words, compare your vision of the word with the spellings given, and you will go a long way toward taming some of your personal spelling demons.

Mark Your Words *(page 243)*

1. The Bible, which is the central book in religious thought, speaks of three virtues—faith, hope, and charity—and says that the greatest of these is charity.

Commas to separate the nonrestrictive adjective clause; double dashes to set off compound appositive that contains commas for noun series.

2. "Did James travel all the way to Concord, New Hampshire, to look for the Joneses' first-edition copy of the story 'The Tell-Tale Heart'?" he asked.

Quotation marks for quotation; comma after *New Hampshire,* as well as before; apostrophe after *Joneses*; hyphen for *first-edition* as a compound adjective; single quotation marks for the short-story title set within double quotation marks; question mark outside the single quotation marks; period, not question mark, at end of sentence.

3. "Did Julie really declare, 'I refuse to make my bed; and I shall never again wash dishes, vacuum rugs, or water plants!'?" asked Jenny.

Quotation marks for quotation; single quotation marks within double quotation marks; semicolon before *and* to separate two independent clauses, one of which contains commas for the verb series; exclamation mark before single quotation mark ending quotation, and question mark before the double quotation mark; period, not question mark, at end of sentence.

4. Although the school is again warning Mary (it's warned her many times before), the brave, wonderfully coordinated young woman wants to try out for the boys' [or *boys*] football team.

Parentheses for parenthetical sentence in the middle of a larger sentence; *it's* as a contraction; comma after parentheses to set off introductory adverb clause; comma for adjective series.

5. Roosevelt brilliantly exploited the political situation by bringing together five have-not entities—the South, which had lived for years in a state of chronic depression (Roosevelt was to characterize it as the country's number-one economic problem); the Roman Catholics, who still formed a minority group in many parts of the country; the blacks, particularly those settled in urban communities; the Jews; and the labor unions. (from Brooks, Lewis, and Warren, *American Literature: The Makers and the Making*)

Hyphen for compound modifier; dash to set off compound appositive; commas to set off nonrestrictive adjective clauses; parentheses to set off parenthetical statement within the larger sentence; semicolons to set off series in which one or more noun phrases contain commas; commas for series of authors; book title italicized or underlined.

Apostrophe Catastrophes (page 245)

1. Use the apostrophe and *s* to indicate the possessive case in singular and plural nouns with an *s* or *z* sound—"the woman's car," "the men's club."

2–4. If a singular noun ends with an *s* or *z* sound, add either an apostrophe and *s* or just an apostrophe, depending on how you pronounce the word. Most of us say *Gus's*, and the punctuation should reflect the oral form of the word. To my ear, either *Jesus'* or *Jesus's* is acceptable, while *Achilles'* seems far more natural than the spluttering *Achilles's*.

5. If a plural noun ends with an *s* or *z* sound, add the apostrophe only—"the babies' diapers," "the Snaggles' house."

6–7. Use the apostrophe and *s* for possessive impersonal pronouns, such as *anyone's* and *everybody's*, but never use the apostrophe and *s* for possessive personal pronouns, such as *its* and *hers*.

8–9. Use an apostrophe and *s* to form plurals only when the application of the regular plural rules would cause confusion—*ideas, 1990s,* but "knows her ABC's and her p's and q's." Modern style favors a simple *s* even after figures, letters, and words used as words, unless confusion would result.

10. Use the apostrophe to indicate contractions and other omissions—*doesn't, o'clock, the class of '93.*

Punctuation Teasers *(page 247)*

1. A clever dog knows it's master.
2. Call me, fool, if you wish.
3. Woman—without her, man is nothing.
4. I saw a man-eating lobster.
5. Mary, Jane, and I went to see the latest Mel Gibson movie.
6. The butler stood at the door and called the guests' names.
7. Other than that, one thought he was not there.
8. Ann Boleyn kept her head up defiantly; an hour after, she was beheaded.
9. *Every lady in this land*
   Hath twenty nails: upon each hand
   Five, and twenty on hand and feet,
   And this is true without deceit.
10. There should be more space between "ham" and "and" and "and" and "and" and "eggs."
11. That that is, is. That that is not, is not. Is not that it? It is.
12. Mary, where John had had "had," had had "had had." Had "had had" had the teacher's approval, Mary would have been correct.

Tools of the Trade

Any good worker needs good tools and the knowledge of how to use them. The carpenter relies on his or her hammer and nails, saw and wood, and plumb bob and square, the dancer on her or his pointe shoes and rosin, leotard and tutu, and barre and mirrors.

Whether or not you are a professional linguist (one who studies language scientifically) or a dedicated amateur, you have probably learned that it is not so much what you know as what you know about the sources that can tell you what you need to know. In this chapter I'm going to pull out the books and journals, most of them reposing on the shelves in my study, that I have personally found to be most helpful to my labors of love in the language vineyard. We are all workers with words, all of us who try to use language accurately and gracefully. My hope is that some of the tools I'm about to unpack will make your wordwork more joyful and precise.

With laudable modesty, the great lexicographer Samuel Johnson once wrote, "Dictionaries are like watches: the worst is better than none, and the best cannot be expected to go quite true." Nowadays, more than two centuries after Dr. Johnson, most watches run quite true, and so do many dictionaries. Just as everyone who wishes to muddle along in the modern world needs to wear a watch, everyone who wants to use words in an informed manner should own a reputable, serviceable, and up-to-date dictionary. The question is which one. Because modern dictionary publishing is a highly competitive business, every imaginable size and type of dictionary is available, from large, unabridged volumes to paperback pocket editions.

The most satisfactory dictionary for all-around use is the one-volume workhorse usually identified as a "desk" or "collegiate" dictionary, containing from 90,000 to 150,000 entries. Don't let the label "collegiate dictionary" scare you off. Collegiate dictionaries are useful to all readers and writers, whether or not they are attending school or are college graduates. Don't be dazzled by the name "Webster" in a dictionary title; the name itself is no guarantee of quality because it is now in the public domain and any publisher may use it.

The desk lexica (one phenomenon–many phenomena, one lexicon–many lexica) I most often use are *Merriam Webster's Collegiate Dictionary, Tenth Edition* (Springfield, MA: Merriam Webster, 1993; updated every few years) and *The American Heritage Dictionary of the English Language, Third Edition*, published in 1992. The Merriam-Webster dictionary houses more than 160,000 entries and 200,000 definitions, and each entry is dated, so that I can easily find out how old a word is and when it was introduced. "When I feel inclined to read poetry, I take down my dictionary," declared Ralph Waldo Emerson. With its more than 200,000 entries, nearly 4,000 photographs, line drawings, and maps, its regional notes, and Usage Panel comments, the AHD III is an epic poem to our native tongue.

Serious scholars and passionate verbivores often plunge into the unabridged dictionaries, which average 450,000 entries and offer quantities of information not available in desk versions. Among the best-known unabridged dictionaries today are *The American Heritage Dictionary of the English Language* (Boston: Houghton Mifflin, 1985), *The New Standard Dictionary of the English Language* (New York: Funk & Wagnalls Publishing Company, 1987), *Webster's Third New International Dictionary* (Springfield, MA: Merriam-Webster, Inc., 1961), and *The Random House Dictionary of the English Language, Second Edition* (New York: Random House, 1987).

An old dictionary is like a whalebone corset, a buttonhook, spats, or a wad of Confederate money—nice to have around but of little practical use. Unless you're a collector, replace old dictionaries with ones published within the past ten years, at least.

In addition to these general dictionaries are various etymological dictionaries that show in detail where words originated, how their forms have changed in English, and how their meanings have developed over time.

In a class by itself is the *Oxford English Dictionary* (Oxford: Oxford University Press, 1988), the most comprehensive dictionary of the English language in existence. It is an undertaking that attempts to record the birth and history of every printed word in the language from the time of King Alfred (about A.D. 1000) to the current date of publication.

It took seventy years to complete the original twelve-volume edition and twenty-nine years to update it in an integrated 22,000-page, twenty-volume second edition that consists of nearly 60 million words. A reduced-type compact edition is now available, complete with magnifying-glass accessory. Volunteer workers from all over the world participated in the massive research, sending the editors more than 6 million slips of paper with recorded usages. What the pyramids were to ancient Egyptian civilization, the *Oxford English Dictionary* is to English-language scholarship—the most impressive collective achievement of our civilization. The difference is that inside the OED pulses something alive, growing, and evolving.

Easier to use and for many purposes just as helpful as the OED is *The Barnhart Dictionary of Etymology* (Bronx, NY: The H.W. Wilson Company, 1988). In one thick volume of 1,284 pages is packed the finest American etymological scholarship that I have encountered. While the Barnhart lexicon contains about a twentieth of the number of words enshrined in the OED, the 30,000 words therein are the ones of greatest etymological intrigue, and the explanations of each word are fuller and more readable. The entries omit the traditional use of abbreviations, symbols, and technical terminology and interweave thousands of linguistic and historical facts to explain the life and times of English words.

Among smaller and more popularized books of etymology, the two most useful to my work have been William and Mary Morris's *Morris Dictionary of Word and Phrase Origins: Second Edition* (New York: Harper & Row, 1988) and Robert Hendrickson's *Encyclopedia of Word and Phrase Origins* (New York: Facts on File Publications, 1987). Within these tomes and the smaller ones in the following selected bibliography repose phrases and expressions that one can't always find in the OED:

Ammer, Christine. *It's Raining Cats and Dogs . . . and Other Beastly Expressions.* New York: Dell Publishing, 1989.

————. *Fighting Words.* New York: Dell Publishing, 1989.

————. *Have a Nice Day—No Problem!: A Dictionary of Clichés.* New York: Dutton, 1992.

Ayto, John. *Dictionary of Word Origins.* New York: Arcade Publishing, 1990.

Barnette, Martha. *A Garden of Words.* New York: Times Books, 1992.

Brewer, E. Cobman (revised by Ivor H. Evans). *Brewer's Dictionary of Phrase & Fable.* New York: HarperCollins, last revised in 1992.

————. *Brewer's Dictionary of Twentieth Century Phrase and Fable.* Boston: Houghton Mifflin, 1992.

Campbell, Grant. *Words: A Potpourri of Fascinating Origins.* Santa Barbara, CA: Capra Press, 1992.

Ciardi, John. *A Browser's Dictionary.* New York: Harper & Row, 1980.

————. *A Second Browser's Dictionary.* New York: Harper & Row, 1983.

————. *Good Words to You.* New York: Harper & Row, 1987.

Claiborne, Robert. *Loose Cannons and Red Herrings.* New York: Ballantine Books, 1989.

Funk, Charles Earle. *A Hog on Ice & Other Curious Expressions.* New York: Harper & Row, 1948.

————. *Heavens to Betsy! & Other Curious Sayings.* New York: Harper & Row, 1955.

Funk, Charles Earle, and Charles Earle Funk, Jr. *Thereby Hangs a Tale: Stories of Curious Word Origins.* New York: Harper & Row, 1950.

————. *Horsefeathers & Other Curious Words.* New York: Harper & Row, 1958.

Funk, Wilfred. *Word Origins and Their Romantic Stories.* New York: Funk & Wagnalls, 1950.

Greenough, James Bradstreet, and George Lyman Kittredge. *Words and Their Ways in English Speech.* New York: The Macmillan Company, 1900.

Hendrickson, Robert. *Animal Crackers: A Bestial Lexicon.* New York: The Viking Press, 1983.

Jacobson, John D. *Eatioms.* New York: Dell, 1993.

Manser, Martin. *Get to the Roots: A Dictionary of Word & Phrase Origins.* New York: Avon Books, 1990.

Muschell, David. *Where in the Word?* Rocklin, CA: Prima Publishing, 1991.

Rawson, Hugh. *Devious Derivations.* New York: Crown Publishers, 1994.

Rogers, James. *The Dictionary of Clichés.* New York: Facts on File Publications, 1985.

Room, Adrian. *A Dictionary of True Etymologies.* London: Routledge & Kegan Paul, 1986.

Urdang, Laurence and Nancy LaRoche, eds. *Picturesque Expressions: A Thematic Dictionary.* Detroit: Gale Research Company, 1980.

Verbatim: The Language Quarterly. P.O. Box 78008, Indianapolis, IN 46278–0008; four issues a year, 1974–93.

Webster's Word Histories. Springfield, MA: Merriam-Webster Inc., 1989.

Word Mysteries & Histories: From Quiche to Humble Pie. Boston: Houghton Mifflin Company, 1986.

One who is fascinated by the origins and development of words will usually want to place that evolution in the context of the history of the English language. The histories I most often read are:

Barber, Charles L. *The Story of Language.* London: Pan Books, 1972.

Barnett, Lincoln. *The Treasure of Our Tongue.* New York: Alfred A. Knopf, 1964.

Baugh, Albert C., and Thomas Cable. *A History of the English Language, Third Edition.* Englewood Cliffs, NJ: Prentice-Hall, Inc., 1978.

Bryson, Bill. *The Mother Tongue: English & How It Got That Way.* New York: William Morrow and Company, Inc., 1990.

Burchfield, Robert. *The English Language.* Oxford: Oxford University Press, 1986.

Claiborne, Robert. *Our Marvelous Native Tongue: The Life and Times of the English Language.* New York: Times Books, 1983.

Crystal, David. *The English Language.* London: Penguin Books, 1988.

Jesperson, Otto. *Growth and Structure of the English Language.* Garden City, NY: Doubleday & Co., 1956.

McCrum, Robert, William Cran, and Robert MacNeil. *The Story of English.* New York: Penguin Books, 1987.

Pei, Mario. *The Story of the English Language.* New York: A Touchstone Book, 1967.

Pyles, Thomas. *The Origins and Development of the English Language, Second Edition.* New York: Harcourt Brace Jovanovich, Inc., 1971.

Robertson, Stuart, and Frederic G. Cassidy. *The Development of Modern English, Second Edition.* Englewood Cliffs, NJ: Prentice-Hall, Inc., 1954.

Shipley, Joseph T. *In Praise of English: The Growth & Use of Language.* New York: Times Books, 1977.

The starting point for anyone exploring the English grown on this side of the ocean is H. L. Mencken's monumental *The American Language.* Mencken's high-spirited encyclopedia of our idiom has been called America's "declaration of linguistic independence" that "put American English on the map." The original work (1919–51) runs to four fat volumes and two supplements; I use the one-volume abridged edition organized by Raven I. McDavid, Jr. (New York: Alfred A. Knopf, 1977).

Other significant and readable explorations of American English include:

American Speech: A Quarterly of Linguistic Speech. University of Alabama Press; four issues a year, 1925–93.

Cassidy, Frederic G., chief ed. *Dictionary of American Re-*

gional English. Cambridge, MA: Belknap Press of Harvard University Press. Volumes began appearing in 1985.

Dickson, Paul. *Slang!—The Topic-by-Topic Dictionary of Contemporary American Lingoes*. New York: Pocket Books, 1990.

Dillard, J. L. *Black English: Its History and Usage In the United States*. New York: Vintage Books, 1973.

———. *All-American English: A History of the English Language in America*. New York: Vintage Books, 1976.

Dohan, Mary Helen. *Our Own Words*. Baltimore: Penguin Books, 1974.

Flexner, Stuart Berg, and others. *I Hear America Talking*. New York: Van Nostrand Reinhold Company, 1976.

———. *Listening to America: An Illustrated History of Words and Phrases from Our Lively and Splendid Past*. New York: A Touchstone Book, 1982.

Hendrickson, Robert. *American Talk: The Words and Ways of American Dialects*. New York: Viking Penguin Inc., 1986.

Hook, J. N. *The Story of American English*. New York: Harcourt Brace Jovanovich, 1972.

———. *People Say Things Different Ways*. Glenview, IL: Scott, Foresman and Company, 1974.

Lewin, Esther, and Albert E. Lewin. *The Thesaurus of Slang*. New York: Facts on File Publications, 1988.

Pyles, Thomas. *Words and Ways of American English*. New York: Random House, 1952.

Schur, Norman. *British English A to Zed*. New York: Harper Perennial, 1991.

Wentworth, Harold, and Stuart Berg Flexner. *Dictionary of American Slang, Second Supplemented Edition*. New York: Thomas Y. Crowell Company, 1960.

Do you fret about floating your conjunctive adverbs, dangling your participles in public, and confusing *who* with *whom, disinterested* with *uninterested,* and "It's me" with "It is I"? With sound scholarship and straightforward common sense, a number of guidebooks catalog and tame the demons of grammar and usage.

By far the most thorough, exhaustive, and realistic elbow book that I own in the area of usage is *Webster's Dictionary of English Usage* (Springfield, MA: Merriam-Webster Inc., 1989). Clearly and readably the articles in this nearly one-thousand-page guide examine the common problems of American usage, such as *fulsome, infer/imply, irregardless, hopefully, bring/take*, subject-verb agreement, and literally thousands of others (including *literally*). After exhaustive research (but not exhausting for the reader), the editors make recommendations for sensible modern usage from the perspective of language history.

The other most dog-eared grammar-usage-spelling-punctuation guides in my library are:

Bernstein, Theodore M. *Watch Your Language.* Great Neck, NY: Channel Press, 1958.

———. *The Careful Writer: A Modern Guide to English Usage.* New York: Atheneum, 1965.

———. *Dos, Don'ts & Maybes of English Usage.* New York: Times Books, 1977.

Claiborne, Robert. *Saying What You Mean.* New York: W. W. Norton & Company, 1986.

Elster, Charles Harrington. *There Is No Zoo in Zoology And Other Beastly Mispronunciations.* New York: Collier Books, 1988.

———. *Is There a Cow in Moscow?—More Beastly Mispronunciations and Sound Advice.* New York: Collier Books, 1990.

Evans, Bergen. *Comfortable Words: Modern Guideposts to the Use of Easy, Simple and Colorful English.* New York: Random House, 1959.

Evans, Bergen, and Cornelia Evans. *A Dictionary of Contemporary American Usage.* New York: Random House, 1957.

Follett, Wilson, and others. *Modern American Usage: A Guide.* New York: Hill & Wang, 1966.

Fowler, H. W. *A Dictionary of Modern English Usage, Second*

Edition, revised by Sir Ernest Gowers. Oxford: Clarendon Press, 1965.

Fowler, H. W., and F. G. Fowler. *The King's English.* Oxford: Oxford University Press, 1931.

Grambs, David. *Death by Spelling.* New York: Harper & Row, 1989.

Heacock, Paul. *Which Word When?* New York: A Laurel Book, 1989.

Hook, J. N. *The Appropriate Word: Finding the Best Way to Say What You Mean.* Reading, MA: Addison-Wesley Publishing Company, Inc., 1990.

Johnson, Edward D. *The Handbook of Good English.* New York: Washington Square Press, 1991.

Montgomery, Michael, and John Stratton. *The Writer's Hotline Handbook: A Guide to Good Usage and Effective Writing.* New York: A Mentor Book, 1981.

Morris, William, and Mary Morris. *Harper Dictionary of Contemporary Usage, Second Edition.* New York: Harper & Row, 1985.

Morsberger, Robert E., and Janet Aiken. *Commonsense Grammar and Style.* New York: Thomas Y. Crowell Company, 1965.

Nurnberg, Maxwell. *Questions You Always Wanted to Ask About English but Were Afraid to Raise Your Hand.* New York: Washington Square Press, 1972.

Quinn, Jim. *American Tongue and Cheek: A Populist Guide to Our Language.* New York: Pantheon Books, 1980.

Safire, William. *On Language.* New York: Avon Books, 1980.

———. *What's the Good Word?* New York: Times Books, 1982.

———. *I Stand Corrected.* New York: Random House, 1984.

———. *You Could Look It Up.* New York: Random House, 1988.

———. *The Fumblerules of Grammar.* New York: Doubleday, 1990.

————. *Language Maven Strikes Again.* New York: Double-
day, 1990.
————. *Quoth the Maven.* New York: Random House, 1993.
Spell/Binder. SPELL, Lake Arrowhead Station 1182, Wal-
eska, GA 30183. Published bimonthly, 1986–93.
Strunk, William, Jr., and E. B. White. *The Elements of Style,
Third Edition.* New York: Macmillan, 1979.
Tarshis, Barry. *Grammar for Smart People.* New York: Pocket
Books, 1992.
Urdang, Laurence. *The Dictionary of Confusable Words.* New
York: Facts on File Publications, 1988.

There are two sides of language—the outside and
the inside. The outside is the practical employment of
words that gets us through our daily lives: "Please pass
the yogurt," "How much does that cost?" and the like.
The inside is the recreational use of language, the part
of us that enjoys having fun with the sounds, meanings,
and configurations of words and letters.

"As long as we have had words, we have had wordplay," says noted logologist A. Ross Eckler. And as long
as we have had wordplay, men and women have exper-
imented with witty and whimsical verbal diversions that
are both true and outré, *outré* being pig latin for *true.* For
the psychically mobile verbivore who enjoys messing
around with words for the fun of it, there is a shelf of
recreational books that play with the sounds, meanings,
and configurations of words—from puns to palindromes, anagrams to antigrams, reversagrams to lipograms, and pangrams to isograms:

Bergeron, Howard W. *Palindromes and Anagrams.* New
York: Dover Publications, Inc., 1973.
Bombaugh, C. C. *Oddities and Curiosities of Words and Literature.* New York: Dover Publications, Inc., 1961 (originally
published in 1890).

Borgmann, Dimitri A. *Language on Vacation.* New York: Charles Scribner's Sons, 1965.

Brandreth, Gyles. *The Joy of Lex.* New York: William Morrow and Company, Inc., 1980.

———. *More Joy of Lex.* New York: William Morrow and Company, Inc., 1982.

Chace, H. L. *Anguish Languish.* Englewood Cliffs, NJ: Prentice-Hall, 1956.

Charlton, James, ed. *Bred Any Good Rooks Lately?* Garden City, NY: Doubleday & Company, Inc., 1986.

Crosbie, John S. *Crosbie's Dictionary of Puns.* New York: Harmony Books, 1977.

Dickson, Paul. *Names.* New York: Delacorte Press, 1986.

———. *Dickson's Word Treasury.* New York: John Wiley & Sons, 1992.

Espy, Willard R. *An Almanac of Words at Play.* New York: Clarkson N. Potter, Inc., 1975.

———. *Another Almanac of Words at Play.* New York: Clarkson N. Potter, Inc., 1980.

———. *Have a Word on Me.* New York: Simon & Schuster, 1981.

———. *The Word's Gotten Out.* New York: Clarkson N. Potter, 1989.

Evans, Rod L., and Irwin M. Berent. *Getting Your Words' Worth.* New York: Warner Books, 1993.

Grambs, David. *Words About Words.* New York: Workman Publishing, 1986.

Hauptman, Don. *Cruel and Unusual Puns.* New York: Dell, 1991.

———. *Acronymania.* New York, Dell, 1993.

Heifetz, Josefa. *Mrs. Byrne's Dictionary of Unusual, Obscure, and Preposterous Words.* Secaucus, NJ: University Books, 1974.

Hellwig, Paul. *The Insomniac's Dictionary.* New York: Ivy Books, 1986.

Hook, J. N. *The Grand Panjandrum and 1,999 Other Rare, Useful, and Delightful Words and Expressions.* New York: Philosophical Library, 1962.

Irvine, William. *Madam I'm Adam and Other Palindromes.* New York: Charles Scribner's Sons, 1987.

————. *If I Had a Hi-Fi.* New York: Dell, 1992.

Manser, Martin, ed. *The Guinness Book of Words.* Enfield, Middlesex: Guinness Books, 1988.

The Pundit. The International Save the Pun Foundation, Box 1050, Station A, Toronto, Canada M5W 1N4; twelve issues a year, 1981–93.

Redfern, Walter. *Puns.* Oxford: Basic Blackwell, 1984.

Sperling, Susan Kelz. *Poplollies and Bellibones: A Celebration of Lost Words.* New York: Clarkson N. Potter, Inc., 1977.

Word Ways: The Journal of Recreational Linguistics. Spring Valley Road, Morristown, NJ 07960; four issues a year, 1968–93.

Dedicated verbivores usually enjoy grappling with word games to strengthen their verbal skills and learn more about language. The following are the most vigorously mind-building books of verbal calisthenics on my shelves:

Augarde, Tony. *The Oxford Guide to Word Games.* Oxford: Oxford University Press, 1984.

Espy, Willard R. *The Game of Words.* New York: Bramhall House, 1971.

Green, Jesse, and Meg Wolitzer. *Nutcrackers.* New York: Grove Weidenfeld, 1991.

Maleska, Eugene T. *Maleska's Favorite Word Games.* New York: A Fireside Book, 1989.

Parlett, David. *Botticelli and Beyond: Over 100 of the World's Best Word Games.* New York: Pantheon Books, 1981.

Shipley, Joseph T. *Playing with Words.* Englewood Cliffs, NJ: Prentice-Hall, 1960.

————. *Word Games for Play and Power.* Englewood Cliffs, NJ: Prentice-Hall, 1962.

————. *Word Play.* New York: Hawthorn Books, Inc., 1972.